"WE WERE THE SALT OF THE EARTH!"

"WE WERE THE SALT OF THE EARTH!"

A Narrative of
The On-to-Ottawa Trek
and
The Regina Riot

by
Victor Howard

Canadian Plains Research Center
University of Regina • 1985

Canadian Cataloguing in Publication Data
   Howard, Victor, 1933-
      We were the salt of the earth!

      (Canadian plains studies, ISSN 0317-6290; 14)
      ISBN 0-88977-037-9

      1. Unemployed - Canada - History. 2. Labor and laboring classes -
Canada - Political activity - History. 3. Labor camps - Canada. 4.
Depressions - 1929 - Canada. 5. Regina (Sask.) - Riot, 1935. I.
University of Regina. Canadian Plains Research Center. II. Title. III.
Series. HD5728.H69 1985   331.13'7971   C85-091245-8

Printed in Canada by Merit Printing Limited, Regina.

This book is dedicated to the memory of
my father

CONTENTS

ILLUSTRATIONS
(Between pages 110 to 111)

Richard Bedford Bennett
Grote Stirling
Relief Camp for Unemployed Single Men, Salmo
"Hut News"
Jacob Penner
Annie Buller
Parade, Kamloops
Thomas Dufferin Pattullo
Arthur Evans
Arthur Evans's Home, Vancouver
Rally of Relief Camp Strikers
Mayor Gerald McGeer
Mayor McGeer Reading the Riot Act, Vancouver
Parade of Unemployed after Reading of the Riot Act
May Day Parade, Vancouver
Mother's Day Parade
Strikers at Woodward's Department Store, Vancouver

ILLUSTRATIONS (continued)

Foreword

The Great Depression still ranks among the worst disasters of the twentieth century, and for Canadians it has become a bench mark by which to measure economic dislocation and social turmoil. Who in recent years has not heard or seen phrases such as "the worst unemployment since the Depression" in the newspapers or on the television screen? Then as now, it was the young and the unskilled who found it most difficult to find permanent employment. It was the young, too, who found it most difficult to obtain "relief," as welfare assistance was then called. No one was eager to grant relief to single men even in their home communities, and when efforts were made to reduce relief budgets they were the first to be cut off. Many took to "riding the rods," drifting across the country in search of work. If so, they became "transients" and could not hope to meet the municipal residence requirements which grew ever more stringent as the Depression deepened.

The plight of these men did not leave the Bennett government unmoved. In 1932, it created a series of single men's relief camps as a means of providing them with useful employment. It is those camps, and the conditions of camp life, which spawned a strike in British Columbia and a march on Ottawa which ended in tragedy on 1 July 1935 in Regina, which form the basis for this book.

Professor Victor Howard is uniquely qualified to write this account of the On-To-Ottawa Trek. He began the research for it nearly two decades ago, when many of the people who had participated in the Trek, or in the events on Regina's Market Square, were still able to recount their experiences. He was also able to consult a number of valuable archival sources, among them the records of the Regina City Police Department which, unhappily, have since been destroyed. As Victor Howard himself notes, the Trek figures prominently in the histories of the Canadian labour and radical movements, of Canadian politics, and of Vancouver and Regina. This perceptive and compelling book makes an important contribution in each of these areas. More than that, it reminds us that the real impact of the Depression of the 1930s cannot be measured in statistics but in more human terms, in the hopes and fears of the Canadians who lived through it.

J. WILLIAM BRENNAN
University of Regina,
Regina, Saskatchewan
August 1985

Preface

AT 8:17 P.M. JULY 1ST, 1935, RIOTING ERUPTED HERE IN
MARKET SQUARE WHEN R.C.M.P. AND CITY POLICE ARRESTED
THE "ON-TO-OTTAWA TREK" LEADERS AS THEY ADDRESSED
TREKKERS AND CITY RESIDENTS. RIOTING THEN SPREAD TO
THE 11TH AVE. AND SCARTH ST. AREA. ENDING NEAR MID-
NIGHT, IT LEFT EXTENSIVE PROPERTY DAMAGE, NUMEROUS
INJURIES, AND A CITY POLICEMAN, DETECTIVE C. MILLAR,
DEAD.

THE TREKKERS WERE SINGLE MEN ENROUTE TO OTTAWA
FROM B.C. TO DEMAND BETTER CONDITIONS IN RELIEF
CAMPS SET UP FOR THE UNEMPLOYED. THEY WERE STOPPED
IN REGINA ON JUNE 14TH BY FEDERAL AUTHORITIES, WHO
FEARED A REVOLUTION IF THE TREK REACHED OTTAWA. AT
A MEETING BETWEEN TREK LEADERS AND THE FEDERAL
CABINET, MISTRUST GREW, AND TREKKERS WERE PROHIBITED
FROM ADVANCING OR GOING HOME. TO BREAK THE DEAD-
LOCK, OTTAWA ORDERED THE LEADERS' ARREST. IN THE
FUROR OF THE RESULTING RIOT, THE FRUSTRATION OF THE
TREK'S FAILURE AND YEARS OF UNEMPLOYMENT WERE
RELEASED.

THE NEXT DAY THE PROVINCIAL GOVERNMENT ARRANGED
FOR THE TREKKERS TO RETURN TO THEIR HOMES.

GOVERNMENT OF SASKATCHEWAN, 1979

This text appears on a historical marker set in front of the Regina,
Saskatchewan, City Police Station. Inside, in a second floor display
case, there is a photograph of the detective who was killed. Nearby, there are a few relics of the struggle, including two clubs which
appear to be sawn-off baseball bats. At the museum on the grounds
of the Royal Canadian Mounted Police barracks, some two miles
away to the west, there is another display of photographs and clubs.

How does one "remember" a riot? Does one "remember" a riot
in the way one "remembers" the North-West Rebellion or Vimy
or Dieppe? Do elderly men who fought on Market Square dress
up in their uniforms, if they were the police, or in their old relief
camp fatigues, if they were Trekkers? Do the two groups of veterans
shake hands in front of the historical marker? In front of the
cameras? Is all forgiven?

The temperate language on that marker suggests that the story
of the Regina Riot is still not clear in the minds of, at least, those
who shaped the description. Something is missing: a point of view,
perhaps. An ideological thrust in the phrasing that would signify
some indignation or resentment. But neutrality for the ages is what
such markers are all about.

For the constables on duty inside the Police Station, the Regina
Riot is only legend, important in the history of their force but, after
all, a part of the past. There are matters of the present that must

be dealt with. The very Police Station is a matter of the present. New, clean, expedient, it occupies the ground on which stood a flat-bed truck on which sat John Toothill, Gerry Winters, George Black and, yes, Arthur Evans, who were there that July evening to launch one more appeal to some twelve hundred Reginans: money and patience, please. As they began to talk, a penny-whistle pierced the summer air, several men leaped from the crowd to arrest Evans and Black, the crowd panicked, the riot was on.

If one is sensitive to the conjunction of time and space, the Regina Police Station extends today across an area which, fifty years ago, churned with violence as men set upon men, as clubs, bricks, rocks, tear gas, police batons, whirled through the air. Along Osler Street to the west of what was then Market Square, along Tenth Avenue to the north, the citizenry who had fled now scurried back and forth, looking for relatives and friends who had not yet run to safety. Minutes later, the riot rushed away west a few blocks, into the centre of the city, where it plunged and gave, plunged and gave, until men had to be shot down so that other men could prevail and restore order.

The Regina Riot was the climax of a strike of relief camp workers which had begun on 4 April 1935 in British Columbia, which had lingered for two months in Vancouver, and which had then taken its participants east by freight train, On-To-Ottawa. The origins of that Strike and Trek and Riot, the character of these events, are what this book is about. It is a narrative, composed from federal, provincial and municipal records, from news reports, from interviews with participants, from sworn testimony, from photographs, from maps, from sawn-off baseball bats. It is the story of an event which figured prominently in the history of the Canadian worker, in the history of the Canadian radical, in the histories of two Canadian cities, and in the history of a certain Dominion government.

This narrative has emerged from my earlier study, *The Mackenzie-Papineau Battalion: Canadian Participation in the Spanish Civil War*, which was published in 1969. It became clear, during the course of that research, that a substantial number of Canadian volunteers to the International Brigades between 1936 and 1938 had taken part in the On-To-Ottawa Trek in 1935. The Trek, as one of them put it, ''had conditioned the men who volunteered to go to Spain to make the decision without much soul-searching.'' An investigation of archive materials, a train ride from Vancouver to Regina, interviews with Trekkers and witnesses, all took place in the spring of 1967, even before the book on Spain had been completed, and while contact with the men was still possible. The research continued intermittently, resulting in a Carleton Library edition of Ronald Liversedge's *Recollections of the On-To-Ottawa Trek* in 1973 and a series of articles in *Canada: An Historical Magazine* in 1974 and 1976. As the fiftieth anniversary approached, it became necessary and possible for me to resume work and then to compose this account.

Over the years, a host of friends, colleagues, government officers, archivists, and certain anonymous well-wishers have, with patience and fortitude, given me encouragement, support and assistance. Two of them, at least, have died since the inception of this project: Ronald Liversedge and James "Red" Walsh. I wish to thank David Carter, Herman Ganzevoort, Bill Gilbey, Irene Howard, Emil and Evelyn Jonescu, Peter Kresl, Peter Levine, Norman London, Brian Long, Ian McClymont, Jim McCrorie, Russell Nye, Mac Reynolds, Richard Seaborn, Gordon Stewart, Tess Tavormina, Lee Thompson, Joe Waldemeir, Norman Ward, Saul Wellman, and Glenn Wright.

I am indebted to the staffs of the Public Archives of Canada, the Saskatchewan Archives Board, the University of British Columbia Archives, and the City Archives of Vancouver for their generous assistance.

Financial and other support for this study has come from the Canada Council, the University of Western Ontario, Michigan State University, and the Canadian Embassy in Washington, D.C.

A substantial grant for publication costs was received from the Regina 1985 Heritage Committee and for this I am most grateful.

Finally, I wish to express my appreciation for the encouragement and assistance given by my editor, J. William Brennan, Department of History, University of Regina, by the Co-ordinator of Publications at the Canadian Plains Research Center, University of Regina, Gillian Wadsworth Minifie, and by Editorial Assistant Jennifer Johnson.

And cheers to Susan, Carrie, Andrew and Jesse.

VICTOR HOWARD
Michigan State University,
East Lansing.
January 1985

Prologue
"We never regretted joining."

— Bill Davis

In the summer of 1934, after working for four years on a Manitoba farm, Bill Davis, a slightly-built twenty-year-old immigrant from England, quit because the crop had failed, went to Winnipeg and from there to a Dominion relief camp on Lac Seul, near Sioux Lookout, Ontario.[1] The project was enormous. Two thousand men dispersed among 15 camps, and living in 384 huts, were supposed to clear the wooded foreshore along 1,400 miles of shoreline across 55,000 acres, so that when the mean water level of the lake was raised 13 feet, by virtue of a newly constructed dam, the timber and the scenery would not be ruined.[2]

The work force comprised single unemployed men and, like Bill Davis, many of the younger fellows who went to Lac Seul soon left, having found the isolation appalling, the food poor, and the black fly a real hazard. From the most distant camps, the "top camps," the only way out was by scow in the warm season and by tractor across the ice in the cold. Davis put up with the uncomfortable conditions for a while, then quit along with a dozen others, and set out by scow, bound south for the railway at Sioux Lookout. Among them, they had a loaf of bread and some bologna.

As the day passed, more men hopped aboard at landings and, since the bread and the bologna could not be multiplied, Mike McCaulay, a camp worker and the acknowledged leader, proclaimed: "When we get to this next camp, boys, we don't move until we're fed." The local foreman did feed his guests, so they pressed on. At 11:00 that night, carrying more than a hundred defectors by then, among them two or three stool pigeons, the scow reached the lake port and was promptly hailed by a police boat bearing a brilliant searchlight. Somehow, the informers fled ashore with ready descriptions of McCaulay and other prominent agitators. "But these guys, they changed clothes, they changed hats, they changed boots, high boots for low boots, rolled-down pants. The police came on the scow and they went round, but the result was that no description they had been given fit anybody...."

Davis and a few others walked to the rail yard where they caught a west-bound freight. "And this is my first experience riding a tender through the night. It was a beautiful moonlit night. Everytime the engineer opened the boiler door, there was this flame reflecting on the clouds and smoke billowing out of the stack. He was blowing his whistle and we were rocking backwards and for-

1

wards. It was quite thrilling."

Going west, Davis joined that restless, frustrated throng of men who traversed Canada in the years of the Great Depression. Many were "new Canadians" and among these were thousands who spoke little if any English, and who had had little employment since they got off the boat. Many of these transients had no skills because they were very young. Many had left home in order to relieve families of the burden of their care.

They roamed here, they roamed there, through and out of the cities, over the Lakehead, back and forth across the scorched prairies, knapsacks strung across their backs, floppy fedoras and soft billed caps tugged low, usually with a pair of goggles attached, pants and shirts and coats frayed, boots and shoes scraped and broken. Quite a few carried a kitten or puppy stuffed in a pocket for company over the long haul.

The railways were an obvious means of transportation, and most of these men made their way atop freight trains, sometimes a hundred or more on the same train, riding the "drag." There was the strain that went with riding on top, cinders in the eyes, chaffed faces, grit driven into hands, arms and legs, bodies rigid with the tension of hanging on. If it started to rain, and by night the ladders up the sides of the cars had iced, men who tried to jump on or off flailed around in the dark, lucky to get their feet under them. Some didn't make it, like the boy outside Revelstoke who lost his leg under a wheel and who lay beside the tracks crying "Leave me alone."[3]

The towns across Canada had their own problems but the men came anyway, looking for food, work, shelter. "Only the man's face turned ugly and he says 'I don't feed no bums!' I said, 'Thanks' and he says, 'Just a minute.' First thing I see is a police dog coming out of the basement door. Boy, I didn't know what to do. Then I remembered my stick. I stood my ground when the dog leaps at me. I step lightly aside and Bingo! The stick lands on his bean. I get out the back gate and put a few blocks behind my heels."[4]

Most towns had missions, immigrant hotels, Sally Anns, where the men could find a meal and a bunk, although these resources were greatly burdened. They also went into "jungles" on the outskirts of the rail yards, where crude huts built of tin sheets, packing crates, boxes, auto chassis, gathered from the dump heaps, were furnished with stinking blankets and mattresses. Ukrainians, Germans, Irish — a little Chinatown in one place — a few Yanks; there were quiet voices in many languages. Maybe there was a fire going and some stew and coffee. Here and there, newcomers, the very young, were jumped, robbed and thrown out. But most times, they were taken in.

Men slept in the jungles, they slept in hostels, they slept in refrigerator cars, they slept in the shade of grain elevators, they slept in the bush, they slept right out on the prairie "till roused by a crowd of children who had come to inspect us. One yelled 'Hobo Hobo, we've got some candy for you,' but as I got up hopefully they took to their heals [sic] and ran for town."[5]

And there was always the chance of an arrest by a railway cop, a "bull," for vagrancy.

Yet there were times when the tedium and the hunger and the anxiety fell away. "Only on top of a box-car can one enjoy the real thrill of. . .the Rockies, enjoy the thrill of mountains towering almost vertically above on the one side and drops to distant valleys and creeks on the other; wondering why the rocks didn't roll down on the train and the train roll over the artificial ledge to the depths below."[6]

Bill Davis came over the mountains in 1934 with his chum, Yorky Burton, went into another relief camp near Floods in British Columbia. There the two boys met a prospector who, like so many of his calling and along with trappers, used the camps as bases from which to make journeys up, say, Silver Creek, to check claims and lines. This fellow also happened to be an organizer for the Relief Camp Workers' Union (RCWU) which agitated against dispiriting camp conditions and the failure of the government to produce a work and wages programme. Davis and Burton signed on. "We were active in wrestling, boxing, punchball and acrobatics and in this way we were active with fellows our own age and so we organized in the bunkhouses."[7]

Word came one day in March 1935 of a major meeting of union delegates in Kamloops, a secret meeting, so his friends elected Bill Davis to represent them. Davis would always insist that he was really a follower, that "I was afraid too many times, you know? And I would freeze up. I wouldn't know what to do." The others did not agree. There was something about this little fellow; scared as he might be, he was also bright, quick-witted and loyal. And so Davis went to Kamloops.[8]

Saturday, 9 March 1935. Hockey Night in Canada. Davis had thought to drop off the freight a few miles outside of Kamloops to avoid the yard police. Because it was still pretty cold in March, he wore an army greatcoat, dyed black, as was the fashion of camp issue; over his shoulder was a knapsack with two or three days' worth of socks and tobacco. Suddenly, Davis walked right into the path of a constable.

''Where did you come from? You just got off that freight, didn't you?''

''No sir!''

''Well, how did you get here? You're from Vancouver, aren't you?''

''Yes sir!''

''Well, how did you come?''

''I walked.''

''You walked all the way from Vancouver?''

''Yes sir!''

''Well, you're one heller for walking, aren't you?''[9]

Fortunately, Davis had run into an officer with a sense of humour, for a minute later, the boy had skipped across the tracks to an empty store at the lower end of Victoria Street. A knock on the door, a word of identification, and Davis entered. His host was seventeen-year-old Morris Rush, secretary of the local unemployed workers' association, who, for the past twenty-four hours, had been scurrying around town, placing men like Davis in friendly homes where they could get some sleep, food and a wash-up.[10]

The next morning, Sunday, 10 March, the sixty or more delegates converged on the store, introduced themselves, many of them familiar names from other camps, other picket lines. They dragged benches into place and settled down for the meeting. They had come from Revelstoke, from the North Thompson River, from Princeton and Hope and Rock Centre and Point Grey and Squamish and from two dozen other towns, hamlets, valleys and hill sides. They were nearly all members of the Relief Camp Workers' Union and they were in Kamloops for two days of talking and planning about the future of those camps and about the future of the men who lived in them. For all sixty delegates, the rendezvous in Kamloops was the climax of years of struggle and agitation and the beginning of a concerted action to persuade or force, if need be, the governments of Canada to realize that the situation of unemployed workers had become intolerable.

One
The Camps and the Union

"We did not organize strikes for the fun of the thing, by any means."

— *Matt Shaw*

The reason Bill Davis and his friends found work so difficult to secure in 1934 was that Canada had been trapped for nearly six years in the worst economic depression in its history. Despite a resolute stand against unemployment made by Richard Bedford Bennett during his successful campaign in the 1930 election, "the first duty of the Canadian government is to provide work for Canadians," the Tories had simply been unable to devise a credible national programme of work and wages which would rescue that considerable portion of the citizenry which had lost jobs, exhausted savings, and lapsed into extended poverty. And there were the successive generations of young people leaving school without skills, finding no opportunity to develop skills. A succession of unemployment relief acts failed utterly to remedy the situation, in part because so little money was allocated, about $140 million; in part because provinces and municipalities were supposed to provide matching subsidies for public works when those very governments were financially disabled, if not, as was the case with some towns, literally waiting for the creditors to walk through the door; in part because the government had little experience with those social services which could rationally disperse the allocations.[1]

Federal funds for relief were channelled into two categories: public works relief and direct relief. The shift in proportions across those early years is instructive, as Ottawa, while conceding more money, at the same time put more and more into direct relief. For Saskatchewan, long suffering Saskatchewan[2]:

	Public Works	**Direct Relief**
1930	$1,464,407.86	$ 454,873.06
1932	$3,754,689.31	$1,837,493.86

Another name for "direct relief" was "the dole." One of the most pernicious policies inflicted on the twentieth century, the dole was surpassed only by war, pestilence, plague and famine in its capacity to reduce the self-esteem of a people. To be on the dole meant that the worker could not find work. To be on the dole meant a means test by which relief officers, who might have little training for the onerous task, set out to make sure that one had no telephone nor bank account nor car nor "superfluous" appliances. In some areas,

5

one did not dare be found buying beer or wine. If the head of a family made more than three dollars a week in casual labour this amount would be deducted from his dole. The dole meant a periodic visit by a case worker who trailed suspicion like a bad smell as he or she interrogated the family, peered into cabinets and behind doors, took notice of any sign of luxury. If the family passed inspection, they would continue to receive assistance. The goods they bought with the dole came to bear the name "pogey." Thus, pogey shoes, pogey flour. The dole was really about humiliation.

One possible solution to this misery might have been a federal system of unemployment insurance. While many diverse interest groups came to support such an initiative, no such insurance was offered to the public until 1935, although the Bennett government had prepared a draft proposal the year before, not that its recommendations proved particularly therapeutic. A family of five would receive little more than eleven dollars a week. Unskilled labourers, loggers, construction and agricultural workers were barred from participation. Moreover, the government would be prepared to contribute only one-fifth of the premium. The cost of the programme for two-thirds of the labour force was estimated to be $50 million per year.[3]

It would seem, consequently, that those who had jobs would not want to jeopardize them by going on strike, but these were turbulent times for labour which was still not that well-organized, if organized at all. And so there were strikes and lockouts for reasons which usually turned on wages and hours or else on demands for union shops.

Year	Number of Strikes	Number of Work Days Lost	Number of Workers Involved
1930	67	71,797	13,768
1931	88	10,738	204,238
1932	111	23,390	255,000
1933	125	26,558	317,547
1934	191	45,800	574,519

Source: F.H. Leacy, ed., Historical Statistics of Canada, 2nd ed. (Ottawa: Statistics Canada, 1983), Series E190-197.

All sorts of disaffected workers went out: garment and fur trade workers in Toronto; miners in Springhill, Nova Scotia, Pictou County, Nova Scotia, and in Estevan, Saskatchewan, where three died in the streets from gunshot wounds; sawmill labourers in Fraser Mills, British Columbia, and furniture workers in Stratford,

Ontario, on which occasion for the first time in nearly a decade, authorities called in the militia.

A particularly militant force in many of these strikes was the Workers' Unity League (WUL), a trade union centre created in 1930 by the Executive Committee of the Communist Party of Canada (CPC). A counter to the American Federation of Labour and the All Canadian Congress of Labour, the WUL derived its form and character from the Red International of Labour Unions, itself a Comintern agency, and it was prepared to serve as an umbrella for an array of national and provincial unions and political and service organizations. The League's founding secretary was Tom McEwen, a CPC veteran, and its executive board included some very prominent and popular radicals: Annie Buller, Martin Forkin, Jacob Penner, Sam Scarlatt and George Drayton. In its six-year history, the WUL assumed much of the agenda of the CPC which had been declared illegal in 1931. At the same time, the WUL organized miners in Alberta, loggers in Ontario, shoe workers in Kitchener and, yes, furniture workers in Stratford. In British Columbia, at least a dozen organizations found affiliation with the League or else were created by that office: the Fishermen and Cannery Workers' Industrial Union; the Truck Drivers, Swampers and Messengers' Union; the Workers' International Relief, which was a coalition devoted to feeding strikers.

The WUL, as Tom McEwen put it, sought to try to get the central labour bodies to recognize unemployed workers as an integral part of organized labour in Canada. With or without the League's sanction, dozens of unemployed workers' associations had sprung up in cities and towns as the Depression worsened. Their members looked after the rights of the unemployed insofar as there seemed to be any rights for this class. Such associations were, in a literal sense, grass-roots, populated by unassuming if vigilant citizens.[4]

When Bill Davis left that Manitoba farm, he voluntarily entered a federal relief camp, and when he left the camp and had crossed the country to the west, he entered still another relief camp where he joined the Relief Camp Workers' Union. Both those camps and that union have their origins in an incident that occurred in Ottawa in August 1932.

In that month, Ottawa watched in some fascination while two distinctly rival and deeply hostile conferences took place a few blocks apart in that city. At the one, the Imperial Economic Conference, Prime Minister R.B. Bennett sat grandly in the chair, his querulous arguments in behalf of Canadian interests quickly proving distasteful to the representatives from beyond the oceans.

Nearby, nearly 600 delegates sent by 200,000 workers met in a huge public garage where they sat on wooden benches and listened to one another call for "a new social order, a workers' state" and for a "united class of workers around the world." This assembly called itself the Workers' Economic Conference.[5]

General concerns and slogans understood, the workers next drafted a set of specific demands which they promptly put into circulation: (1) a workers' non-contributory unemployment insurance bill; (2) a seven-hour work day and a five-day work week; (3) repeal of those tariffs and taxes which inhibited the rise of the standard of living; (4) repeal of Section 98 of the Criminal Code which dealt with membership in illegal organizations; (5) the release of Tim Buck and other Communist Party leaders from Kingston Penitentiary; (6) exemption of poor farmers from taxes, debts and rent payments. And, not to forget Mr. Bennett's guests, self-determination for India and an early cessation of shipments of food and war materials to Japan.

A committee of seven workers met with the Prime Minister on 2 August at 12:15 P.M. at which time Mr. Bennett promptly dismissed the demands.

At 2:00 P.M., the workers' conference began a demonstration in front of the Parliament Buildings. Civil servants crowded to the windows of public offices to watch police move into the throng, prodding the delegates along, cracking one or two heads, until, after twenty minutes, the marchers had cleared off.

The two groups of conferees now left Ottawa, both clearly exasperated by the imperious and contentious manner of the Canadian Prime Minister. Wrote Neville Chamberlain, the British Chancellor of the Exchequer, "Most of our difficulties centred around the personality of Bennett. Full of high Imperial sentiments, he has done little to put them into practice."[6] The one "official" assembly dispersed around the world. The other went home, too, to Verdun and Thunder Bay and Edmonton and Toronto, there to organize other committees and parades and to plan still more confrontations with Mr. Bennett.

Not long after, the Chief of the Canadian General Staff, Major General A.G.L. McNaughton set out across Canada on an inspection of military districts. Perhaps General McNaughton went forth already concerned about the tens of thousands of unemployed Canadian men, among whom surely were many veterans of World War I. Perhaps, too, he appreciated the wear and tear on these hapless people. Most certainly, when he arrived back in Ottawa, he knew that the presence of this itinerant mass posed a real threat to peace, order and good government. Witness the Workers'

Economic Conference. Witness the dissident political elements in the country which might well recruit these thousands of unemployed into conspiracies of agitation and disruption. Although the leadership of the Communist Party languished in the penitentiary, the rank and file remained intact and lively. Their capacity for making nuisance seemed undiminished.

In early September, General McNaughton passed to the Department of Labour his recommendation for the creation of a system of relief camps whose function would be

> to restore and maintain the physical condition and morale of these men [by providing] for the care of such as were medically fit in camps where their condition, both physical and mental, could be improved by the provision of good food, adequate clothing, comfortable accommodation, proper medical care, recreational and educational facilities, and a small cash allowance, in return for a measure of work on undertakings to the general advantage of Canada, the main purpose of the Scheme being to care for these men until they could be absorbed into industry as economic conditions improved.[7]

Another month passed. On 6 October, at the occasion of the opening of Parliament, Prime Minister Bennett told the General that Cabinet was interested in the relief camp proposal. Might McNaughton's staff be able to have a design ready for review by the next morning? All that night, McNaughton's people worked away on the original draft of the "Unemployed Relief Scheme" which was meant, in its first assignments, to put two thousand citizens to work repairing the citadels in Québec and Halifax and clearing land for TransCanada airports at Trenton and Rockcliffe. Cabinet quickly approved Order in Council P.C. 2248 on 8 October 1932, and the Scheme was launched. The cost per camp worker per day had to be kept to one dollar of which twenty cents would be a cash allowance.[8]

But there were complaints. The Civil Service Commission worried that camp supervisors could be hired without its scrutiny. The Treasury Board said that the camp men themselves were civil servants and thus 10 percent of their cash allowance had to be deducted. Finally, the Department of Justice ruled for the Scheme, declaring that this was an emergency enterprise exempt from standing directives and regulations.[9]

Because General McNaughton believed that the Department of National Defence (DND) had the experience, the facilities, and the support services required to deal with large contingents of men, the camps immediately came under its jurisdiction although with regular consultation with the Department of Labour. Supervisors and foremen, however, were definitely civilians.[10]

A single, unemployed man made his way into a relief camp after applying to the Employment Service or to a relief officer and then after passing a medical check which confirmed that he was free of contagious disease and hardy enough to do manual labour. Once in camp, he was issued work clothes, shaving gear, a towel, a bunk and three square meals a day, plus that twenty cents daily cash allowance which was never intended as wages but only as an allowance for tobacco and the like.[11]

The government was supposed to provide free medical care, including surgery, free dental care in the case of extractions, and repair of dentures broken on the job. Spectacles would be repaired or replaced if damaged at work.

Consideration was given to leisure activities by the officers and the workers. Donations from charities were directed into the Unemployment Relief Comforts Fund and these monies purchased sports equipment, books, magazines and the occasional radio. Even so, the men often had to improvise their own checkers and checkerboards and borrow horse shoe sets from farmers. If a camp had a radio, it was the custom for men to huddle around for the evening news and then scamper back to their bunkhouses with a summary.

Frontier College teacher-workers lived in camps and conducted classes in reading and writing, languages, mathematics and history.

If a man died "while on the strength of a project," and 237 did die during the history of the Scheme, a maximum of seventy-five dollars could be allocated for funeral expenses, including purchase of a cemetery plot.

In return, the relief camp worker spent eight hours a day, forty-four hours a week, clearing brush, laying out airstrips, constructing barracks, lengthening and widening roads, carving railway grades, digging sewage systems, raising telephone poles and power lines, and planting trees, crushing rock and erecting fences.

In the four years of the Scheme's existence, 170,248 men moved through the camps (though many moved through more than once and under different names), each spending an average of 107 days in residence. They generated 18,156,213 man-days of relief, the total expenditure finally being $24,517,012.[12]

From the beginning, General McNaughton paid close attention to the achievements of the relief camps. While he came under increasing criticism from organized labour, from radical movements and from the public, the General never doubted that the camps could and did succeed in their purpose.

Unions complained, understandably, that the assignment of camp men to building projects undercut their own constituency, and deprived the employed of jobs. McNaughton replied that only a very small percentage of this sort of work, 2.5 percent in fact, was taken up by the relief camps.

The public thought a twenty cents daily allowance a shame; it scarcely gave a man a chance to save money to re-enter society, but the government simply couldn't afford to pay wages; if it could, the camps wouldn't have to be there in the first place. The camps, recited General McNaughton, were meant "to meet an emergency situation and to care for many thousands until they could be reabsorbed in industry and not to set up a wholly new and socialistic substitute for the ordinary methods of organization of the economic life of the country."

To the charge from the left that the camps were really nascent para-military units, the General responded: "It is neither the intention nor would it be either advantageous or practicable to make use of the personnel on unemployment relief projects as soldiers...There is no ulterior purpose." But quite a few observers thought that, indeed, the Dominion government had an ulterior purpose. In short order, the Relief Camp Workers' Union would seek to counter that purpose.[13]

Under the Unemployment Relief Scheme, 123 works projects were launched across Canada. Many of these took up one camp site each, though in Alberta and British Columbia, where extensive highway construction occurred, an individual project might entail as many as a dozen camps. British Columbia was the busiest of the provinces with 53 projects on which 61,832 men worked.[14]

The Employment Service of Canada in British Columbia had its offices at 411 Dunsmuir Street in Vancouver where Colonel D.W.B. Spry served as Administrator of Relief for Single Men. Although Spry regularly reported to W.A. Gordon, Dominion Minister of Labour, he also collaborated with the District Officer Commanding Military District Eleven, Major General E.C. Ashton, who had overall supervision of the camps in that province. To the Dunsmuir address came thousands of unemployed men from all parts of Canada and, finally, from around the world, to register for assignment to a camp.

In 1933, the first complete year of the Scheme's programme in British Columbia, 31,562 men registered with Spry's office, among whom 11,430 were Canadian-born, 8,846 Commonwealth, 930 American, 1,540 Swedish, 946 Chinese, 1,267 Norwegian, 308 Hungarian, 17 Mexican. Of these, 8,418 were actually dispatched to camps, 2,383 of that number being "foreigners." Obviously, registration did not automatically mean assignment. Many were turned away for medical reasons which was understandable, since prolonged periods of unemployment not only damaged the morale but weakened the body through malnutrition, pleurisy, bronchial and gastro-intestinal disorders. No doubt because they knew they would fail the examinations, many registrants never appeared for the check-up. Many more never returned to 411 Dunsmuir for further processing after having registered.[15]

The men assigned to the camps laboured on projects which, with the exception of highway construction which was defined by the province, were all conceived by the DND's Directorate of Engineer Services in Ottawa. But while they laid out airports at Yahk, Salmo, Lytton and Oliver, the British Columbia camp workers most particularly worked on road and highway development. Forty of the fifty-three projects comprising 101 camps were so assigned. In DND nomenclature, the number of the project was indicated, followed by the name of the nearest town, followed by the specific camp number, thus: 55 Hope-Princeton Number 210.

Project 117 at Squamish on Howe Sound, launched on 9 October 1933 and terminated on 31 May 1935, was supposed to build 7.65 miles of road between Squamish and Britannia Beach. The DND took over a provincial relief camp in the area, added another 1,792 square feet of living quarters and, on an average day, 88 men were set to work clearing 50 acres of roadbed, of which 2.4 were actually cleared, and excavating 33,000 cubic yards of earth, of which 8,087 were actually excavated. Only 64 square yards of road were ever surfaced. Man-days at work: 21,177. Expenditures: $53,432. The slow progress was attributed to the "heavy country" and to inadequate equipment. More than likely, the reason the project closed down on 31 May 1935 was that the camp men had gone on strike into Vancouver.

More prominent and extensive projects about the province were 55 and 56 at Hope-Princeton, involving 10 camps, 59 miles of highway, an expenditure of $792,434 and a duration of exactly 3 years; 101 Big Bend-Revelstoke involving 16 camps which stretched north from Revelstoke along or near the Columbia River, an expenditure of $232,075 and a duration of 2 years. Camp men came to know of similar projects at Point Grey, at Spence's Bridge and at Hope-Boston Bar, the last of which generated 329,888 man-days of work.[16]

Each project had at least one supervisor, often a civil engineer, each camp had a foreman, a store or supply clerk, at least one cook and a number of "gang" bosses, chosen from among the camp men. More often than not, the first men onto a campsite laid out the bunkhouses, mess halls, store rooms, privys, parking areas for the trucks, cut trails or marched through the snow in column rank to beat down the trail. They had, meantime, been issued a pair of lumberman's boots, a mackinaw, a greatcoat, leather and woolen mittens, summer and winter caps, socks, underwear, trousers, shorts and a nightshirt; 58,114 of those last were issued.[17]

The camp men were constantly complaining about the food served them. In fact, the daily ration was that prescribed for the "Permanent Force" per man: one pound each of bread, meat, and potatoes, six ounces of fresh vegetables, three ounces each of bacon and sugar; two ounces each of beans, jam and butter; one ounce each of cheese and powdered milk; one-half ounce each of split peas and salt; one-third ounce of coffee; one-quarter ounce of tea, and one-thirty-sixth ounce of pepper. An enterprising cook might do wonders with such a ration; he might barter with farmers and grocers nearby; he might persuade the men to contribute money for extras; or he might not do any of these.[18]

For all the carefully measured portions of beans, jam and butter, for all the caps, peaked, summer, and caps, peaked, winter, and for all the apparent attention to yards of dirt excavated, and for all of General McNaughton's good intentions, the camp system in British Columbia had its problems. Not every cook knew how to cook. Many tents and bunkhouses lacked stoves. A second blanket was as scarce as a steak dinner. Gang bosses betrayed their men. Store clerks absconded with the recreation funds. Foremen proved feckless and incompetent. The work itself often seemed ridiculous: "building a culvert that will never be of any use. Some of those who know this land say that the floods that come down the creek in the spring will undo all that we are doing. Ten teams scraping around in the dust."[19] The bad weather, the isolation, the Scheme.

During the history of the Unemployed Relief Scheme, its military and civilian officers, from McNaughton down to the newest foreman, said again and again that if a man had a complaint, he had the right to make it known to the immediate authority, but he must do so on his own. "It was a definite rule that committees, combinations or mass protests, would not be regarded or considered."[20] If ever a rule was made to be broken....

The Department of National Defence, during the four years it managed the Scheme, recorded 359 occasions in all the camps in Canada of strikes, riots, demonstrations and "disturbances."[21] Of these, some 160 occurred in British Columbia, the first on 23 June 1933, at one of the 55 Hope-Princeton camps when ten men created a disturbance because of insufficient clothing. All ten were promptly discharged. Four days later, nearly 400 other men from the project walked away in sympathy and set out for Vancouver. Their march was quickly dispersed by local police. Thus it began and so it went on, month after month, with men refusing to work because of stoppage of the tobacco ration or poor food or sympathy for discharged friends. Thirty-five men would be dismissed from this camp, 8 from that one, 6 from another, 63 from still another. Once in a while, a complaint struck home. On 27 November 1933, at 55 Hope Number 210, almost the whole camp struck over allegations that the foreman, the store clerk and the cook were habitually drunk and inefficient. Forty-six workers left, apparently for good, but an investigation resulted in the resignation of the foreman and the discharge of the clerk.

The year 1934 was the most troublesome for the British Columbia camps: one hundred disturbances, riots and strikes, with twenty-seven occurring in December as the men prepared to walk out and into Vancouver for a major demonstration before provincial and dominion authorities. These authorities, General Ashton in particular, were under no illusion as to the real reason for so many outbursts. With the first appearance of the federal relief camps in the province, an organization calling itself the Relief Camp Workers' Union had come into being, proceeding thereafter to recruit the camp men into its ranks, in support of its policies of agitation and disruption.

With the designation of the Unemployed Relief Scheme in 1932, the Workers' Unity League found an opportunity for recruitment which even in its most blessed dreams it could not have invented: hundreds and then thousands of unemployed men conveniently isolated in camps with infiltration by covert organizers remarkably easy.

While the WUL could take credit for formalizing the RCWU, an organization bearing the name Relief Project Workers Union sent representatives to the League's British Columbia district office in the early summer of 1933, requesting affiliation. The exact origin of the Union is obscure; it may have been in existence a year before, formed by men living in provincial relief camps before the majority of these came under federal jurisdiction.[22] In any case, William Pegg, the League's district secretary, called a meeting in July 1933, where the business of constructing a charter and constitution took place. The aims of the Relief Camp Workers' Union:

> To organize all relief camp workers into the Union. To promote and lead the struggles of the relief camp workers for higher living standards. To rely upon the principles of Trade Unionism and the democratic decisions of the membership to forward our policy

of struggle and if need be, to use the form of strike if so decided. To actively support all measures that will give the right of franchise to all camp workers. To give assistance to all workers in their struggle for Non-Contributory Unemployment Insurance, adequate old age pensions, compensation for disability, sickness, etc. In the spirit of the Trade Union movement to resist all efforts to enforce our participation in Imperialist War.[23]

The RCWU was forthwith given a seat on the League's district council, and it had its own provincial organizer, a secretary, a treasurer and an educational department. Insofar as there was a national Union, the British Columbia chapter was far and away the most industrious and, in time, the most notorious. In fact, there is only sketchy evidence of a nation-wide organization. There would be talk of an inter-provincial conference of the Union in the summer of 1935, but the On-To-Ottawa Trek forced its cancellation.

With the creation of a headquarters staff in Vancouver, the identities and, to some extent, the personalities of RCWU members and functionaries become specific. The original secretary was a boilermaker named Malcolm MacLeod. With him in those first months were Ernest "Smokey" Cumber, Ronald Liversedge, John Matts, and Matt Shaw. All of these men had experience and skills which they now devoted to the Union. Liversedge, for example, had served in the British army in World War I, having enlisted at the age of sixteen in a Yorkshire regiment. Wounded at Ypres, he was given sustenance by a German prisoner of war who shared a canteen of cold coffee and various revolutionary precepts with the boy. A conversion of sorts took place on the edge of the battlefield. Soon after demobilization, Liversedge joined the Communist Party, emigrated to Australia, returned to England in time to take part in the 1926 General Strike, emigrated to Canada where, in 1933, in his early thirties, he found his vocation as a propagandist for the Union. There were many like Liversedge in those ranks: "returned men," veterans of the war who were not yet at peace.

These early organizers lived in rooming houses about Vancouver, but their business address was 52½ Cordova Street, near the Canadian Pacific Railway (CPR) station. There they secured a desk and a chair from the Single Men's Unemployment Association which had been around for two or three years and which functioned, in one respect, as did its counterparts across Canada, as a fraternal centre where a man might find help in obtaining a meal or a bed, or conversation, or assistance in tracking down a friend thought to be in the area. In return, he might be asked to help on a picket line or with the distribution of leaflets. Down and out as these men were, "a cheerful spirit pervaded all activity; comradeship was very real."

Malcolm MacLeod lived in a housekeeping room in a hotel on Dunlevy Avenue and it was here, more so than at 52½ Cordova Street, that union business was carried on. Organizers regularly reported to the modest room, slept there, as many as ten at a time, brought food purloined from the camps, once in a while even contributed money so MacLeod, who received no salary, could pay his rent. The hotel was owned by a Japanese émigré whose chief concern seems to have been for his two dollars a week and not for the stream of strangers who trooped through the lobby, looking for MacLeod.

There were two other workers' organizations with which the RCWU allied itself. The Canadian Labour Defence League (CLDL), an affiliate of the WUL though senior in its career, gave itself to the support and protection of workers under arrest. A national group with a large membership, the CLDL was led by Methodist minister, Winnipeg General Strike veteran, former Manitoba MLA and Communist Party stalwart A.E. Smith, known to all as "that grand Christian character."[24]

Also active in Vancouver as well as across the country was the Worker's Ex-Servicemen's League (WESL), clearly an alternative to the Canadian Legion, and a refuge for the "returned" men. Many relief camp workers belonged to the RCWU and to the two Leagues at the same time.

All three organizations contributed material to the *B.C. Workers News* and to the *Relief Camp Worker*. The *Relief Camp Worker*, in particular, found its way into every camp in the province, either by post or in the knapsacks of couriers. Its pages conveyed articles on camp conditions, on union meetings and programmes, on economics. Camp men sent in letters filled with gossip about the bad food, the inadequate first aid supplies, the makeshift bunkhouses or tent compounds, the busybody townspeople who tried to recruit them into militia units. John Matts drew stern cartoons for edification and amusement. "His workers were always depicted as upright, honest, clear-eyed, strong-jawed specimens of humanity and his police were always depicted as the neanderthal type in boy scout hats, clutching a big club in big hairy paws."[25]

The editor of the *Relief Camp Worker* was Ronald Liversedge of Yorkshire and Ypres. Under his guidance, union members scurried about Vancouver, borrowing typewriters, scrounging stencils, courting printers. The newspaper eventually had its own office on

West Hastings Street where police constables appeared regularly to pick up copies for their files.

And so the Relief Camp Workers' Union went to work recruiting members, documenting the inadequacies of the camp system, organizing protest. On the occasion of National Unemployment Day, 6 March 1934, the RCWU saw to it that copies of a petition were sent to provincial authorities from such camps as those at Kitchener, Yahk and Squamish, bearing the increasingly familiar demands for abolition of the Department of National Defence jurisdiction; recognition of camp committees; reinstatement of evicted men; adoption of the British Columbia minimum wage; adoption of full and free unemployment insurance; the use of porcelain dishware instead of tin. That same week, in obvious celebration of the holiday, more than six hundred camp workers from seven projects walked off their jobs. All were back in a day or so; none was discharged.[26]

When the union deemed other mail-in campaigns necessary, it had no difficulty in securing the signatures of colleagues from the Workers' Unity League or the Coastwise Longshoremen and Freight Handlers' Association or the Boilermakers and Shipbuilders' Union. Denunciation of Section 98 of the Criminal Code was a favourite pastime.

The harassment of camp policy and authority by work stoppage had become an obvious tactic: there were a hundred incidents in 1934. There does not seem to have been any attempt to prevent men from going into the camps, no picketing of the Dunsmuir office, for example, no propagandizing against registration.

On 12 August 1934, twelve union delegates met in secret near Salmon Arm to assess the achievements and the failures of the organization after a year of activity. The secretary of the gathering was Malcolm MacLeod who might be presumed to have set the agenda. The *Relief Camp Worker* subsequently published the minutes. Lest one think that these plain men conducted their affairs in a haphazard untutored manner, those minutes reveal very close attention to parliamentary procedure, to properly filed reports, to motions seconded.[27]

Prominent on the agenda was the matter of membership, which was very unstable. This could be attributed, in part, to the seasons, for men did leave camps to work in the orchards and fields when the weather was mild. But someone complained, even so, that "the younger men keep going and coming. Every payday brings a wholesale stampede down the line for the harvest and intermediate jungle points.''

This drain on human resources could be checked by more and better trained organizers who would know how to assemble and educate the camp men, forge them into a militant unit. But once "the agitational work had penetrated," the organizers had a real problem maintaining the men in the ranks of the union. The delegates at Salmon Arm agreed that this crucial lapse was the result of "leftism" among certain organizers and workers, that is to say, an arrogant display of ideology which violated the democratic ethic which the union sought to inculcate.

This distaste for "leftism" expressed by men who may be assumed to have been "left" in their orientation and sentiments has to be seen in the larger context of international communist strategy at that time. The proclamations of the Sixth Comintern of 1928 had become obsolete. The enemy was no longer just capitalism with its more or less reluctant supporters, the socialists, the trade unions, the liberals. With the confirmation of Adolph Hitler as Chancellor of Germany in 1933, the enemy was now fascism, the most drastic force in the fifteen-year-long counter-revolution directed at the Soviet Union and Communism. If the official message would not be forthcoming until the Seventh Comintern in 1935, still the shift had already been signalled. In the struggle against fascism, the Communists would willingly unite with all left and liberal elements to form a United Front. In British Columbia, that meant a coalition across the Communist Party, the CLDL, the WESL, the Co-operative Commonwealth Federation (CCF). The Salmon Arm committee put its imprimatur on the policy with its recommendation that the struggle against the relief camp system be integrated with the struggle against fascism. In subsequent issues of the *Relief Camp Worker*, announcements and advertisements inserted by the Canadian League Against War and Fascism, a premier organization within the United Front, affirmed this association.

The struggle against fascism may or may not have interested the average relief camp worker. If he joined the RCWU, it was most likely because he wanted to protest the camp conditions and to argue for work and wages programmes. The Salmon Arm meeting presumably appreciated this, for its delegates issued one more challenge to their colleagues: walk away from the camps in a massive demonstration and take their concerns and demands to Victoria and set them before the provincial government. Though this instruction was also published in the *Relief Camp Worker*, the authorities made no effort to prevent such an exodus.

And so, in the first week of December 1934, several hundred British Columbia camp workers descended on Vancouver to wait there while a committee of six took the ferry to Victoria. On 8 December, these six, led by a Saskatchewan youth named Matt Shaw, who was the Union's new secretary, obtained an audience with Premier T. Dufferin Pattullo, a considerable person in the Canadian Liberal Party. Although Premier Pattullo was the author of a "little New Deal" for British Columbia, the contradictions between philosophy and action became painfully clear when he faced Shaw. Pattullo told Shaw that he did support a work and wages policy, but he also asserted that the province had no money to implement this policy. That was that. On the other hand, he would look into the allegation that the names of camp men evicted had been placed on a "black list" so that subsequent registration would be denied them. Pattullo also agreed to authorize the issue of scrip and to provide lodging for the strikers waiting in Vancouver. Finally, he would recommend to Ottawa that a commission of inquiry be formed to appraise the camps in British Columbia.[29]

If the Shaw delegation came away only slightly mollified, Prime Minister Bennett read the Premier's concessions as foolish inconsistency. The grant of scrip and lodging positively encouraged the men to opt for short-term residence in the city. Moreover, there was absolutely no need for a commission of inquiry since the public could visit the camps anytime it wanted or needed to. This exchange may be said to mark the first volley in a quarrel between Pattullo and Bennett that would grow and expand in intensity and bitterness through the winter and spring of 1935.[29]

In any case, the walkout collapsed quickly due to poor organization and sour weather. Most, if not all of the strikers, went back to the camps although they took their time about it. The week ending 11 January 1935 saw 555 men shipped out, the week of 18 January another 393, inordinately high figures even for a winter month.[30] Matt Shaw came away from the experience thinking that "We had been kicked around in this political football game which the civic and provincial and federal authorities had been playing."[31]

The federal authority, Mr. Bennett, now turned his attention away from the particulars of British Columbia to the situation of the country as a whole. In an astonishing series of radio broadcasts early in 1935, the Prime Minister proposed "to nail the flag of progress to the masthead," to assert a programme of reform "and in my mind, reform means government intervention. It means government control and regulation. It means the end of *laissez faire.*" On the matter of unemployment, "if the worker is able and willing to work, but can get no work, provision must be made for his security in a decent way. By this, I do not mean the dole. The dole is a rotten thing."[32]

No doubt, many Canadians thought Mr. Bennett was quite sincere. No doubt many thought he was only preparing for the general election which he must call that year. The relief camp men have left no record of their reaction to those broadcasts, though quite a few must have listened to one or more of them since the camps usually had radios provided for recreation.

In February, the *Relief Camp Worker* announced the creation of five Union sub-districts in British Columbia by which recruitment and reorganization might be expedited: Salmon Arm, Revelstoke, Nelson, Princeton and Hope. By the end of that month, those sub-districts had identified delegates and issues that would be sent forward to a conference to be held at Kamloops on 10 March. That assembly, it was understood, would plan another strike for the spring season. This time, the organization would be in place, the weather bountiful. [33]

Two
The April 4 Walk-out

"Isn't that a pessimistic view to take of it?"
— *Regina Riot Inquiry Commissioner*

The Kamloops meeting had been called by the district organizer for the Workers' Unity League, Arthur Herbert Evans, nick-named "Slim." Although, for the most part, Evans kept in the background throughout that weekend, there was little question that he was the guiding force. "I was elected not as a member of the Workers' Unity League but simply because that conglomeration of people assembled there wanted a leader...because in the opinion of the workers I had more experience than most of them...."[1] More experience indeed. A month shy of his forty-second birthday, Evans had spent twenty years in the radical labour movements of Canada and the United States. In 1935, Slim Evans was one of the best known labour organizers in Western Canada.

Born of Anglo-Irish parents in Toronto in 1893, Evans apprenticed as a carpenter, a craft to which he returned on and off over his lifetime. He left home between ages nineteen and twenty, drifted west and then south into the United States, where he seems to have made his first formal commitment to labour struggles by joining the Industrial Workers of the World in 1912. That same year, Evans was arrested in Kansas City for, as he put it, reading the Declaration of Independence at a meeting about free speech, one of the Wobblies' perennial interests. He received a three-year sentence, one year of which he served. In 1913, after a saunter across the Dakotas and Montana, Evans arrived in the Ludlow, Colorado, area, where he took part in the quarrel between miners and mine operators which erupted into one of the deadliest labour battles in American history. From October 1913 through April 1914, miners and militia fought it out in a series of skirmishes and pitched gunfights which took many lives, including those of miners' families, and injured countless others. At some point, Evans has said, he was struck by machine gun bullets. "How did I get in the way of the machine gun bullets? I do not know how I got in the way. They got in my way." One bullet struck a shin bone and inflicted a wound which never quite healed. Evans's limp was noticeable. It is unlikely that Evans crossed paths with young William Lyon Mackenzie King who had come into the employ of the Rockefeller family at this time and who visited Ludlow after the disasters.

21

Once recovered, Evans remained in the northwest of the United States, still engaged in labour organization, until 1916 when he returned to Canada where he found occasional work as a carpenter and as a miner. With the creation of the One Big Union (OBU) in 1919, Evans finally found his vocation as a union official, for a time as OBU district secretary of the coal mining department in Alberta and eastern British Columbia and then as business agent for the Drumheller Valley United Mine Workers. But the parent union, the United Mine Workers of America, brought charges against Evans in 1923 for "fraudulent conversion" of members' dues totalling $2,554.10, which, in fact, Evans had kept for local relief instead of sending the funds to the international headquarters. An unrepentant Evans skipped bail and fled to Seattle where he was soon apprehended. He was returned to Canada and spent a year in the penitentiary at Prince Albert.

Married since 1920 to a miner's daughter, Ethel Jane Hawkins, Evans next moved to Vancouver where he took up work as a carpenter, became active in carpenters' unions thereabouts and, in 1926, joined the Communist Party of Canada. "Well, I have been a Communist much longer than I have been in the Communist Party."[3] From Vancouver, Evans watched events to the East: the arrest of Party leaders in 1931, the Estevan strike later that same year. In 1932, the Workers' Unity League named him its British Columbia district organizer, in effect, a transfer from a similar job he had held with the National Unemployed Workers' Association which the League had helped form. Evans received no pay for this work; his travel expenses were reimbursed from collections taken up at the numerous meetings he visited around the province. This may be the reason why, on 9 March 1932, the Department of Relief for the City of Vancouver opened File E-574 for Arthur Herbert Evans.[4]

At the time he went on relief, Evans indicated that his last employment had been on odd jobs about the city and that he owned a house at 27 East Forty-second Avenue, valued at four thousand dollars and bearing a fifteen hundred dollar mortgage. (The case workers immediately recognized the applicant as "the Communist leader.") Thereafter, until late September, Ethel Evans, and not her husband, made occasional applications for relief and for groceries. On 12 July, she acknowledged that Evans had disappeared. "She does not know where he is and has heard nothing from him." This situation prevailed until 20 September when an irate and "very belligerent" Arthur Evans appeared in the relief office, complaining of visits to his wife by the staff checking on his absence. He was advised that he should have written his wife, upon which Evans "stated that it was none of [their] business."

Whether he had spent the summer looking for work or, what is more likely, in the field in behalf of the WUL, in November Evans accepted an invitation from Princeton miners to set up a local of the Mine Workers' Union of Canada, a League affiliate, to help combat unjust policies and manoeuvers of the coal operators. Evans was promptly arrested under the notorious Section 98 of the Criminal Code which forbade membership in an unlawful organization, among other things. After some weeks, he was released on ten thousand dollars bail and his trial set for June 1933. From then on, Evans apparently devoted much of his time to gathering support for his defence. In April 1933 he was kidnapped from a friend's home in Tulameen by an angry squad of vigilantes who put him on a train for Vancouver with the expected warning not to return. Evans detrained at Mission and went right back to Princeton where he was rearrested and thrown in jail.

By this time, the Vancouver relief office had reached the conclusion that Evans was exploiting their good services to care for his family while he "engaged in propaganda work." Nonetheless, Mrs. Evans continued to make periodic, though by no means regular, inquiries about relief which seem not to have been rejected. In July, she, too, "disappeared" but returned a month later explaining that she had been with her dying mother in Drumheller.

Arthur Evans was sentenced to a year in Oakalla Prison on 16 September 1933 and, a day or two later, Ethel Evans checked in to the relief office where a file was then opened in her name. In January 1934 she reported that she had been given a foreclosure notice on the property at 27 East Forty-second Avenue, but she was also told that the relief office would contribute five dollars a month plus 20 percent of the asking price for another dwelling. Then, on 24 April, because she had not yet found an alternative, a case worker went to Mrs. Evans's house "accompanied by Sheriff Cochrane and Deputy Sheriff Robertson who had protection of the Vancouver City Police while they removed applicant's goods and chattels" into the street.

The reason the police turned up, more than likely, was that for the past month a picket had occupied the front porch, steps and lawn of the Evans's home, men conscripted, no doubt, from 52½ Cordova Street. There is a photograph surviving of this detail: some thirty-five men posed for the camera, one holding up a sign which says: "Picket Line on Comrade Evans' Home." But the guards made no protest when the sheriffs arrived. "Everything was orderly."[5]

Mrs. Evans continued to argue with the relief office about another dwelling although no resolution is evident in the office's files. On 26 June 1934 she reported that her husband would not be released from prison until the end of the year.

Evans emerged from his third incarceration in mid-December, just as the walk-out had collapsed in Victoria and Vancouver. He promptly returned to his duties with the WUL and so he came to Kamloops.

There Arthur Evans stood, a tall, extremely slender man with light brown hair parted in the middle, grey eyes, a notably square, almost forbidding jaw; he was clad in the carpenters' overalls which he habitually wore. Evans conducted himself with a dignified bearing, a gentleman, one follower thought,[6] "a quiet spoken man" reported a Vancouver relief officer.[7] But when called upon to speak for the cause of labour, Evans drew from an intense, profound anger, a class-hatred impeccable in its credentials and guaranteed to strike awe:

> I owe allegiance to this country but not to parasites who own this country at the present time. . .those that own the mills, mines and factories and all the good things of life that are in this country. . .I am very patriotic to this country. I want to see it become a beautiful place for people to live in, but not for those men that take these utilities and close them up, who close up mills and factories, and have elevators filled with food stuff to overflowing with every good thing, and denying the possibilities of sharing in these good things to the people who are not given work.[8]

And now the Kamloops conference.[9] First, greetings came from RCWU secretary, Ernest "Smokey" Cumber, who had replaced Matt Shaw after the December strike. Under Cumber's direction and according to parliamentary procedure, the delegates elected James "Red" Walsh as permanent chairman, Gerry Tellier also known as Winters, as recording secretary, and Charles Sands, whose real name was Walthers, as sergeant at arms. The minutes of the meeting do not indicate any other candidates or any opposition to this slate.

Evans presented greetings from the WUL as did friendly observers from the CLDL and the Young Communist League (YCL). Then Cumber made his report.

There were, at that time, about one thousand RCWU members in the province. Moreover, contacts were being established across the country so that an inter-provincial conference could be held that summer. "Good prospects for the future..." Next, the sub-districts came forward to testify.

Salmon Arm: Six camps organized. "...a strike was absolutely essential to hold the men in ranks...it should be called before the men answered the call of spring."

Revelstoke: Number 501B has a firm base in organization: however, its storekeeper "went south with $200 and so they are cutting down on the rations." There are 115 men in that one camp, the largest in the sub-districts. Three Mile West Camp is making good progress in recruitment.

Nelson: Though some camps are still weak, progress is being made. Mail contacts are good.

Hope: Uneven success but progressing. An economics class has been established.

Princeton: The men are very militant with good reason because the area has been noted for its "fascist" tendencies i.e. in the communities. Federal mail to camp workers is being opened so the men have to create an inter-camp communications system.

All in all, these were not very encouraging reports to a gathering which was intent on a massive strike from those very camps. Obviously, the organizing had not gone forward over the previous months. Or at least, it had succeeded only in the Revelstoke and Princeton units.

The reports were accepted, however, and the first day's meeting ended with greetings from two RCWU men who had just arrived from Alberta, penniless but enthusiastic.

The next morning, 11 March, Arthur Evans conveyed his belief that a strike was necessary and that, the assembly willing, it should take place on 4 April, three days after payday, so that each man would have some money to take along. Their destination: Vancouver.

Red Walsh resumed the chair, guiding the discussion of numbers, transportation, exit routes, supplies, the call for assistance from the CLDL, the YCL, the WESL and the many friends in Vancouver where the camp men would reassemble: fraternal clubs, civic groups, churches, trade unions, ethnic halls. The camp men must be fitted out, clothing repaired or replaced somehow, provisions secreted from the foremen. It was understood that many men would not walk out or, at least, would not want to. Pressure must be brought to bear. "Say a hundred men were in a camp and sixty wanted to go and they were the loudest. The rest went along." The younger men were generally enthralled with the idea. "We couldn't care less where we were." But there were quite a few older fellows to be considered: the miners and trappers and loggers who used the camps for bases. These would be discouraged from joining up.

In the midst of this protracted discussion, Charles Sands, the sergeant at arms, felt obliged to speak up. Sands was a fifty-two-year-old veteran of German communist movements, with four years' residence in Canada. Six feet four inches tall, at two hundred pounds, with a full red face, brown hair and eyes, Sands walked in a distinct slouch. This posture, it was said, was intended to hide his height, which seemed like a good idea for a revolutionary on the move. Sands tended to stutter when he was excited and now, suddenly, he burst forth to the amusement of the men gathered there who knew that Sands regularly invoked some article of radical testament by which a tactic might be enriched. A favourite text was A. Lozofsky's *The World Economic Crisis: Strike Struggles and the Tasks of the Revolutionary Trade Union Movement.* The pamphlet was known to many of the delegates, but Walsh had never heard of it or its author.

As Walsh spoke to the gathering, Sands began yelling out: "What of Lozofsky? What of Lozofsky?" Walsh shrugged off the question, but Sands persisted. "Well, Comrade Walsh, in this or that situation, Comrade Lozofsky says we should do this or that. And again." Until Walsh whirled on him and screamed back, "Comrade Sands, if Lozofsky knows so goddamn much, why the hell isn't he here speaking for himself!"

The men broke out in a roar of laughter, fuelled as well, by the sight of the diminutive Walsh, scarcely five feet five inches tall, staring down the giant Sands.

Walsh would later tell this story on himself, no doubt because he had a salty, unassuming sense of humour. He had other virtues as well. In his early twenties that year, as a youth Walsh had come from Ireland to the United States with two brothers who found work on New York City building construction. After he lost one then the other brother in falls from skyscrapers, Walsh left for western Canada where he caught on with the unemployed movements. A man of great intelligence, charm and stamina, not to say wit, Walsh became one of the leaders of the expedition in the weeks and months to come, his rich baritone brogue itself a legend.

The final action taken at the Kamloops conference involved the adoption of a set of demands which derived from those first given to Prime Minister Bennett at the Workers' Economic Conference in 1932 and those provided Premier Pattullo in December 1934: (1) that work with wages be instituted at a minimum of 50¢ per hour for unskilled workers and trade union rates for skilled labour on the basis of a six-hour day, a five-day week with a minimum of twenty work days per month; (2) that all workers in the camps be covered by the Compensation Act and that adequate first aid supplies be carried on the jobs at all times; (3) that the National Defence and all military control with the system of blacklisting be abolished; (4) that democratically elected committees be recognized in every camp; (5) that there be instituted a system of noncontributory unemployment insurance; (6) that all workers be given their democratic right to vote; (7) that Section 98 of the Criminal Code, Sections 41 and 42 of the Immigration Act and all vagrancy laws and anti-working class laws be repealed.

Publicized constantly over the next three months, these demands would be presented by Evans to Prime Minister Bennett in a stormy interview that marked the climax of the On-to-Ottawa Trek.

The Kamloops conference now moved to adjournment with a public rally. A collection of $2.42 was secured and turned over to the two Alberta men to help them make their way across the mountains.

The meeting had been convened in secrecy but a public rally at its close suggested that secrecy was no longer required. In fact, the *Relief Camp Worker,* in its 19 March issue, published the minutes of the sessions along with a call to all union members to take part.

More than likely, a copy of that newspaper formed part of the report turned in on 22 March to Colonel W.W. Foster, Chief Constable of the Vancouver City Police Department, by an informant lodged in the camps.

> *Twelve camps organized near Hope. Men out to raise hell. Don't underestimate. From all camps, men to march to Vancouver on April 4, 5, 6 for mass meeting to be held on April 7. A number of good agitators leaving Vancouver in next two weeks to prepare. Burnaby unemployed and longshoremen and loggers to join. Men may burn camps when they leave. Tim Buck arrives in area March 23. Speaks Vancouver March 28. Hold meeting in area and stay for a few weeks. Tom Carr and others recently released from Kingston are with him. Also Sam Carr. Difficult period in April. Governor General in province. Strikes in several areas.*[10]

There is more to be said about the presence of undercover agents in the ranks of the camp workers, but analysis of this appraisal on the eve of the strike is in order. First, the men were not exactly out to raise hell since to do so would jeopardize the whole expedition. Discipline and restraint were the orders of the day. In this way, the men could gain and keep the esteem of the public.

Tim Buck did give a speech in Vancouver that month but he did not take part in strike matters, then or later, except as a publicist of sorts. Yes, the Governor General was in the province but then everybody knew that. There was no general policy about burning the camps since to do so would have meant immediate arrest. There is no evidence that a large contingent from Burnaby enlisted. But, most certainly, April would be a difficult period.

General E.C. Ashton of the Eleventh Military District visited Premier Pattullo on 25 March to brief him on the nature and magnitude of the forthcoming "general disturbance." Pattullo replied that there was a lot of popular support for the men and reiterated his wish that a commission of inquiry be set in motion at the federal level.[11] Later that day, Pattullo wired Ottawa of his concern and recommendation. Prime Minister Bennett, ill from a respiratory affliction which led to a mild stroke, cerebral ischemia, had turned over his office to Minister Without Portfolio, Sir George Perley. The senior Tory in Canada was down and out for weeks and only completely recuperated while on a state visit to England for the Silver Jubilee in late April. He would not return to the floor of the House of Commons until 20 May. As a consequence, the Vancouver relief camp strike, through most of its history, would be monitored in Ottawa by Perley, McNaughton, Grote Stirling in the Department of National Defence and W.A. Gordon in the Department of Labour.

Thus, the first exchange between Pattullo and Perley. Pattullo: "Citizens are generally sympathetic...as they believe system devastating both to morale and character." Again, the premier pleaded for a commission of inquiry. And more: "...it is incomprehensible that your Government will not make provision so that these men can be put to work on a basis of reasonable wages." Give us the money, Pattullo concluded, and we will do the work, that is, take care of the unemployed, carry out public works projects and thus "remove young men from invidious environment and improve morale generally."[12]

Perley promptly replied that citizens of British Columbia could visit the camps at any time to make their evaluations and publish whatever advice or recommendations they saw fit. Then Sir George sought to remind Pattullo that

> constitutional duty of maintaining law and order in B.C. rests with your government. If you state you are unable to discharge your constitutional obligations and seek Federal assistance, it will be furnished when requested as by law provided.[13]

His gorge really up, Pattullo fired back this message on 27 March. The gauntlet was thrown down.

If your government is under impression that every Ukaz issued by your government is accepted by the public generally, your government is labouring under grave delusion... Your government is facing adverse public opinion under a system which is generally and I think properly condemned. It seems almost useless to continue this correspondence in light of your wires but officers in your service know seriousness of conditions and if there is riot, bloodshed and destruction of property, responsibility will rest upon your government.[14]

By "officers in your service," Pattullo presumably meant General Ashton and his associates, though Ashton did not, by any stretch of the imagination, endorse Pattullo's requests or his invective.

Two days later, Grote Stirling, Minister of National Defence, rose in the House of Commons, flourished a copy of the 19 March edition of the *Relief Camp Worker*, and read aloud these words: "Let us go forward in the coming struggle with the only weapon that gets results, that is, organized militant action!" Stirling then said: "I think that is sufficient evidence to demonstrate that we are face to face with a definite organization of men who are desirous of raising trouble so considerable that it may be handled but with difficulty."[15]

In the interval between 10 March and 4 April, the RCWU went about the business of preparing for the walk-out. As Chief Constable Foster's agent predicted, a number of "good agitators" left Vancouver and moved inland to meet with local organizers. Another cadre remained behind, arranging sleeping quarters, drafting publicity, sounding out friends and acquaintances for their support. Matt Shaw, for example, made it his special task to refreshen the memories of citizens about the December evictions and strike and the promise of the commission of inquiry.[16]

Up country, camp workers worked discreetly to facilitate the exit. Along roads leading to top camps, trees were undercut so that they might be easily shoved across the lanes to prevent pursuit. Old tents were dragged into the bush and cut up and sections reserved for knapsacks. Men scrutinized freight and passenger train schedules and scouted likely points for hauling logs and ties across tracks in case they had to force trains to stop for them.

Some of the old miners who had made the camps their homes were told that they had better not come. One fellow we called "Tin Pan Bill" said, "No, I'm coming with the kids." Bill had a pack. He was short and I swear his pack was taller than he was. He had everything in it: gold, all kinds of junk he'd gathered over the years. He never dumped it out; he just kept putting things in. He would be given new underwear and he'd

feel it was too much trouble to put it on so he'd shove it in
his pack. When he got into town, a couple of young fellows who
were looking after him, got him to a hotel to take a shower and
to change his underwear.[17]

The movement from the camps into Vancouver took a few hours
or it took several days, depending on the distance travelled and
the degree of dispatch with which a group could find transportation.
The first contingent to arrive hurried down from Squamish on 2
April. But for most, the ride in was tiring and slow. The three
hundred or so men from the Revelstoke area, those numbers
dominated by very young, very loyal and very excited fellows, rode
a freight through rain and snow, "a miserable bloody trip" that
still did not daunt them.[18]

A week before the walk-out, Red Walsh left Princeton armed with
a prospector's license, a loaf of bread and some bacon parts in his
pack, bound for the line of camps that stretched north towards
Merritt. After a day of hitchhiking, Walsh quit the road at a point
midway between two camps, struck overland for a half a mile until
he found a bare knoll on which he built a signal fire. One striker
who joined Walsh minutes later was Irven Schwartz who
remembers that Walsh

stood there and just spread his hands out and said in his way
of talking, he had a distinct "bronx" accent, "All right, in
the morning we pull the pin and giv'em the works."

Walsh walked ahead to the top camp where he found that the
men had already cut telephone lines and had thrown trees across
the road. Apparently, the foreman had turned the few trucks over
to the strikers: "If I say no, you'll take them anyway." There
weren't enough, though, so Walsh ordered the packs and bedrolls
stored in these and then began the long walk to Princeton, taking
out camp men as he passed by. According to Nels Madsen, one
of the "foreigners" in the camps, by the time the column reached
Princeton, it contained several hundred men who tramped along
four abreast.[19]

In Princeton, Walsh billeted his men, over four hundred now,
in the Legion and Community Halls, threw pickets around taverns
and brothels and set about catching a train. The Princeton
newspaper apparently erupted the next morning with an attack
on the strikers who, its editor thought, were led by Communists.
In high dudgeon, Walsh went to the man and threatened to picket
his business unless he published a retraction. "We'd pull the thing
down around his ears, you know. He wrote a kind of apology the
next day, but he didn't go all the way."

Walsh was approached by the madam of a brothel who told him that one of the camp workers was in attendance. In fact, he was a cook from a nearby camp. Walsh found out that the man had not gone on the strike and so told the madam who threw the miscreant out.[20]

The *Relief Camp Worker* carried on 12 April an article dated the fifth and sent from Princeton by Walsh, in which he described the attempt there of "two or three agents of the Bosses...to create dissension and confusion in our ranks by furnishing booze in order to create quarrels." To thwart such efforts and to alert the townspeople to the strikers' desire for restraint, Walsh circulated a poster castigating the two agents, one of whom was called "Salvation Jim," and calling attention to the "solidarity and discipline that has been evidenced by us during our stay in Princeton."[21]

Finally, a freight pulled in (railway ties were draped across the tracks for insurance) and the strikers from Princeton climbed aboard. The fact that some of the cars had recently carried fertilizer seemed not to matter. Off they went, north to Merritt and beyond to the crossing of the Thompson River at Spence's Bridge. There the train paused while the men filed into the village for a quick meal. When the food ran out, Bill Hammill, a baker, now a camp worker and always a pretty good scrounger, accepted a ride in a police car to Lytton where he secured extra provisions. The train paused again at Ruby Creek, a few miles from Hope, where the men waited for a seaboard train to pick them up. Hammill formed a food committee which borrowed boats and chugged back and forth across the river to Hope for food and tobacco.[22]

At Coquitlam, the men spent a few hours sleeping in a round house. Before dawn, they mounted for the last lap, police officers shining their flashlights on the train's ladders so the men could climb in safety. In this way, the men from Princeton went on strike.

The last to arrive in Vancouver were sixty-four men from Nelson who were taken off a freight for trespassing and thrown in jail. One fellow scrawled on his cell wall: "In memory of 64 camp workers" and when the guards came to quarrel about this, one took a pail of slops in the face.[23]

General Ashton's office had been busy with its own preparations for the walk-out. Camp foremen were warned that the strike was organized by subversive elements who might just burn the camps behind them. "Certain loyal camp personnel" were hired as "special watchmen" at ten dollars a month to guard stores left behind. An inventory of "forces available in Vancouver for special emergency duty" counted 325 municipal police, special reserves and provincial police.[24]

Ottawa, in a gesture that was simply too late, not to say hypocritical, on 28 March authorized an order in council which created a commission of inquiry into the conditions of the British Columbia camps, this coming one day after Perley's wire to Pattullo in which he urged that any citizen could appraise the camps! The commission consisted of the Honourable W.A. MacDonald, a retired provincial supreme court justice; C.T. McHattie, vice-president of Gault Bros. Ltd.; and the Reverend Edwin Braden, pastor of the Ryerson United Church in Vancouver.[25] The first testimony was taken by the MacDonald Commission on 4 April from General Ashton who rationalized the administration of the camps by the Department of National Defence and who also commented on the notorious blacklist. "Under our regulations when a man is discharged for cause, his name has to be reported and these men are listed under various heads e.g. refusing work, continual trouble making, agitating. . . ." A year before, Ashton added, this policy had been revised so that a man could be readmitted if it was felt that he would not create further disturbance.[26]

Among the camp workers interviewed that first day was eighteen-year-old Vincent LeGrandeur, a two-year veteran of Salmon Arm, who testified to the presence of fourteen-year-old boys: "Their voices hadn't even broken." One could hear them "squeaking" clear across the campsite.[27]

The weather in Vancouver that first week of April 1935 was sunny and temperate, just above freezing at night to mid-50s in the afternoons. Spring was on the way. The *Sun* and the *Daily Province* carried advertisements for winter wardrobe sales as well as news and advice about gardening. The Athletic Park Baseball League, four teams in all, began its workouts. Best of all, Lord Bessborough, the Governor General, and his family, were in Victoria and would soon come to Vancouver for a farewell visit before their return to England.

In Vancouver newspapers that week, one followed the adventures and antics of "Apple Annie," "Alley Oop," "Tailspin Tommy" and "Out Our Way." One listened on the radio to the Biltmore Hotel Dance Band, "Myrt and Marge," "Amos 'n' Andy" and "Kate Smith's Star Review." Shirley Temple appeared in "The Little Colonel" at the Capitol, Will Rogers in "Life Begins at Forty" at the Orpheum, Clark Gable and Claudette Colbert in "It Happened One Night" at the Dominion, and Fred Astaire and Ginger Rogers in "The Gay Divorcee" at the Stanley.

If one eschewed such frivolity, he might prefer to hear Tim Buck speak at the Arena before a crowd of eight thousand. "In the present crisis, there are two things for the working classes...submit to fascist control or put up a struggle for a Soviet Union in Canada."[28] Buck became passionate as he described the riot at Kingston Penitentiary during which, he charged, an attempt was made on his life by guards who clustered on the tier below his and shot up into his cell. Buck saw this coming and threw himself to the floor which is why he could be in Vancouver that week. A mild-mannered though self-assured man, Buck led the audience in cheers as the Young Pioneers marched in behind a drum band. And then he introduced Smokey Cumber, the RCWU secretary, who announced the 4 April walk-out.

Two municipal officers must now be introduced; it was their responsibility to cope with the relief camp strikers over the next two months. The mayor of Vancouver that spring, and he had been mayor for just a few weeks, was Gerald McGeer, a lively, ambitious, rather original politician. At the moment, Mayor McGeer, a Liberal, was in the East, attending a Dominion Mayors conference and, thereafter, accepting speaking engagements where he announced that he was considering running for Parliament in the autumn general election. Mayor McGeer would prefer a British Columbia seat "but if necessary I am sure I would have no difficulty in getting a seat either in Alberta or Ontario."[29] McGeer would soon be back in Vancouver to welcome Lord Bessborough.

The other prominent city authority who figures in this story was Colonel W.W. Foster, Chief Constable. Colonel Foster was a long-time veteran of militia affairs in the province and a member of the Distinguished Service Order for his heroism in World War I. A man of dignity, sound judgement and administrative skill, he and his force sought and usually succeeded in matching the restraint and discipline which Arthur Evans encouraged among his men.

The relief camp men, in time, came to an appreciation of McGeer and Foster which, while not exactly esteem, was certainly a recognition that the two did hold the line. The same day the trek departed for Ottawa, these officials turned to deal with a longshoremen's walk-out.

On 5 April, the first delegation of camp strikers to seek out city authorities found Colonel Foster. Accompanying Matt Shaw were Bill Davis and Gerry Winters, recording secretary at the Kamloops conference, whose real name was Tellier and whose brother, Lou, also on strike from Revelstoke, bore the *nom de guerre*, Summers. The Telliers' fond hope, of course, was to be arrested together so they could tell the constables that they were Summers and Winters and, by golly, we're brothers![30]

Foster told the trio, "I don't think any intelligent citizen will not agree that a system which offers to young men such as yourselves no hope for any future, but life in a camp is entirely wrong." But Foster made it clear that the provision of food and shelter was not Vancouver's responsibility. The sympathy and the caution were characteristic of Foster's attitude towards the strikers for the most part.[31]

Behind Shaw, Davis and Winters, an elaborate organization of camp men and townspeople began to settle into place in that first week. This persisted throughout the strikers' stay in Vancouver and, in a modified version, accompanied the On-to-Ottawa Trek. On 9 April, an intelligence report to Foster indicated that fourteen hundred strike cards had been issued to the camp men — that is, cards which gave the men individual identification numbers, group numbers and division numbers. This same report cited the strike headquarters' assertion that there would be eighteen hundred strikers in the city very soon. [32] In those early days, there may have been as many as eighteen hundred present but that figure diminished as the weeks went by, crept by, actually, as the slow pace of negotiations, the growing warmth of the weather, prompted young men "to answer the call of spring."

The relief camp strikers were met by Arthur Evans and by Perry Hilton, a burly cook who had been chiefly responsible for organizing the reception.[33] Working with the basic unit of a bunk-house group of a dozen or fifteen men, Evans fashioned a series of four "divisions" of about four hundred men each. These divisions appear to have been created around the more populous sub-districts of the RCWU, with the Revelstoke Crowd forming one and the Princeton 400 another. One may have been deliberately filled with men on the black-list, though if this was the case, they would not have been in the camps at this time, but already in Vancouver on the streets.

The divisions were numbered 1 through 4 and each had its own headquarters here and there along Hastings and Cordova Streets, in the Ukrainian Labour Temple, in the Orange Hall, in the east end of downtown Vancouver, near the railyards, near the Victory Cenotaph. Each division had a chairman who served as general administrative officer; a captain or marshal who took the men into the street when ordered and who looked after discipline; and a secretary. Each division appointed a finance committee which issued meal tickets along with a bed ticket, if needed, at the daily meetings held around 1:30 P.M. Each division also boasted a publicity committee, a food committee responsible for collecting and dispersing donated goods; a card committee and a bumming committee which solicited funds from the citizenry.

Where did fifteen hundred men sleep and eat? Soon after the strikers settled in, an undercover agent described the premises at 318 Cordova Street, whether an entire building or a suite of rooms, is not clear, in which as many as two hundred men slept: "All using one wash basin and one toilet. This is not sanitary and should be locked up by the Health Department."[34] Doubtless, men slept in similar large congregations at labour temples, and individually in boarding houses, cheap hotels and even in private homes with friends and relatives.

Meals were taken at a myriad of small cafés which featured Chinese food and Canadian cuisine. The White Lunch chain was popular. The strikers received two fifteen-cent meal tickets each day which were funded by donations from the public. In the second month of the strike, those donations diminished and the men went hungry.

Each division meeting each day had an agenda of the sort described by Bill Davis:

> The agenda usually started with a report on the success of the strike or failure so far. Then the reports of the finance committee, so much money collected, so many tickets issued, so many meals taken, so much food and clothing collected, so many movie tickets issued.[35]

Someone or some group, perhaps friendly theatre managers, saw to it that the strikers got a break from the routine of agitation and demonstration. Admission, for the most part, was twenty-five cents before 6:00 p.m. and thirty-five cents thereafter.

As for the men who led these divisions, the chairmen and the captains, it appears that a variety of strikers took their turns in these posts, men who, for the most part, had already proven themselves as RCWU organizers or camp stalwarts. Red Walsh ran Division 1 for a time, but so did Perry Hilton. An enigmatic figure named Jack Thomas led Division 2. What is remembered about Thomas other than his leadership is that, sometime after the On-To-Ottawa Trek, Thomas hanged himself. Ernest Edwards was chairman of Division 3 but was replaced by Steve Brody and Robert "Doc" Savage. Division 3 was supposed to have been the unit with the blacklisted camp men in its ranks.[36]

The names of these division officers are thought to be their legal names. The same cannot be said for a considerable number of strikers in Vancouver that spring. Many had, for years, moved in and out of the camps and on the road bearing aliases. It was not uncommon for a man to drift across the country, sign into a camp, receive an issue of clothing, work for a month and then slip off, sell what gear he could, move to another province and start over again under another name. Presumably, some notorious organizers saw cause to change names. Possibly, young men changed names to spare their families any embarrassment should they be arrested. The Tellier brothers, Summers and Winters, took this step out of waggish humour. Charles Sands, né Walthers, must have had serious reasons from the moment he entered Canada. And though undercover agents often sent in long lists of names collected at meetings and rallies, particularly near the end of the strike, even these cannot be said to be reliable. The thousand strikers who left Vancouver in June and on the On-To-Ottawa Trek were later joined by another eight hundred or more as they approached and reached Regina. How then to prepare a roster? Still there is something poignant about their anonymity: Carl and Alfie and Dan and Burt and Mike and Red and Smokey and Matt and Slim and Tin Pan Bill.

If we can't know all their names, we can have a pretty good idea of how they appeared in the streets of Vancouver. Here is the description of Charles Sands who gained notoriety, and thus the interest of the police, because he was appointed captain of the pickets who watched the railyards for defecting strikers: "brown felt hat, crown full up; grey pullover Canadian jacket for a shirt; brown pullover coat with zipper fastenings; camp trousers, dark grey with reddish thread throughout; brown camp boots; grey camp socks."[37] Change that hat for a soft cap and the jacket for a dyed army coat and Bill Davis comes into focus. The strikers did not necessarily wear the most distinctive outer garments taken from the camps; many had kept their street wear and so they sported suits, jackets, hats of all sorts, cowboy hats, trainman's hats. With food and shelter more important, it can be assumed that they had little chance to shop for extras. That one basin at 318 Cordova Street no doubt saw service as a laundry.

Above the divisions was the Strike Committee, composed of about eighty men, fifteen or so from each of the divisions, plus Smokey Cumber, Evans and a few of his intimates. The Strike Committee served as a parliament from which came the major and many of the minor decisions regarding tactics and strategies. Divisions could refer ideas and requests to the Strike Committee. Its chairmanship rotated every two weeks or so with Red Walsh sitting there for a time, as did another veteran named Tony Martin, as did Tom Forkin, brother of WUL executive officer, Martin Forkin.

Matt Shaw, the best known of the relief camp men around Vancouver, took naturally to the chairmanship of the Publicity

Committee of the Strike Committee. In the spring of 1935, Shaw was aged twenty-five, with a seven-year tenure on the roads in the relief camps of Canada. He had been "Matt Shaw" for three years, born John Surdia in Saskatchewan. "But Matt is stronger with the newspaper apart from the fact that changing one's name usually gives one a new lease on life... it has a certain effect among people who may be prejudiced against names that sound foreign." Shaw came to the union out of a deep anger at never having had a chance to learn a skill and because the camps in British Columbia were so wretched. In Beaver 333, he found the water polluted, the food scarce, and a sick and unattended worker. Hot cakes were called "sweat pads." The men ate old "buffalo" meat. Months after the strike, Shaw sat through an interrogation by royal commissioners.

Shaw: The biggest quarrel was working for 20¢ a day, eight hours a day with nothing ahead of us but a blank wall, day in and day out...

Question: Isn't that a pessimistic view to take of it?

Shaw: In this camp, the food degenerated to such an extent that it was unfit for human consumption.

Shaw was everywhere during the Vancouver strike, a major force in the publicity unit where he wrote and published daily bulletins with a circulation that often reached twenty thousand. Quite a few of these were sent over to the North Shore and to the waterfront, but not specifically into the suburbs "because you couldn't expect hungry men to go to a distant district distributing leaflets over long hours."[38]

It was Shaw who gained an interview with Lord Bessborough whose private railway car stood in the Canadian National Railway (CNR) station. Shaw walked with the Governor General for ten minutes explaining the origins of the strike and soliciting from his companion a promise to convey the demands of the camp workers to Ottawa.[39]

Attached to the Publicity Committee was the Invitations Committee, charged with assigning speakers to address trade union, civic and other public gatherings, acquainting the audiences with the conditions which provoked the strike, summarizing day-to-day events and resolutions. Evans coached the speakers, "showing them how to present their case so our points would be brought out as fairly as possible." Bill Davis joined this committee and found himself fielding invitations not just to speak but to join a Vancouver family for a meal or to be their guest at the movies. Davis did not compose letters or speeches with particular facility "so they gave me the job of handling details, seeing that all the t's were crossed, the allocation of speakers, the reports and so on. . .[40]

Crucial to the success of the strike was the Action Committee, a collective of delegates from forty-two civic, fraternal, labour, political, ethnic, religious and educational groups who first met at the Lumberman's Hall on Hastings Street on 7 April. The CCF sat next to the YCL, the Socialist Party next to the CLDL, street car workers, longshoremen, the Mother's Council. This last group was one of the more remarkable of the era: a United Front of Vancouver women whose common devotion was to the correction of the social afflictions around them. It was this Mother's Council which dubbed the strikers ''Our Boys.''[41]

At the apex of this vast scheme, Evans located the Strategy Committee comprised of himself, Red Walsh, Doc Savage, Mike McCaulay who had brought Bill Davis down from Lac Seul, Stewart ''Paddy'' O'Neil, who was also with the WESL, and Gerry Winters. The Strategy Committee was, without doubt, *the* policy-making element within the strike.

The Vancouver relief camp strike was on. The organization in place. Evans and his men ready to launch their protest, despite the horoscope which had appeared in the *Sun* on 10 March, the first day of the Kamloops meeting where it all began:

It will be wisdom to stick closely to your own knitting and not attempt to untangle the snarls made by other hands.[42]

Three
April in Vancouver
"Now, won't you leave the store?"
— Deputy Chief Constable Alfred Grundy

All sorts of witnesses to the strike now began to come forward. The *Sun* and the *Daily Province,* of course, put their reporters into the streets. Interest groups monitored the progress of the demonstrations and negotiations. The authorities sought to keep abreast of events. What was often more important was the *anticipation* of events. What the authorities did not know by virtue of conversations with strike leaders, they endeavoured to learn from reports issued by undercover police officers and informants. The Vancouver City Police Department (VCPD) and "E" Division of the Royal Canadian Mounted Police (RCMP), located in Victoria, regularly received messages and briefings from these sources. The RCMP passed such material on to General Ashton's office which, several times a day, communicated information to Ottawa gleaned from these reports, as well as from the press and personal observation. Ashton does not appear to have had his own men in the ranks of the strikers, perhaps because no request for aid to the civil power had been forthcoming, either from the province or the municipal government. (For that matter, no such request was ever made throughout the history of the strike, the Trek or the Regina Riot.)

The reports that survive are of two kinds. One group was provided to "E" Division by a pair of RCMP constables, L.H.A. Graham, a six-year veteran of the force, who joined the CLDL, and Eric Kusch, four years in service, who dogged the strikers for two months and who wrote the actual narratives based on his and Graham's observations. Kusch's reports are neatly typed, coherent expositions set down on official forms, signed by Kusch and counter-signed by J.F. Phillips, Assistant Commissioner commanding "E" Division, who sent a copy to General Ashton. For the most part, the reports contain units of information characterizing daily activities and presented in an impersonal tone.[1]

The second group was sent to Colonel Foster's office. These reports are dated but unsigned, typed on plain paper. Their style is colloquial, abounding in incomplete sentences, drafted overall in an intimate voice not found in the RCMP documents. Recall the report received by Colonel Foster on 22 March: "Twelve camps organized near Hope..." The agent's "information" is actually a blend of alleged facts, speculation, advice and gossip. In pretty much the same format, it eventually made its way to General Ashton who passed it on to Ottawa, although this Foster to Ashton to Ottawa route does not seem to have been a regular connection. Was this agent the same fellow who wrote in a later message, ''. . . after a year with these fellows, mostly Eastern toughs, I know their minds pretty well''? Was he the same man who wrote "I was at a Communist meeting on Saturday night and am now a full fledged 'inside' member of the party''?[2]

There is no way of knowing the number of authors of the VCPD reports, that is how many agents and informants there were. There may have been only one in the camps prior to the strike, but it stands to reason that the Chief Constable had the manpower and the initiative to deploy more once the camp workers came into Vancouver, although it is conceivable that these turned their messages over to a colleague who then condensed them into daily digests, as Constable Kusch did.

Were these men actually police officers or were they paid informants — or volunteers, for that matter? The likelihood is that the reports were drafted by constables who drew on their own observations and experiences but who also had contact with informants, strikers who liked to gossip, dissidents who became increasingly impatient with the progress of the strike or, again, paid informants.[3] Among these last, if the word "paid" can be said to accommodate more than financial reward, there may have been a number of penitentiary parolees who were released on the condition that they infiltrate the strike and spy on the camp workers.

Both the RCMP and the city police, if indeed they were, provided descriptions of rallies, lists of names of strikers and associates, names of organizations implicated. There is no way of knowing whether any of them ever really influenced the course of the protest, even if one could exclaim that he was "a full fledged inside member of the party." Nor is it evident that any deliberately sought to or succeeded in compromising the strike, except in passing along information that might have enabled McGeer to better prepare for this or that manoeuvre or tactic. Two electrifying moments — the incursion into the Hudson's Bay Company store and the eight-hour-long occupation of the City Museum — went ahead as planned and took the authorities completely by surprise.

These reports will be used throughout this history, both for the information they contain, much of which can be confirmed by other sources such as daily newspapers and by the appearance of the same information in the two groups, and for the opinions and advice found there as well. Of course, an extensive *caveat* has to be appreciated with respect to this material.

As for the strikers themselves, they had always assumed the presence of "stool pigeons," knowing that their ranks were sufficiently fluid that penetration could scarcely be avoided.

Curiously, after all this attention to the strike in Vancouver, none of the governments, municipal, provincial or federal, sent agents with the Trek as it left Vancouver. Not until the march reached Moose Jaw did the RCMP slip an officer on board. More than one Trekker thought there were constables along from the outset but apparently this was not the case.

Most of the strikers had reached Vancouver by 8 April, with the group detained in Nelson showing up on the twelfth. A number of camp men took advantage of the exodus to go east over the mountains, never having intended to join the strike. In any case, there were more than enough to warrant the first rally on Tuesday, 9 April, at Cambie Street Grounds, a small park quite convenient to the Cordova/Hastings neighbourhood where the men lived. The Grounds would become the regular point of daily assembly for announcements, rallies and parades.

The principal effort of this maiden gathering was the dispatch of a telegram to Mayor McGeer at the suggestion of Dorothy Steeves, a CCFer, who had joined the Action Committee.

Mass meeting of 3,000 demand your government grant immediate relief to camp workers here. Demand secession [sic] police terror and guarantee safe arrival of all strikers to Vancouver.[4]

One might ask, what police terror? The only known incident of police intervention that involved arrest had occurred at Nelson. On the other hand, constables at Coquitlam had actually shone their flashlights on the ladders of the freight cars so that the Princeton group could ascend safely. This kind of inflammatory language was a permanent feature of protests such as this, signs of a hostility which needed little rationalization.

After the rally, the strikers and their audience of friendly townspeople walked from the Grounds to the City Hall and back again, in good order. Among them was a VCPD informant who reported later that the strikers had thus far collected about fourteen hundred dollars which, if issued at the rate of forty-five cents per day per striker — that is, two meal tickets and one bed ticket — would scarcely last another three days.[5] The *Sun* discovered that 841 meals were bought on Monday the eighth and 1,168 on Tuesday the ninth.[6] If these figures are accurate, and if each man is counted for two meals, then about one thousand had been fed across those two days and about six hundred dollars had been disbursed.

This money, for the most part, had been donated by longshoremen, $800; the crew of the motor vessel, *Unicana*, $10.25; the Women's Auxiliary of the Lumber Workers in Lake Cowichan, $25; *Piggly Wiggly*, $100. The United Association of Journeymen, Plumbers and Steamfitters called to say that "after endorsing a resolution, they are very sorry that their financial condition is such that they cannot contribute money."[7] Obviously, some major effort had to be made to replenish the strike treasury.

Meanwhile, Pattullo and McGeer exchanged information and advice, the nature of which indicated that while these two men might belong to the same party, they did not necessarily see eye to eye on every manoeuvre. McGeer sent along a pair of letters from the Dominion Mayors Conference, from which he had just returned, wherein mayors and premiers were urged to attend another conference in Montréal on 22 April to discuss the lack of response on the part of the federal government to the mayors' earlier request that they "take over the entire responsibility for unemployment relief." Pattullo replied that he had already approached Ottawa regarding unemployment, that negotiations were proceeding and that, moreover, "municipalities are creations of provincial legislatures." He, and not McGeer, would deal with Ottawa. In any case, Pattullo didn't think the meeting in Montréal would add any weight and so he would not take part. What the premier could have meant by negotiations with Ottawa is not clear since his exchange with Perley in late March certainly implied the opposite.[8]

Undaunted, McGeer next wired Grote Stirling, Minister of National Defence, urging that "all men in good standing leaving camps will be returned to camps immediately upon application." If they aren't sent back now, McGeer insisted, the strikers would "be provided with good reason for demand for subsistence pending their return," which return might take weeks. Stirling disagreed. Regular readmission procedures must be retained although the physical examination would be limited to examinations for infectious or contagious diseases. "Otherwise, we are faced with possible reentry to camps of men responsible for present disorder... Reentry without careful elimination of agitators would certainly result in disturbances on a greater scale at a later date which it is to your advantage as much as ours to avoid."

McGeer concluded this exchange with another plea for readmission pending the report from the MacDonald Commission and a lengthy call for federally funded public works projects that would, so far as Vancouver was concerned, "completely eliminate 75% of our unemployment troubles and pave the way for a restoration of prosperity."[9]

On Friday, 12 April, a little more than a week after the strike had begun, the first demonstration other than a parade in the streets took place. Foster's office had been alerted to the prospect of striker divisions marching into, through and around the larger department stores: Spencer's, Woodward's, Hudson's Bay. In fact, Spencer's was the only target for several hundred men who spent about one hour-and-a-half tramping up and down the aisles. But they departed peaceably, no damage done, no arrests made. Yet it was a harbinger.[10]

Foster also knew that Evans planned to send his men out on Saturday, 13 April, for a tag day, a license for which he had refused. Tag days were not unknown in the towns of Canada; organizations of all kinds regularly, though under permit, went into the streets to solicit donations for this or that charity enterprise. Without a license then, the relief camp men, at 7:00 A.M. on Saturday, moved out across Vancouver, Burnaby and New Westminster, hopping public transit where necessary, all wrapped up in paper streamers describing their cause, decorated tin cans held in one hand, and in the other, dozens of small paper tags with strings attached on which was printed "When do we eat?"

Ronald Liversedge, now with Division Three, recalls the excitement.

> The tag day headquarters was a large room up a flight of stairs on Hastings opposite the City Hall, which was then in the Holden Building. Here were the general staff with maps of all the city streets and intersections, lists of taggers, times of shifts, volunteer workers from the Vancouver unemployed preparing cans, girls ready to count the money as the full cans came in, blackboards on the walls to list the amounts of different periods during the day, the inevitable coffee makers and hovering above all the activity with a word here and a suggestion there, Slim Evans, with a happy smile. . . .[11]

Crucial to the success of the tag day were flying squads of strikers in borrowed cars who sped to this or that neighbourhood to replace taggers or to catch up full cans or to treat with police who, by and large, stayed out of the way.

When the counters back on Hastings found that four thousand dollars had been collected, Evans sent word for a pair of city constables to come and guard the money and, no doubt, to bear witness to the final moments of the day when $5,500 had spilled in and Arthur Evans capered about the office chanting "Moscow Gold! Moscow Gold!" The constables, amused or not, took receipt of the money and hauled it to the police station where it was kept until the following Monday when Evans opened a checking account in a bank, giving the dispersal of the funds thereafter to a colleague named Marsh, who kept the books.[12]

All in all, a grand, a gala day. When interviewed by the *Sun*, J. Grattan, a WESL delegate to the Action Committee, said:

> *We do not want to give the impression that this is any act of defiance to the authorities. The fact remains that men must be fed and there are 1,750 men in Vancouver who will have nothing to eat by tomorrow. We feel that we have the public with us and are using this means of appealing to them.*[13]

The next day, a Sunday, more than five thousand strikers and citizens marched across Vancouver to Stanley Park and then back to Cambie Street Grounds. In the front rank was a huge banner: WE THANK YOU FOR OVER $5,000/FORWARD TO VICTORY. *Sun* columnist Bob Bouchette wrote "If a crowd of homeless, hungry men by the sheer force of demonstration can attain their objectives, what is to stop the main body of the public from doing likewise?"[14] Of course, the strikers had not attained their objectives, not yet anyway.

Rather more quietly but with just as much good nature, the MacDonald Commission made its way about the relief camps, interviewing men who had stayed behind. The Commissioners heard complaints about cramped living quarters, about bad-tempered foremen, about the food, naturally, "eggs of dubious character." Once in a while, Chairman MacDonald waved camp officers out of the room so that witnesses wouldn't feel intimidated. In one camp, the men just sat and stared at the Commission and never uttered a word. Once, Arthur Evans bustled in waving a pair of khaki camp trousers made by Gault Bros. of which Commissioner McHattie was an executive. "Naturally" cried Evans, "he is partial to the camps." But McHattie was also Chairman of the Board of the Vancouver Welfare Association which is presumably why he was appointed in the first place.[15]

Much later, after the Trek, Evans stated quite simply that, yes, conditions of camp life varied, that small nuisances appeared here and there "but what we were mainly concerned with is the hopelessness of life. It is the hopelessness of life these people are kicking about, not the camp conditions."[16] Still, it was the camp conditions that the MacDonald Commission was charged with assessing, not such larger issues as hopelessness. Judge MacDonald commented early on that "A competent foreman and a good cook seem to be the main ingredients of a contented camp."[17]

The major newspapers in Vancouver, prompted by the success of the Tag Day, came forward with their first editorials on the strike. The *Sun:* "There are three main inequities of these relief camps that do violence to every human instinct: (1) absence of a regular wage and the feeling of individual well being that goes with a regular wage; (2) absence of feminine companionship; (3) the food . . . economic crisis or no economic crisis, men were not meant to live forever in camps that offer only a bare subsistence."[18]

The Daily Province professed sympathy, thought the strikers had made their point and now they should go back to the camps. The question for these men was not "When do we eat?" but "When do we earn our bread by our self-respecting labour?"

The papers also published letters from readers which, no doubt, were also inspired by the Tag Day. One writer thought that the disregard of the strikers by the city was simply "dastardly."[20] Another, in some confusion evidently, called the strikers "Bennett's stooges."[21] And one veteran of World War I thought "It was strange that they don't want these boys now. But if war broke out, who would want them then?"[22]

The Canadian government might or might not have wanted the strikers back in its camps at that moment, but there was another organization in Vancouver that, rumour had it, planned to deploy the camp men in its behalf. On 9 April, General Ashton notified Ottawa the "longshoremen reported to have decided on a strike if camp workers remain in the city and will assist as pickets." The next day, he further advised that the longshoremen had planned a sympathy strike for the relief camp strikers on the eleventh though, as it turned out, this gesture never took place.[23]

Throughout the two-month course of the relief camp strike in Vancouver, Ashton and Foster were constantly aware of the possibility of a general strike, in the main organized by the Vancouver and District Waterfront Workers' Association (VDWWA). May Day, the revolutionaries' holiday, seemed a likely moment. Such a massive adventure never materialized but the longshoremen did go out on 4 June, the day after the On-To-Ottawa Trek left the city.

The VDWWA emerged in 1923, paradoxically, as a company union created to break a movement launched against the Shipping Federation of British Columbia by the International Longshoremen's Association. Thereafter, the VDWWA maintained its alliance with the Federation which was, itself, an amalgam of shipping and other waterfront business groups. In 1934, the union and the Federation signed a three-year agreement which gave the Federation the right to oversee regulation, employment, dispatch and wages and which prevented the VDWWA from joining any strike by any other union. In early 1935, the VDWWA began to protest these clauses in the contract. The arguments had sufficiently escalated by the time the relief camp workers arrived that local authorities feared the longshoremen might just co-opt the strikers' own initiatives. In any case, the VDWWA provided financial support to Evans, and in other ways demonstrated their sympathy and interest. Towards the end of May, the waterfront workers began to make their own move to a strike, at which time the Shipping Federation mounted a public campaign of denunciation.[24]

For the moment, the relief camp strikers were content to count their receipts from the Tag Day and to complete the organization of divisions. The week following passed rather quietly perhaps because Evans feared any disturbance on the eve of the Easter holiday, 21 April, which might turn the city against his men. Prime Minister Bennett was attending the Silver Jubilee of King George V so Evans wired the monarch and ''brought to the attention of His Majesty the King the fact that two thousand camp strikers had been sentenced to starvation in Vancouver by Mr. Bennett....''[25]

The men did gather on 19 April at the Arena, along with three thousand townspeople, to listen to a host of speakers from the RCWU, the WUL, the CCF, and the CPC. The message to all: The strike must be extended to all relief camps in the nation, then on to a general strike! The United Front must be encouraged! After these ideas had been asserted and reasserted, a more homely call: If anyone can feed or house a striker, please telephone TRINity 4328 (which the VCPD identified as the office of the CCF Unemployed Section on Hornby Street).[26]

If General Ashton could report all quiet in Vancouver that week, he obviously made reference to the camp men. The same could not be said for his relations with some of his colleagues. For the time being, McGeer had to be content with the insistence that any men who wanted to return to the camps had to follow standard procedures. But then Ashton learned on 14 April that Judge MacDonald had cabled General McNaughton suggesting that strikers in ''good standing'' be allowed to return ''without new application'' and that this concession be granted quickly so that he could announce it the next day when he resumed interviews. McNaughton then replied to the Commissioner that (1) there was no way of ascertaining which strikers were in good standing; (2) the agitators and ''agents of subversive organizations'' must be weeded out first; (3) those who did apply for readmission would be "promptly and sympathetically" dealt with. In a confidential message to Ashton, McNaughton wondered just how Judge MacDonald would expect to identify men in good standing other than by registration. "It seems to us that he may be endeavouring to find a way round a possible refusal by the Province to take responsibility of nominating individual men for readmittance." Ashton confirmed that, indeed, Premier Pattullo "definitely refuses to submit requests or assume any responsibility."[27]

Judge MacDonald's plea could be turned aside with relative ease, but the same could not be said for the next petitioner, General J.H. MacBrien, Commissioner of the RCMP, who had come to Vancouver that week to make his own inspection. A former member of the North-West Mounted Police, a hero of World War I, one-time Chief of the General Staff, General MacBrien had his own notions about dealing with the strikers. After interviewing Foster and after meetings with civic leaders, MacBrien concluded that a state of crisis existed in Vancouver and that, therefore, the strikers, men in good standing *and* agitators, must be returned to the camps forthwith. According to MacBrien, Vancouverites felt that the camp system had run its course and that work and wages programmes had to be established. If the striker funds ran out, MacBrien had been led to believe, the men might either raid cafés and force their own arrests or else simply turn themselves in to the police and take jail terms over the camps. Whether or not he told MacBrien, Ashton was pretty sure that the camp staffs would not endure a return since many had become notably fed up with the abuse dealt them by camp workers.[28]

Commissioner MacBrien turned his recommendations over to Grote Stirling, Minister of National Defence, who referred the matter to McNaughton who wired Ashton that he should "suggest [to MacBrien] danger expressing opinions contrary present policy Dominion government, as defined telegrams sent by Acting Prime Minister to Premier Pattullo which have been repeated to you. Show these telegrams to MacBrien for his information. Acknowledge and report time this information given to MacBrien."[29]

If McNaughton seemed just a bit testy, his memorandum on the controversy written on 19 April made absolutely clear that his patience, in this respect, had been severely strained.

> *I said that I was very anxious that MacBrien should not weaken our position by giving out a lot of half-baked ideas; that I was particularly upset [that he had not] had the courtesy or the good sense to obtain information on the situation from General Ashton himself. . . .*[30]

After composing this note for his files, McNaughton went into a cabinet meeting whose single topic was a lengthy exposition in defence of the camp system as composed by McNaughton and read by Sir George Perley. One crucial argument was that the nation could not afford a public works scheme on the scale envisioned by Pattullo, McGeer, Evans and MacBrien. Fifty million dollars a year was the conservative estimate.

McNaughton went from the meeting to the telephone and gave Ashton the sum and substance, plus this message for his maverick colleague: "Tell him the Government is very upset with him." Ashton: "He spoke as if he didn't give a damn." McNaughton: "He is in for serious trouble." MacBrien soon thereafter returned to Ottawa.[31]

But pressure was still on Ashton. A struggle among miners, owners and police in Corbin, British Columbia, erupted that week, with injuries on both sides. Ashton thought this misadventure derived from the same subversive control as the relief camp strike. With the prospect of still another explosion on the waterfront, "my feeling is Vancouver is danger point and if not firmly and efficiently handled may cause spread throughout Canada."[32] McNaughton responded:

> I share your opinions but until Provincial authorities request aid as by law provided, responsibility for dealing with situation rests with them. This includes choice of method. Anxious that any advice given Attorney General [of British Columbia] by you should not be susceptible interpretation Dominion dictating their action at this stage.[33]

While Vancouver when to Church on Easter morning, 21 April, camp workers and supporters came together across a series of four meetings, all of which apparently were attended by the VCPD. At 10:00 A.M. in the Rex Theatre, an audience learned that the Action Committee would "lay plans," although what these entailed the witness did not explain. But he did move among the assembled and heard "men grumbling. No account of monies collected or paid out. The men have complained about this before. Were told they would be given it at next meeting."

That afternoon, in rapid succession, citizens and strikers heard a speech on the United Front and then from a Corbin miner named Doran who spelled out the exact nature of that struggle a few days before. According to his account, "The police were the first to start." The report from Corbin was followed by an announcement from the Strike Committee to the effect that it had now made plans: "Force city or province to grant relief"; "bring out balance of camps into city"; "force negotiations." The VCPD certified that "Kelly

[Joe Kelly, an RCWU activist] and four others leaving tonight or tomorrow to bring in other camps."

Finally, at 8:00 P.M. that Sunday, about three hundred gathered on West Hastings to hear representatives from WESL and CLDL draw "a beautiful picture of Russia."[34]

Given the events of 23 April, just two days later, when a division of strikers invaded the Hudson's Bay Company store and Mayor McGeer had to come forward and read the Riot Act, the Strike Committee's plans may or may not have been relevant. Did they hope to force negotiations by tempting riot and disorder?

If the VCPD's count can be trusted, the Sunday gatherings were sparsely attended and then as much by citizens as by strikers. It rained that day and perhaps the men kept inside, lounging on their bedrolls, standing or squatting in groups in the various halls, hunched over coffee cups, peering out into the quiet streets. The union offices, the cafés frequented by the camp workers, were located in the working class district of the east end of downtown Vancouver, a lonely stretch of blocks on an Easter day.

The strikers of a squad and division tended to stay together, to eat, sleep and march together — clans, of sorts. The contrast which many detected between the temporary existence which they had led for years and the relative security of the permanent middle class in Vancouver was painful to perceive. In a letter to the *Sun,* a striker expressed some of this pain. Because they were assured of only two meals a day, many of the men stayed up late at night, strolling about the neighbourhood or gathering in rooms to talk. The later they stayed up, the later they would sleep in the morning and in this way, they could ignore one meal since rations were not handed out until the division meetings at 1:30 P.M. But the walks brought them into contact with people who were apparently comfortable and well-fed. "There is no laughter in our hours," this fellow wrote, "no hope in our young lives." And, consequently, "we see red and we think red; we who should be the pride of the nation are the derelicts."[35]

On 23 April, at 3:45 P.M., one division of strikers marched into the Hudson's Bay Company store and, within the next half-hour, forced a fight with police and contributed to the destruction of several thousand dollars worth of display cases and notions and sundries. If the men had been grumbling a few days before, if the young letter writer had seemed bored, now they had revived, now they had created an incident.

On that Tuesday, an hour after division muster, an estimated fourteen hundred camp strikers left their several meeting halls, gathered at Water and Carrall Streets and "commenced to march."

Their elected path took them through the wholesale grocery area where efforts to enter stores were discouraged by city constables who had immediately begun to walk, in the manner of parade marshals, on each side of the column. The marchers, four abreast, trailed along the sidewalks to Cordova and from there to Hastings and then to Georgia Street where they made one complete circuit of the Hotel Vancouver, then returned to Georgia, to Granville, where some three hundred of them, said to comprise Division Three, dove into the arcade entrance of the Hudson's Bay Company store and onto the main floor, surging across the vast room to the Seymour Street side.[36]

On the way, police had darted ahead to Spencer's, Woodward's and the Hudson's Bay to advise staff of the approach of the strikers. The first two immediately closed doors, but when Constable G. Lyons notified the Hudson's Bay floor manager, Mr. Frayer, of the threat, he was told that Frayer "did not deem it necessary to close doors as he expected strikers would march in an orderly manner as on their previous visit" on 12 April. So much for tradition.[37]

Once, inside, the men sought to snake walk through the aisles, but Lyons and his colleagues moved quickly to halt this manoeuvre. Now, near the centre of the room, Malcolm MacLeod, raised on the shoulders of his comrades, spoke out loudly to the customers and clerks who had scurried to the mezzanine or otherwise stood in the stairways,

> briefly stating the strikers' demands and announcing that they would use peaceful measures to obtain these, but should they fail to move the government officials by peaceful measures, they would adopt more strenuous methods. He ordered the marchers to stay right there where they were until the authorities saw fit to consider their case.[38]

Deputy Chief Constable Alfred Grundy walked among the men until he came to a spot where further passage was obstructed by bodies. "I told them that some of them might be men, to stand on their hind legs, so they all did to make a passage clear." The men told Grundy they wanted "to bring [their concerns] to the attention of the public." "Well," said Grundy, "you have obtained your object; now won't you leave the store?"

Grundy edged over to the Seymour Street exit to join up with several other officers who had just entered, speaking to strikers who were nearby and asking them to leave. About twenty men started to depart but then voices cried out "Hold fast boys!" Grundy found himself jammed against "a solid wedge" then broke away to go to the aid of Inspector Charles Tuley under attack by a man wielding an iron bar. "Well, I had a scrap with the same fellow and there was a few blows struck, and officers came there and picked up this fellow and wanted to know if he should be arrested. I said no, he has got enough."[39] Tuley, as it turned out, had been struck down by an iron railroad brake shoe pin about one inch by eighteen inches; twenty or more of these were recovered by store clerks after the melee.

Suddenly, a glass display case toppled over, whether deliberately kicked in or accidentally smashed by the surging crowd, is not clear. J.E. Boyd, a passerby, did claim to have seen Jack Lawson, a division officer, knocked down by constables, stagger to his feet and lurch into a show case "just like a punch drunk fighter."[40] Other cases went off like firecrackers and then three aisles were laid waste, men cursing, police batons thudding, bonbons, shoes, notions flying through the air.

Acting Inspector F.R. Lester turned back into the crowd to chase the men out. When the display cases went down

> at the same time, I was hit on the top of the head with some heavy weapon, which caused my face and tunic to be covered with blood. Several of the officers were injured at this time, so we went to work with our clubs and cleared the store of the strikers. A citizen then caught me by the arm and brought me to a room where I had my wound dressed and the blood washed from my face.[41]

J.E. Boyd, who saw Lawson go down, remembered the faces of the strikers just before the fight began: "Some of them seemed like as if they were trapped, and there were others that were more of a pugnacious type that wanted to fight it out, and there were others that wanted to go away, and I saw them try to slither, to pass by the policemen peaceably."[42]

But most of the division stayed intact and spilled into Seymour Street, running east to Dunsmuir, towards the Victory Cenotaph. At the first corner, Constable Robert Tisdale saw six men trying to overturn an automobile. "Have some sense, fellows, this don't get you anywhere doing this." Their rage up now, the six jumped Tisdale, struck him over the head several times with rubber hoses, kicked him to the ground, broke his teeth and cracked two ribs.[43]

The camp men surged up to the base of the Cenotaph and then halted, their ranks now swollen by townspeople, among them Harold Winch, MLA (CCF), who jumped up beside the monument to join Joe Kelly, Arthur Evans and Matt Shaw. Each spoke quickly and briefly to the crowd, calling attention to "the display of police strength about them in the square." A delegation of twelve men was promptly recruited and sent up the street to the mayor's office. Behind, the nervous throng watched as Colonel Foster arrived.

What this officer saw most definitely left him unsettled; "a great mass of citizens were around, and the Police Force outside circling right around the Square, and the R.C.M.P. facing down, and the City men and the mounted policemen behind them, and the police facing the square."[44] A few minutes went by and then Matt Shaw, who had led the group to City Hall, burst among them with this news: after being turned away by Mayor McGeer, the delegation had been arrested and charged with vagrancy! Shaw had escaped because he had persuaded police that since he was on relief in Vancouver, he could not be called a vagrant.[45]

A second squad, led by an irate Winch, hustled off to demand the release of the other men, but it ran into McGeer who had driven over from his office. There, alongside the Cenotaph, McGeer read the Riot Act.

> Our sovereign Lord and King charges and commands all persons assembled immediately to disperse and peaceably depart to their habitations or to their lawful business upon pain of being guilty of an offense on conviction of which they may be sentenced to imprisonment for life.

As far as Colonel Foster was concerned, this pronouncement was intended to warn citizens to get away from a dangerous situation; to protect the city in case there was damage so that everybody had full warning; to protect the police force. Because the crowd was so large, constables walked about reciting the implications of the Riot Act to those who might not have heard McGeer's voice. The act was binding for one hour.[47]

Winch appeared again and urged the crowd to disperse. There was a moment's wait as the strikers moved into columns to march away rather than depart singly as the police preferred, but this order was reasserted and the camp men began to drift off.

The strikers scattered for a time to pick up an evening meal. Few seemed to be in the vicinity when, at 10:00 P.M., there were details of constables raiding RCWU offices on Hastings and Cordova, removing quantities of posters and leaflets. An hour later, however, the men had gathered at the corner of Hastings and Carrall, shouting, chanting, milling about, obviously angered by the raids. Two windows in a hardware store were smashed, several policemen struck and kicked, several strikers injured.[48] Harold Winch showed up, saw men in street clothes carrying batons beating other men to their knees. Winch came away having been hammered on the shoulders by one of these assailants, though whether they were police or strikers, Winch did not know. Then the crowd melted away into the night.[49]

Wasting no time, Matt Shaw had departed Victory Square that afternoon to draft a letter proclaiming the day's events, twenty-five thousand copies of which were printed and given to the strikers who were urged to sell them for five cents apiece and to keep one cent of that amount for tobacco.[50]

Wasting no time, Mayor McGeer departed for Victory Square and went off to draft a telegram to Sir George Perley describing the fracas and insisting that "This unfortunate incident due entirely to your government's ineffective policy of administering unemployment situation. I appeal to you to authorize return of men to camps without further delay..." McGeer concluded with still one more call for a conference of provincial, federal and municipal leaders to "meet national unemployment crisis."

Perley and his associates waited twenty-four hours to reply. While pleased to learn from the press that the city had met its duties in the affair, Perley took "definite exception" to McGeer's insistence that it was all Ottawa's fault. Once those camp men had left the camps, they became the province's responsibility. On the other hand, Perley agreed that "Vancouver is being victimized by an organized attempt to capitalize for revolutionary purposes conditions of Depression which now exist." The defeat of such organizations was of paramount importance, but that was also the responsibility of the province unless and until the province asked Ottawa to intervene. In closing, "I remind you that all cities are created by province and in our opinion your telegram should have been sent to the Premier of British Columbia."[51]

Very likely Sir George meant for McGeer to appreciate that he understood the Mayor was trying to capitalize on conditions of the Depression in forcing home his criticism of Dominion responsibility. And very neatly, Sir George turned the issue of national concern into a problem of municipal law and order and provincial jurisdiction. Insult for insult.

Wednesday, 24 April, passed quietly, as police and strikers rested, tended their wounded. Inspector Tuley and two of his constables had suffered fractured skulls; Constable Tisdale, beaten down in the streets, spent three weeks in the hospital and emerged permanently crippled. Jack Lawson and one other striker were in jail on charges of malicious damage, two more from the evening assault arrested for attacking an officer. As for the group seized in front of the Mayor's office, among them Red Walsh, Bill Davis and Mike McCaulay, when they appeared before Magistrate Wood, their lawyer, Gordon Grant, made a point "well taken" by Wood, that the men were simply not "wandering abroad," as the vagrancy law prescribes, but obviously were on their way back to the Cenotaph, on an errand, as it were. Wood set the men free.[52]

The day following, the first significant meeting between the city authorities, the strikers and interested intermediaries took place in McGeer's office. General Ashton was there, along with Angus MacInnis, MP, Harold Winch, MLA, Jack Price, MLA, Colonel Foster, three members of the Trades and Labour Council, J.H. McVety, Percy Bengough and Ted Jamieson, and four strikers, Arthur Evans, Smokey Cumber, John Matts and Peter Neilson. From Ashton's summary to Ottawa and from minutes taken by McGeer's aides, the following discussion can be reconstructed.

Evans read off the seven demands, then added that until they were put into operation the "intolerable conditions obtaining in the relief camps" couldn't be corrected. McGeer indicated his sympathy, but made it clear that there were no city funds available to maintain the men and that in any case, the city would not provide the needs of the strikers without the permission of the Province "which could not move without the approval of the federal government."

Already, it is apparent, Evans and McGeer were talking about apples and oranges, national crises and city problems. If Evans's demands could be met only by the Dominion, it had been the Dominion's argument that the city's problem could be solved only by the city and the province. The needs of the strikers were twofold: immediate relief and resolution of the seven demands. McGeer and Pattullo might, just might, meet the first; only Ottawa could take care of the second.

The strikers next laid into the MacDonald Commission, Evans particularly incensed by the implications of the Gault Bros. connection. Matts and Evans then suggested that the city pay transportation to Ottawa for a delegation of strikers and that the city maintain the rest of the men on relief until the party's return. McGeer, of course, refused the second request. Prophetically, this was the very compromise offered by Ottawa two months later when the Trek stopped in Regina.

A general discussion of the respective jurisdiction of province and dominion ensued during which McGeer, "to show his personal stand in the matter," reviewed his own attempts to bring Ottawa around to his argument for work and wages programmes.

Matts asked whether relief would be forthcoming should the men promptly agree to go back into the camps. McGeer said yes, and that the men could be moved out of the city in twenty-four hours. At this Evans indicated that he would not let the seven demands stand in the way.

McGeer, without previous consultation with Ashton, set out his terms. If the men submit to physical exams: (1) the men would be provided with immediate transportation and needs; (2) the Mayor would personally support the remedying of camp conditions and the establishment of a work and wages programme to take the place of the present unemployment relief system and to secure the support of the Mayors conference in that regard; (3) the city would assist in financing a delegation of three strikers to Ottawa to place claims of men before the federal government; (4) in the case of a black-listed man, he would have an opportunity to have his case heard and determined by the MacDonald Commission.

Although Ashton made no comment on these offers in his report to McNaughton that evening, he did indicate that he had refused to endorse an ''aside'' from Angus MacInnis that ''camp committees in the future be permitted.'' It can be assumed that Ottawa was incredulous. The Mayor made no reference to two key demands asserted by the Dominion: that the men register first and that every effort be made to separate the agitators from the ''men in good standing,'' however these were to be identified. McGeer could finance a delegation if he liked, but Ottawa had no obligation to meet with it. While McGeer's support of work and wages was widely known and his use of the Mayors Conference for whatever gain regarded with some cynicism, he simply had no right to extend the terms of reference of the MacDonald Commission which was a Dominion instrument. Clearly, McGeer had overstepped his authority. There had not even been a representative from Pattullo's office at the conference.[53]

Arthur Evans left with the Mayor's terms, saw to their distribution at Cambie Street Grounds and in the division headquarters and set about formulating a set of counter-proposals which barely acknowledged McGeer's plan: (1) until the MacDonald Commission reported in, the city would place all of the strikers on relief; (2) the strikers did accept the Mayor's offer to send a delegation to Ottawa; (3) all RCWU property taken on the night of 23 April would be returned; (4) all strikers arrested on that date would be released unconditionally.[54]

Except for the likely gnashing of teeth, Mayor McGeer seems not to have made a public evaluation or response to Evans's rude dismissal of his terms except to send a note to a rally at Cambie Street proclaiming that ''the strikers were being controlled by subversive organizations.'' As a matter of fact, while the issues remained in the forefront, the specific proposals and counter proposals quickly faded away as new incidents, new strategies and new resolves took their places, across the next days and weeks.

The ferocity of the fights at the Hudson's Bay Company store and on the streets that night, the growing rancour fuelled by the cross purposes of McGeer and Evans, may have inspired undercover agents to pick up the pace. Reports began to come in in increasing numbers and in expanded detail from the VCPD and the RCMP agents.

The VCPD's man went to some lengths to represent the Cambie Street rally held the afternoon of the Mayor's meeting. Joe Kelly sat in the chair and introduced Cumber and Evans who described McGeer's offer and who promised full discussion at division meetings the next day. After a reminder of what happened when they went back to the camps after the December walk-out, the strikers vowed not to return at McGeer's recommendation. The VCPD agent then closed with a characterization that was certainly libellous.

> *How Communists work in meetings: The first thing is to set up Strike Committee, which must contain large numbers of Communists, who receive instructions from [George] Drayton, Evans, etc. So agendas are framed with resolutions, etc. to bring before General Meeting. In this meeting, there are what is called Fractions (Communists) distributed, [whose] function is to see that agenda is carried as laid down, so any one (irrespective of political or religious beliefs, as they call rank and file democracy) [who] gets up in argument or [is] not to their liking, shout sit down, throw him out, reactionary stool pigeon, etc. Through this method a few rule and intimidate.*[55]

Whether the VCPD agent was using this particular meeting as an example or whether their infiltrator was generalizing about all striker gatherings is not made clear. Would Evans and company allow such patent abuse at public events, which the Cambie Street rallies were, where the press as well as friendly or curious citizens might be in attendance? On the other hand, the division assemblies were closed, as were occasional meetings of all the strikers in one or another of the theatres thereabouts.

As for the Strike Committee which was composed of representatives from the divisions, if these men were elected, it is possible that those doing the nominating knew whom to identify. But there were many free spirits in the ranks who, even at the outset, would have watched and wondered and perhaps put up their own candidates. The names of the men on the Strike Committee have never been published, not even in agents' reports, nor is the manner of election or selection known.

Both the VCPD and the RCMP agents filed reports of an assembly that same evening at the Moose Hall on Burrard Street sponsored by the CCF Women's Group. Mrs. Elizabeth Kerr chaired the meeting and introduced Mrs. Ada Crump, of the provincial Parent Teachers' Federation, and Smokey Cumber. Prominent on the agenda was an announcement regarding arrangements for the rally to be held at the Arena on Saturday evening, 28 April, under the auspices of the CCF. A unique tag day would be laid on for Saturday, not a solicitation for money but an advertisement for the rally. The tags handed out would be marked "Are Our Sons Criminals?" Citizens who took tags would be asked to sign a petition against the camps and to come to the rally with money.

The other major announcement had to do with a one-hour long "general strike" by area unions sympathetic to the RCWU, particularly the longshoremen. This would take place on Monday, 30 April. The RCMP learned "that there will be a walk-out by high school students. . . in conjunction with the general strike. . ."

Both the VCPD and the RCMP agents found the rally orderly, "considerable enthusiasm being displayed."[56]

The *Sun* quoted one CCF woman as saying, "We've had enough of commissions, delegations and petitions. Now, we'll take over," — "we" presumably meaning the CCF women.[57] Coincidence or not, another meeting had taken place on that busy 25 April. Delegates from seventy-two women's clubs in the area gathered at the Hotel Georgia, across the street from the Hotel Vancouver, and light years from the Cambie Street Grounds. When they had finished their business, they sent a small representation to Mayor McGeer bearing this resolution:

> Citizens cannot understand why no action has been taken to clear up relief situation. The protest of camp men is a logical outcome of policy extending over three years, which has deprived our Canadian men of hope and self-expression. Yet no adequate program has been offered. We believe these men to be worthy citizens only desirous of reestablishment. The influence of present policy is such that it imperils the welfare of all Canadian citizens.

> Resolved:
> 1. That without further delay the Dominion government exercise its undoubted powers in a statesmanlike way to provide such a program that these men will be absorbed in normal community life within a short definite period of time.
> 2. We strongly urge that immediate temporary relief be provided pending adjustment of present difficulty.[58]

While the women waited in his office, Mayor McGeer drafted a telegram to Sir George Perley, citing the delegation as "representative of best citizenship in our city" and expressing generally the public sympathy for the strikers. The Dominion must call a conference "through which some practical solution can be developed."[59]

No doubt McGeer must have been delighted to have these women in his office after having endured the skeptical or disapproving or wondering expressions on the faces of strikers, politicians and generals the day before.

As for the strikers, their morale began to waver. On the one hand, two hundred recruits were thought to have come into Vancouver since 22 April, probably in response to Joe Kelly's expedition; financial support arrived from friendly unions and from anonymous citizens.[60] But on the other hand, as the first month of the strike came to a close, as plans for a mammoth May Day parade were being drawn up, more than a few camp men began to drift away, not in great numbers, but enough so that pains had to be taken to keep them in the ranks.

Indeed, there was another dispute going on some distance from Cordova and Hastings and the Victory Cenotaph and the Mayor's office those days. It was a domestic quarrel. It was the matter of the Picket Committee whose chairman was Charles Sands. Sands's men were charged with patrolling the railway yards on the lookout for camp men seeking to leave the city. Whether a fellow had word of a job or was homesick or craved the mountains or was tired of the strike and wanted to get away, the only real options he had were walking, catching a boat or jumping on a freight, assuming he lacked fare. And since it was imperative that the ranks of the strike be kept intact, unyielding, then it was just as important that defectors be discouraged and examples set.

Arthur Evans said later that the work of Sands's committee was "Not preventing them going but they were informative, and asking them to stick in Vancouver. . . . If force was used it was done without the sanction of the main body of the strikers."[61]

During the first week of the strike, Sands came to the Strike Committee and won from it the right to organize his pickets into a unit set apart from the divisions. Given its assignment, the committee needed all the flexibility and freedom from daily routine that it could secure.

The essential information about the career of this picket committee came from various VCPD reports and memoranda from Colonel Foster. Red Walsh, long afterward, provided an anecdote that not only illuminates the moment but also throws light on the discipline of the strikers and on their capacity for violence.

Sands's physical description appeared earlier in this book: German émigré, aged fifty-two, six four in height. Behind him, "twenty 6' 6" thugs" who were on duty with Sands every night from 9:00 P.M. until 9:00 A.M. When Sands slept, it was at the Beaver Rooms, though his office was at 31 Cordova Street. His men were dispersed among the CPR yards, 10:00 P.M. until 2:00 A.M.; the CNR yards, 1:30 A.M. until 5:00 A.M.; and to the Great Northern Yards around 11:00 P.M. when the stock train left.

Sands checked at the Cordova Street headquarters regularly for reports from pickets at New Westminster, Port Mann, Coquitlam, BCE Bus Terminals, as well as messages from the day pickets.

If a fleeing striker was apprehended without some sort of safe conduct pass from his division, then the pickets moved quickly to drag the culprit off the train and escort him back into town. And here is Walsh's story: On one occasion three strikers managed to jump aboard a rolling train before they could be stopped. Sands and some of his men climbed up on the roof of the car and rode to Port Hammond, all the while hammering on the top and sides with boards. At Port Hammond, they leapt down, broke open the door and started to clamber in. Sands was promptly struck over the head with a 2x4 as he went after the escapees. But the men in the car were outnumbered, and shortly they were pulled outside and badly beaten.

It should be added that the camp men were discouraged from seeking reinstatement in the camps. Sands saw to it that pickets strolled back and forth in front of the Employment Service office.

But as tough as he was, the chairman of the picket committee was vulnerable, according to a VCPD report: "This fellow Sands can be deported. He told me so the other day."[62]

The Vancouver area and British Columbia caucuses of the CCF had, from early April, pitched in to give the strikers a hand, to help them with the Action Committee, otherwise to take part in rallies, parades, negotiations, whenever possible. This was as it should be because the principle and ethic of a United Front were in place. Angus MacInnis, Dorothy Steeves, Harold Winch, Dr. Lyle Telford, were among the best-known leaders or personalities of this party, which included Grant McNeil.

Yet there was a mood of uneasiness with respect to this alliance between the CCF and the strike leaders. The CCF had organized a mammoth rally at the Arena for Sunday evening, 28 April. That afternoon, at Cambie Street Grounds, Grant McNeil told a group of strikers and citizens that "there seems to have been a difference between the Communists and the CCF...anyway it has been patched up. . . we are out to help the camp strikers, not for a political purpose.''[63] But not every striker was convinced.

The VCPD agent seems almost spellbound by the ''difference'' which he analyzed at great length in memoranda prepared on 27 and 28 April. Evans and his men, Communists or not, were very worried about the extent to which the CCF might just be using the strike for their own profit.

> The CCF, it is felt by the Reds, are using the B.C. strikers to fight their political battles against Victoria and there is a strong feeling in the ranks that we should not be tools of the CCF such as parading on Sunday night to the Arena and letting the CCF run the meeting. The CCF are taking too keen an interest in the whole thing for the Left Wing radicals liking. I have never seen so many women running around. One would think it was election night. The petitions the CCF women are getting the citizens to sign asking McGeer, Victoria and Ottawa to close the camps are supposed to have 5,000 signatures on them by 6:00 P.M. tonight.

At this point, the VCPD man shifted from a factual representation to a more personal note.

> I would like to express my opinion, sir. If the CCF are trying to absorb the Communists, they are, by their speeches, breeding dissatisfaction among the people. . . . To ignore constitutional authority for their own political ends. Every time they express their opinion against the mayor, police or anyone in author- ity, they like to hear hissing and boos, which is not doing good at this critical time. But they do tell the strikers to keep cool, use intelligence, and they will win their strike by public support.[64]

The VCPD agent seems almost to regret the CCF's transgressions, if indeed, that is what they were. Perhaps he expected a decorum which was not forthcoming. As for the CCF absorbing the Communists, the history of conflict between the two parties throughout the decade too often revealed that compromise of the CCF was a particular ambition of the Communists.

In his report of 27 April, the agent expresses considerable alarm over the prospects for violence in the next few days. Money is running out. May Day is approaching. ''The situation here in Vancouver looks very black today with all governments turning the relief strikers down.'' He is sure that ''There will be hell to pay. . . There is sure to be a lot of trouble next Monday. . . . Troops should be kept in readiness and martial law might have to be declared. . . Vancouver is now a seething cauldron of discontent.''

And, yes, he claims, the strikers are armed: "318 Cordova. Baseball bats, about 12 pounds of lead. In a great many of the packs there is [sic] billys." (The room where two hundred or more sleep at 318 Cordova Street is called "the baggage room" probably because so many packs are stored there. Has the VCPD agent, at some risk, been poking through them?)[65]

Saturday, 28 April. The women of the CCF have been at it for two days, preparing for the great rally at the Arena, arranging the programme of speakers, drafting their colleague, Sarah Colley, as leader of the parade to the auditorium, handing out tags, circulating a petition which calls for humane treatment of the camp men and abolition of the camps themselves.

That afternoon, the strikers gathered at Cambie Street. Malcolm MacLeod introduced Paddy O'Neil, who extended encouragement from WESL, as did other delegates from the Provincial Mother's Council and the Young Communist League. A veteran radical named Bob Kerr stepped forward to remind everyone that it was the Workers' Unity League which made this strike possible, thank you, that plans were set for a "General Strike" of one hour's duration on Monday and for a May Day parade on 1 May.

A man named Jack Taylor was next introduced. Taylor was the *nom de guerre* of Muni Erlich, a Communist Party functionary, recently arrived in British Columbia, already spotted by the VCPD: "32 years, 5' 11", 155, eyes brown, hair black and curly, wears no hat, blue overcoat, blue serge suit." Taylor expressed outrage at remarks made on the radio the night before by Mayor McGeer, who proposed that the Communists were the organizers of the strike and that they were intent upon revolution. Taylor is supposed to have exclaimed that "the Communist Party was not ready for revolution yet but may be a little later."

With Grant McNeil's disclaimer about CCF opportunism and Matt Shaw's brief chat about the rally at the Arena, the meeting came to a close.[66]

The camp men returned to the Grounds around 6:30 P.M., two divisions lined up on the west side, two on the east. They had been told that they would set out first for the Arena, with the CCF women next and then a gaggle of clubs, union delegates, sympathizers, citizens last. But Sarah Colley now approached Smokey Cumber and asked him whether the women could walk at the head of the column. Smokey said all right and off they went.

The RCMP had witnessed this exchange: "Again the CCF leaders proved themselves masters of manoeuvres and sent Mother Colley to Cumber to ask him for the head of the line for the women. Cumber agreed...."[67]

Off they went. Two hundred and sixty women in front, followed by twenty-seven hundred strikers and friends. Another ten thousand, it is estimated, flooded along the sidewalks, banners up, singing, cheering. The Arena was quickly packed with sixteen thousand spectators, the largest political rally in Vancouver history to that date.

The chairman was Robert Skinner, the CCF party president. The agenda included Sarah Colley, Matt Shaw, Harold Winch, Dr. Lyle Telford. The audience was kept in a perpetual state of excitement by the announcement of a $1,181 contribution from the streetcar union, by the proclamation from the waterfront workers that all unions were being canvassed about a general strike, and by the repeated call from Harold Winch: "Is Mayor McGeer in the audience?" A most popular speaker was Arnold Webster, a CCFer and a school teacher. "Addressing himself to the youth particularly, he said, 'Under capitalism, you have no future' and pointed out the significant fact that as the depression deepened so the cost of militias and police forces will rise." So the evening passed with many occasions for cheers and, whenever McGeer's name was called, for boos. And then the crowd departed, perhaps just a bit weary after two hours of speeches and noise.[68]

Later that night, according to the RCMP agent, there was a very private meeting held among the Communist Party stalwarts in the strike executive. If the constable was not there himself, he learned of it shortly and evidently from a source that was extremely close to Evans's circle of intimates, perhaps a source that was at the meeting.

"Chagrin is being registered by the Party 'Poobahs' over their failure to check the tag-day manoeuvres of the CCF." Evans was the first to appreciate that his men were being used by the CCF, in particular by Dr. Telford that evening at the Arena. The incident of the CCF women leading the parade "behind a Woodsworth banner" was reviewed, as was the presumably deliberate attempt to humiliate Smokey Cumber by allotting him just ten minutes to speak at the rally.

According to the RCMP man, Evans was then confronted by two party functionaries, Jack Taylor and one Disnitski, though what their complaints were exactly is not made clear. There was a "wrangle" however. Evans exploded and told the two men "to get out and rustle themselves a job so that they might be in a position to study the working 'plugs' psychology after doing some work themselves. Evans told them very bluntly that they were isolated from the masses because they were and are afraid of the criticism of the rank and file."

Returning to the matter of the CCF, Evans argued that if the strikers had refused to walk with the CCF women in front, then Winch, Telford, Skinner and company would "turn to their followers and scream. There you are! We told you so! The Communists ask us to come in on a United Front and then turn around and sabotage the movement!" Evans had a point. So the night wore on and then the meeting broke up for a few hours only to resume Sunday morning.

Disnitski and Taylor turned to other matters, particularly the Corbin miners' dispute. Taylor directed Malcolm Bruce, a veteran radical and an Evans supporter, to go to Corbin and gather information. Bruce refused "point-blank" and added that Taylor was the one who should go. "Ulrich (Taylor) protested that with conditions being favourable for a general strike he could not be spared from Vancouver." "Oh," said Bruce, "I can be spared from Vancouver but you are too valuable a man to send to the sticks." Whether Bruce won his point is not known for the antagonists went their way to Cambie Street for yet another meeting of the strikers. The RCMP agent was there.

To add to Evans's troubles, a leaflet had been circulated that weekend which described his arrest in Drumheller years before and which charged that Evans "was responsible for the loss of a good deal of public sympathy for the striking camp boys." The origin of the leaflet was not indicated. Evans, as angry as anyone had ever seen him in public, began to defend himself but Jack Stevenson, a striker and chairman of the rally, interrupted to announce that the divisions had voted to retain Evans as their leader. As a further vote of confidence, Stevenson proposed that Evans lead the parade planned in conjuction with the present meeting.

> Evans was given the platform and being in a highly inebriated condition, delivered a rather foul and profane address to the crowd. He vehemently protested against the underhanded way these leaflets had been published against him, labelling the contents and references to his character as just so many lies. He is quoted as having stated "This is some of 'Jeremiah Jesus' McGeer and his God Damn gang of fascists working."

The RCMP agent walked in the parade to the Longshoremen's Hall on Dunlevy Street, Evans indeed at the head, pausing at every corner to question spectators: "If they approved of 'Jeremiah Jesus' McGeer reading the Riot Act and if they did not, to join the parade."[69]

Whether Evans was drunk or not, and the local press did not remark on this matter at all, the RCMP agent has given us a portrait of a man under considerable stress. Evans may have been overwhelmed by the contradictions of the weekend and the strain of holding his men together over the past month.

On the one hand, the Arena rally had been eminently successful; on the other hand, it demonstrated the degree to which the CCF had the capacity to grab the limelight and inadvertantly provoke a bitter quarrel among strike leaders and party functionaries. And now this leaflet! The co-ordination of strike tactics, the unrelenting attacks by McGeer, Pattulo and Bennett, the anxiety over funds, the failure so far to ignite a general strike, the approaching May Day celebration with the very real tensions it generated, all of these had to be borne by Arthur Evans.

After this eccentric procession made its way back to the Grounds, the crowd heard more speeches from the WUL's Bob Kerr, who revealed that the Action Committee was about to draft a referendum for the trade unions in the city regarding a general strike on 1 May, and from Oscar Salonin of the VDWWA who described that group's negotiations with the Shipping Federation. Thirty-five high school students next moved to the front of the assembly as their representative joined the others on the rostrum to announce that the youngsters would join the one-hour General Strike on Monday and otherwise hoped to bring out three thousand more of their classmates for the May Day festivity.[70]

The VCPD agent had been sure of chaos and disorder that weekend but, in fact, it had been a relatively mild period so far as public apprehension of the strike was concerned. Vancouver was not quite a seething cauldron. And, as it turned out, the one-hour strike on Monday was another orderly affair. A thousand or so longshoremen, seamen, loggers, students took part. A crowd of camp men marched along the waterfront calling on stevedores to join in. And so April passed. [71]

Vancouver had long since become accustomed to the strikers on parade, snake dancing through the streets, drifting around Cambie Street Grounds, tagging, bumming, hectoring the authorities. Cordova and Hastings became a tourist's obligation. Ron Liversedge writes of the nightly departure of the 10:10 seaboard freight with hundreds of townspeople coming to watch Sands's committee at work.

> The smart serious pickets strung out in pairs along the track from Carrall east to Gore Avenue, the precision with which they boarded the moving train, the very thorough combing over which they [Sands's men] gave the train from stem to stern, the occasional flying human bundle hitting the dirt at a quick

> run...and then Victoria Avenue, the 'piece de resistance',
> where, with the train going at a speed too fast for anyone to
> board, the pickets dropped off one by one on light and nimble
> feet.[72]

But Vancouverites, rich, middle-class and poor, also had other diversions as the spring moved along. The Governor General and his family had departed, their places in the society columns now taken by the Baden-Powells, dressed in scouting uniforms, father, mother, daughters. There was a marvelous long-running trial in England involving a Vancouver couple: she was supposed to have killed him. City fathers sought to get the area moving again by opening mines and by seducing tourists from the prairies to come West. And will Mr. Bennett be knighted whilst he is at the Jubilee? In the charming way Mr. Laurier had been honoured years before during a visit to London? Will Mr. Bennett in fact leave office when he returns? How is his health, anyway? And the eleven-mile walking marathon around Stanley Park is just a few days off.

Four
May in Vancouver
"Well, what do we do now?"

— Red Walsh

Recall that Colonel Foster was in receipt of a report from an agent dated 27 April in which it was urged that "Troops should be kept in readiness and martial law might have to be declared," all this in anticipation of a May Day parade organized by the striker's Action Committee.[1] There is no evidence that Foster was alarmed by this prognosis nor that martial law was ever considered during the history of the strike. In fact, in a letter sent to Mayor McGeer on the morning of 1 May, the Chief Constable declared: "There is no reason to suppose that during the parade or at the Park [Stanley Park] there will be any acts of violence...It is possible that, excited by inflammatory speeches, smaller groups in the city, towards evening, may be troublesome, but every preparation is being made to meet the situation."[2]

Foster sought to meet the situation in this fashion: the parade itself would be escorted by six motorcycle officers and two cars filled with constables. Seven squads of five men each would stand by, armed with tear gas. Ten detectives were posted as scouts along the parade route and in the park itself. Fifty-five mounted officers, two more cyclists and 290 patrolmen were dispersed among the Beatty Street Drill Hall, the City Police Station and the Provincial Police Station. Finally, twenty-one plainsclothes officers mingled in the crowd at Stanley Park.[3]

And here is the May Day Parade. Some seventy-five hundred strikers and friends departed Cambie Street Grounds at 1:30 P.M.: the CPC, the CLDL, the CESL, the VDWWA, the Seafarer's Industrial Union, the Food Worker's Industrial Union, the Carpenters and Joiners, the Boilermakers, the Fishermen and Cannery Workers, the Mine Workers, the Lumber Workers, the Farmers' Unity League, the Women's Labour League, the Friends of the Soviet Union, the YCL, the Worker's Sports Association, the Young Pioneers, the Student's League of Canada, Finnish, Scandinavian, Chinese, Japanese, German, Ukrainian and Italian Associations. Plus nine hundred public school students who had skipped school. There is no record of discord or even competition regarding procedures in the march. In fact, the CCF seems not to have been present as a unit nor even on the speaker's stand at the Park.

Out front, two pipe bands, and a fife and drum corps. Many, many banners announced the unions and clubs. Young Pioneers wore red scarfs and tams and walked behind their own band. Here comes the Worker's Sports Association, beautifully dressed in white duck trousers, white singlets, red sashes and crests decorated with the hammer and sickle. Two floats: a mock-up of a relief camp tent. A replica of the Cenotaph with a striker dressed and masked as Mayor McGeer reading the Riot Act.[4]

The parade passed Detective Vince who was scouting at Pender and Hastings, passed Detective Hichens who was scouting at Georgia and Granville. On down Georgia to the Park. The number of marchers doubled along the way. Another five thousand waited at the Malkin Memorial Shell. As each detachment, union, club, band passed in, its name was called out over a public address system.[5]

Jack Taylor, Evans's nemesis of the previous weekend, opened the ceremonies, calling for cheers in his "yiddish English" as the RCMP report put it. Taylor celebrated the Red Army and the Soviet Union. The throng sang the *Internationale* and observed a two-minute silence for revolutionary martyrs. A Jugoslav orchestra played the Soviet Funeral March. Arthur Evans came up to plead the case of the relief camp strike. He was followed by Pete Munro of the Street Railwaymen who described his recent visit to Russia. And then, according to the RCMP, "many persons, including a fair percentage of the longshoremen, who had on that day gone on strike in sympathy with the r.c. strikers for the period of one day, filed out of the crowd and left the park." One stevedore told the RCMP that his chums were "thoroughly disgusted with the meeting as they hear nothing but 'bally ho' of the Russian Soviet and Communism." Nonetheless, Oscar Salonin of the VDWWA told the crowd that his organization was in support of the camp men.

Thereafter, a veritable swarm of representatives from organizations in attendance trooped across the stage for brief comments or acknowledgements: the IWW, the Chinese Workers' Protective Association, the B.C. League Against War and Fascism...Matt Shaw wound up the affair with a brief thanks for donations from the longshoremen and the boilermakers. By 5:00 P.M. the ceremonies had closed and the relief camp workers had withdrawn in good order, returning to Cambie Street Grounds.[6]

Despite the crowds, despite the banners, the pipe bands, the red tams, the floats, the Jugoslav orchestra, and the exhortations from the platform, Chief Constable Foster was pretty sure that the day had fallen flat for the strikers. The other unions, though represented, did not turn out in strength. The promise of a general strike which had haunted the authorities for days was not kept.

Foster's constables came away having heard complaints from relief camp men that the city police were a lot tougher than they had been led to believe and that, moreover, Mayor McGeer was "another great disappointment" in that, he too, stood up to Evans. In doing so, McGeer had earned that paradoxically flattering sobriquet: "Dictator."

> ...a great number of men from the camps see that they are not getting anywhere and even Evans, the communist leader, said it might be necessary to make the best arrangements they could and let the camp strikers return and then organize for a 100% strike in July....[7]

Colonel Foster concluded his report to the Mayor with a judgement and a recommendation that were as severe as any he had yet offered. There was no reason to be concerned about trouble since his men could handle that. But:

> every effort should be made to disassociate the men from the camps from the communistic leaders, as there was a real tragedy yesterday in seeing a parade consisting of notorious criminals, foreigners of a low type, communistic organizations intent upon destruction, and with them, large bodies of young men looking for an opportunity in life, together with a certain number of school children whose presence indicated that they are starting out under most unfavourable conditions.[8]

Just who the "notorious criminals" were, Foster did not say. Nor did he explain what "foreigners of a low type" signified, although one might infer an Anglo-Saxon attitude rising to the occasion. If the criminals were really criminals, then why weren't they arrested? Or is it that Foster was urging a label not unlike the strikers' designation of McGeer as "dictator"?

Bob Bouchette, columnist for the *Sun,* had quite a different and certainly a more charitable estimate of the day. He noted that the city had granted a license to use the Malkin Memorial Shell so long as the paraders did not talk politics.

> They certainly did talk politics. The good old time denunciations that we had heard over and again during the past twenty years, and they had a thoroughly good time doing it. They sang the Internationale and they had band music, presumably revolutionary....[9]

And the *Daily Province* dubbed the parade "a shrewd exploitation of the sympathy which exists in the country for the men," which is what it was.[10]

On 3 May, Angus MacInnis wrote Mayor McGeer from his office in Ottawa that "On May 1, just before leaving Ottawa, I had a talk with Grote Stirling, Minister of National Defence, in which I tried to convey to him the situation as I saw it in Vancouver.... Unfortunately, Mr. Stirling and other here believe that it is altogether a result of agitation. For some reason, they will not see or cannot see the naturalness of what has happened and what must happen until the men in the camps are allowed to live like human beings."[11]

"The result of agitation." MacInnis could not know that Mayor McGeer was increasingly leaning towards the view, no doubt encouraged by Foster, that agitators were taking control of the strike, even though he continued to sympathize with the main body of camp strikers in his city, and just as he continued to assault the Dominion government for its refusal to give any kind of assistance to his city. As the next weeks passed, McGeer would step up his campaign against the Communists whom he identified as directing the affairs of the RCWU for nefarious purposes: Evans, Taylor, Bruce and the others.

McGeer faced still another problem: The appearance in Vancouver recently of hundreds of unemployed men, not camp workers, but itinerants who clogged the already overburdened relief system and who provided ready recruits to the strike leadership. Just how many did join up is not known. Disaffected strikers were still seeking to leave the city and perhaps their places were taken by this new breed. But there is no indication that a sizeable growth in the ranks took place at this juncture.

According to a signal sent to Ottawa by General Ashton on 4 May, the camp men themselves were becoming increasingly impatient with the course of the strike. They had even asked for and had been given permission to hold a meeting at which only the original strikers would be included. "This is interpreted as an effort to break away from outside control," presumably the Communist Party and the CCF. Neither intelligence reports nor the press confirm that such an assembly did occur.[12]

The CCF returned to the fore on Sunday, 5 May, Jubilee Weekend, with a huge Youth Rally in Hastings Park. Dorothy Steeves and Lyle Telford were there as were the Reverend Andrew Roddan of the First United Church, the Reverend Wilberforce Cooper, rector of St. James, and Bill Davis from the RCWU. Conspicuously absent, the *Sun* noted, were the three thousand school children who had been expected. Absent as well were Evans and his circle of associates who dispatched the young and amiable Davis in their stead. The chagrin over the 28 April Arena rally had not yet dissipated.[13]

The city's Jubilee Parade passed elegantly on 6 May, the only distraction being the appearance along the way of strikers who tagged spectators.[14]

The coming week was to go by quietly with respect to public demonstrations. Around this time, the RCWU decided to send men into the residential neighbourhoods bearing petitions urging negotiations with the authorities. Ron Liversedge and his friend Pete Neilson were assigned a corner near the University of British Columbia, "a quiet lovely suburban backwater, a street of laburnums and lilac-draped lawns." Guiltily relieved to find no one waiting for them, the contrast between lilacs and camp sweaters being grotesque, the men decided to wait for five minutes. Promptly, and to their dismay, out from a nearby house emerged "a tall old tweedy gent with a couple of ancient, satiny ladies" who prevailed upon Liversedge and Neilson to make their presentations, "a mass public meeting with an audience of three and two speakers." After a half-hour of this, the tweedy gent said he would not sign the petition because "he did not believe in embarrassing the Prime Minister" though he did sympathize with the strikers. The ladies likewise commiserated but felt the men should have stayed in the camps "until the government found something better for us to do." With that, they gave Liversedge and Neilson streetcar tickets for the trip downtown, shook hands and went back inside.[15]

The strikers had organized a straw poll that same week, circulating ballots about the city, urging them on shoppers: Do you wish to abolish the relief camps and are you in favour of granting immediate relief to the strikers? Twenty-seven thousand six hundred and forty-six ballots were cast, of which 26,972 said yes to both questions, 512 voted for abolition and no to relief and 162 were spoiled. Mayor McGeer cabled his good news to Sir George Perley:

> This report indicates that public opinion in Vancouver is overwhelmingly against relief camp system and equally in favour of work and wages programme. In view of nationwide unemployment problem, I urge you to consider development of plan under which men can be put to work for reasonable wages.[16]

Perley was quick to reply that the Dominion could not set up such programmes for one particular group or in one province only. The expense was simply too great. The scheme of work and wages "might result in retarding the gradual but steady revival of business."[17]

On Friday morning, 10 May, Mayor McGeer granted an interview to a striker delegation of seven men: A. Renaud, R. Rogers, G. Swazey, N.F.I. Cunningham, V. Wadlinger, R. Savage and John McEllagott, who "purported to represent 2,000 men." If "R.

Savage" is the Robert "Doc" Savage who had been a division officer, then he is the only one of the seven about whom something is known. Given the substance of the interview, the point about the constitution of the delegation is important. None of the more familiar leaders was there, not Evans, nor Shaw, nor O'Neil nor Walsh, not even Bill Davis. The plaintive quality of their questions and requests causes one to wonder whether they really represented all the strikers or the Strategy Committee.

First, of course, they asked for relief. McGeer, of course, told them that while they had his sympathy, the city was in poor shape financially and couldn't help them in this respect.

Then, one of the strikers, not named, "wished to know if the City would put them on as Special Police at $3.00 a day." Who are "them"? All the strikers? The seven standing before the Mayor? What would be the function of such Special Police made up of strikers (or ex-strikers, as the case may be)? Was the query agreed on prior to the interview or was it spontaneous?

McGeer explained that the Dominion government would supply all police and military protection "to keep peace and order in the city."

Someone asked whether it was not true that there was a city statute that provided relief for anyone who had been in Vancouver for thirty days. McGeer said there was not.

Well, what if the community said give them relief?

"No possibility" unless the Civic Charter was changed and only the legislature could do that and the legislature was not then in session.

Then John McEllagott, late of Boston Bar Number 108, offered this assurance:". . .they [the strikers] had no intention of starting anything; feeling that if they did their next camp would be one surrounded by barbed wire. They felt that if they again returned to camp, they could be forgotten."

All in all, a most curious session, the strikers' questions and comments appearing meek and mild, lacking the force and anger that Evans would surely have exerted, even if to no avail. Again, one has to wonder who authorized such a visit.[18]

Meanwhile, Colonel Foster was receiving and conveying to McGeer reports of the growing restlessness in the ranks of the camp men. The plan for a General Strike did not seem to be progressing. The Action Committee had set up classes in public speaking for strikers who would then go among the unions in the area "to broaden out the strike," the implication being, perhaps, that these unions were not naturally turning themselves to such a mass walk-out.[19]

The City had given the CCF women a permit to hold a Mother's Day Parade to Stanley Park on Sunday, 12 May, and so off they went, three hundred women and fourteen hundred strikers. In one of the prettier sections of the park, the women formed an enormous heart which encircled most, if not all of the men. After that, the ladies passed among their visitors, arranging them in groups of two or three and handing out street car numbers and addresses for Sunday night dinners. Ron Liversedge thought it all "very touching. The unity and resolve of the people of that time not to submit to abject misery gave one a feeling of deep pride in working people." No one seems to have objected to the "exploitation" of the strikers on this charming occasion.[20]

But for all that, the frustration continued. By 16 May, all the strike funds would be exhausted. The longshoremen and the street railwaymen had pledged donations later in the month, but in the meantime, how would they pay for food and lodging?

Matters were certainly not helped on Monday, the thirteenth, at the regular meeting of the Vancouver School Board, when a delegate from the provincial parent teacher federation offered a resolution in support of the strike. Replied Board Chairman George Cunningham:

> ...we must remember that the school board has been the recipient of a lot of criticism over the children's part in the May Day Parade. If we endorse the resolution now, it would seem, perhaps, in the eyes of certain interested parties that we were part and parcel of the group endeavouring to use the children for propaganda.

The resolution was defeated.[21]

A week later, at a meeting of the Board, an irate Vancouver resident, Charlotte Cole, presented a letter demanding an investigation of school faculty to determine communistic activities in the classrooms. It was "an appalling and soul shaking state of affairs." School children marched in Stanley Park behind the Red Flag. There was no Union Jack in evidence, that's for sure.[22]

The City granted a permit to the strikers who proposed to meet at Cambie Street on 16 April and then proceed past but not stop at Mayor McGeer's office. A delegation would step aside and wait on the Mayor. But that morning, Colonel Foster learned, presumably from his agents, that "Communists have urged making use of this parade as an opportunity to defy the police and start trouble." The parade, Foster said, *would* halt in front of City Hall, Evans would make a speech. Traffic would be blocked and police would be assaulted as they tried to move the marchers along. The hope was that it could later be shown that the police really started the trouble.

To meet this threat (apparently Foster declined to cancel the permit to parade), the Chief Constable issued a list of orders placing an RCMP detachment on Beatty Street, forty dismounted provincial police at the city station, two cars armed with tear gas guns and bombs, twenty-five VCPD men hidden out of sight at city hall, plainclothesmen all over the area, rooms overlooking city hall "safe guarded," close observation of Evans and his colleagues.

> There must not be any display of force until necessary and every effort will be made to avoid a clash, but any attempt to deliberately defy the law must be firmly dealt with.[23]

The obligatory rally began around 2:00 P.M. where the strikers were told that only fifty-six dollars remained in the strike fund. Then Dr. Lyle Telford, a CCF supporter and a frequent speaker at rallies, came forward and delivered himself of remarks, which, according to the VCPD report, were nothing short of inflammatory, if one in the crowd happened to be a communist or a striker:

> Comrades, fellow workers, friends, enemies, stool pigeons, agents provocateur: the crisis has arrived, but he hoped everyone would use their head and intelligence, not to be led by stool pigeons or agents to cause trouble, thereby lose public sympathy which you have gained. The CCF and our followers are behind you. They are intelligent and believe in the change of government by constitutional methods, not by riots and chaos. Otherwise you will find that the state is ready for any emergency, that you will be the cause of innocent people getting hurt, yourselves also, with no advantage whatever, but a set back.[24]

George Black, a WESL representative and chairman of the rally, interrupted at this point to remind Telford that the Action Committee still existed and that if any organization wanted to help, they should join that group. Malcolm Bruce further embarrassed Telford by denouncing his plea for passive resistance.[25]

The delegation bound for McGeer's office had already left on its mission but Evans sketched out the parade route and, contrary to the terms of the parade permit, told the crowd to circle city hall until the delegation emerged. Once there, the marchers commenced to snake dance, jamming traffic. When the delegation came out, its leader, Sid Skinner of the lumberworkers, jumped on McGeer's official car and started to make a speech. Immediately he was whisked off by constables who then threw a cordon around the delegation and marched them, and the camp workers, back to Cambie Street where Skinner reported that McGeer said he could not help them, he had no authority nor funds, but that he would dispatch a cable to Grote Stirling asking Ottawa to assume responsibility.[26]

Thus the afternoon, so filled with alarm, came to a close more or less peacefully and the strikers retired once more and the police dispersed. But, claimed the RCMP:

> *Many of the strikers taking part in the above parade came fully prepared for trouble: some of them having their hats well padded and carrying concealed lengths of pipe, rocks, etc.*[27]

The cable which McGeer sent to Ottawa as the delegation looked on described the scene outside his office, passed along the injunction that Ottawa appoint a "competent commission to settle dispute between provincial and national governments and the relief camp strikers... responsibility of situation must rest with those who alone have power to remedy it, namely the national government of which you are head."[28] This message was sent to "The Right Honourable R.B. Bennett," who was back in Canada and, after two months recuperation, in his office. Said Bennett in an interview at this time:

> *The House meets Monday [the 20th] and God willing, I will be there but I am not going to expose myself to efforts that will destroy me... I do not want to boast that I am fit for anything nor do I want to indicate that I am not fit. I must feel my way.*[29]

Presumably not interested in sparing the Prime Minister "efforts that will destroy me," Arthur Evans next launched an expedition which resulted in the one real victory the strikers enjoyed during their two months in Vancouver. While Colonel Foster had warning of the trouble on the sixteenth, he seems to have had no notice that on Saturday, 18 May, a division of strikers intended to seize and occupy the Vancouver City Library and Museum.

This was the plan. Division One would march to Spencer's Department Store and create a diversion, whether or not they gained entry. Division Two would go to Woodward's Department Store for the same purpose. As it turned out, both units got inside, some scuffling and head thumping occurred and then the police forced the men out into the streets.[30]

Division Three, led by Steve Brody, was to march up Main Street to the Library, dodge in, run upstairs to the Museum proper:

> *One big room with angles and alcoves and corners crowded with historical, artistic, cultural and anthropological exhibits and artifacts, some good oil paintings and taxidermy, most of which was irreplaceable.*[31]

Ron Liversedge thought the room uniquely suited for defence: one front exit with a grill across it and a narrow stairway to the lobby, one rear door leading into a small stairwell.

As Division Three pushed into the building, a striker told Ruth Corbett, a clerk working near the front to "Get out!"

Corbett replied: "We don't have to get out because it already belongs to you. It is a public museum."

Strikers: "Get out!"

So, for the rest of the day and into the evening, Corbett sat on the front steps, preventing curious children from going up to peek inside "because I didn't think it was right to have children looking at that sort of thing, and I stopped them."[32]

The museum curator, H.L. Nelson, joined Corbett in the street while Librarian E.S. Robinson remained inside on duty throughout the entire siege. In fact the library remained open to patrons until 4:00 P.M., about two hours after the ordeal began.[33]

Immediately they had the museum secured, the strikers jumped to a telephone and began to call friends, the police, the press, union halls, the CCF offices. Shortly, calls came back recounting the movements of the other two divisions down the street. Naturally, a food committee had been designated at the outset and these men began to lower baskets on ropes to friends below. Ron Liversedge:

All the bake shops for blocks around were sending bread, pastries and pies; the stores, delicatessens and the cafes were contributing. From the White Lunch down the street came gallons of cream cans filled with hot coffee. People in the crowd below were sending up tobacco and cigarettes and candies and chocolate bars. Later in the evening when many of the boys in the museum began to suffer headaches (probably from over-eating and smoking) a request via the basket quickly brought over a half dozen bottles of aspirin tablets. We were overwhelmed with good things.[34]

Lou Tellier recalls that the men found a book about World War I which contained horrifying pictures of mutilated men and over which the younger strikers hung in amazement.[35]

Colonel Foster arrived and, unexpectedly joined by Oscar Salonin of the VDWWA, stood chatting with the strikers hanging out of windows and peering through the grill.

I pointed out to them that their conduct was extremely foolish, that they had done anything but a clever thing in placing themselves in the top part of the building, because all that was necessary to do, and I had the men with me who could do it, who could easily flood the building with gas. . . . I told them they would have to stay there. . . . until I had gone a little further into the matter. . . .[36]

The Chief Constable left in search of the Mayor; a striker deputation led by Joe Kelly also set forth. The crowd outside, estimated at two thousand, carried on in high humour. From the VCPD:

> *A parade was led to the library, back to Victory Square, then after waiting around for a while, Evans suggested we go to City Hall, shouting "We want relief." Singing "Hold the Fort," then zig zagging from one side of the street to another, also circling street cars, holding up traffic, which had to be rerouted, back to Victory Square. [Jack] Taylor spoke then. Everyone in the press, by whispering campaigns, runs down the leadership of the Communist Party. But I am here to tell you the C.P. organized you in the slave camps, drew you out of them to Vancouver, kept you under their control to your first victory today. We have not finished. We will still carry on. . . .*[37]

Heretofore, Taylor, Evans, Bruce, any figure deemed to speak for the Communist Party, had persisted in telling the strikers and the city that the Party supported the strike, definitely, but did not control it. If the VCPD information is accurate, Taylor was conceding quite an authority and responsibility at a time when the city was first beginning and McGeer had already started to look again at the leadership, to question the motives of the leadership, to distinguish between the Communists said to be in charge and the rank and file who were thought to be naive young men.

Ron Liversedge later claimed that Mayor McGeer was found resting at the Vancouver Yacht Club.[38] He was hustled to his office where he met with Foster and Joe Kelly. Foster remembers saying to the Mayor that " . . . if there was any possibility of getting any kind of reasonable settlement as far as the City was concerned, of course it was the correct thing to do. . . . On the other hand, this City could not long support an attitude of contempt for law. . . . "[39] Foster and McGeer then came up with eighteen hundred dollars to be given to the strikers for relief over the weekend. The money, McGeer thought, would probably come from the Police Commission Emergency Fund.

Foster and Kelly returned to the Museum and presented the decree to Brody and company who took a vote and found the division ready to vacate the premises. But first Curator Nelson came in at the strikers' invitation and checked for damage and loss. Though Liversedge reports that Nelson found "nothing out of place, nothing broken or disturbed in any way,"[40] in fact, the curator later indicated that one case had been broken, about one-half pound of placer gold had been removed along with an old bible which was returned the next day. Liversedge also claims that the men offered to leave a clean-up squad behind but that Nelson waved this offer aside. Nelson put it afterwards that the Museum was "filthy."[41]

The siege lifted, the strikers left the Museum to a great cry from friends.

> In the dusk of an early spring evening, as far as we could see, in any direction, and jammed right up against the building, faces, thousands of faces, and then a roar of greeting; it was like a physical shock. . . Every one was filled with pride and joy at our victory.[42]

In a cable to the Prime Minister that weekend, Mayor McGeer gave vent to his indignation and humiliation. At the most, the message may have acted as a cathartic, since Ottawa again refused to accept responsibility.

McGeer to Bennett:

> Never in the history of the Dominion of Canada has blind brutal lawlessness been more in existence than it has been during the last month in the city. Our funds are therefore exhausted and we cannot do anything more than we have done. We cannot force the relief camp strikers to go back to camp. We cannot force them to be orderly and peaceful.[43]

Bennett to McGeer:

> It was only at the request of the provinces that the Dominion undertook the care of single homeless men in camps as a measure of assistance and it is an indispensable condition of our coopera- tion that the men to be thus cared for should be nominated by the provinces, subject to our selection of those eligible. No powers of compulsion have been exercised by, or are vested in the Domi- nion, and in consequence, the men are free to leave camps at any time. Having done so, their care devolves on the province.[44]

Had the provinces, in fact, requested that the Dominion erect the camps? General McNaughton had come forward with the idea three years before and there is no evidence that he proceeded from conversations with provincial premiers or their advisors.

Unfortunately for McGeer, the weekend was not over so far as nuisance and disturbance and intrusion were concerned. On Sun- day, the nineteenth, the Mayor appeared at an evening service of the First United Church upon the invitation of the Reverend Andrew Roddan to comment on the strike situation in the city. Word of this event circulated. When McGeer arrived a few minutes before 8:00 P.M., he found dozens of representatives from the Women's Labor League, the CCF and the strike, sitting in pews, booing, yelling catcalls, exclaiming "Read the Riot Act, Gerry!" Most of the "offenders," as the RCMP called them, were women.

McGeer sat in a side room until his critics departed, apparently under their own power. Out front, they waited while McGeer gave his talk and then slipped out of a rear exit to his car. The crowd, suspicious and dubious when the word came that he had left, hung around until 9:45 P.M. at which time the Reverend Mr. Roddan invited them to send two search parties through his church.

Next, two women came up and proclaimed that the protest was in response to the proposal made by McGeer and endorsed by the Vancouver Ministerial Association that the strikers return to their camps pending negotiations. Roddan read a letter ostensibly from the RCWU denying any complicity in the embarrassing episode. The VCPD agent, forever skeptical: "The letter was just to pull the wool over the public's eyes," although he did acknowledge that strikers did not really appear in numbers until "the crowd collected outside to razz McGeer."

The RCMP had been told by one woman present that evening that the protest was really directed at "Gerry's predilection for the pulpit as a means of putting forth his electioneering propaganda . . . . The women were so gratified with their success in discomfiting Mr. McGeer that they plan to attend church as regularly as he does."[45]

The euphoria generated among the strikers by the Museum seizure must not have lasted long. The RCMP agent reported in early the following week with a story about a split between what he called "left" and "right" factions. "Right" wanted to break from the present leadership; Evans and company, the "Left," exercising "considerable intimidation," argued for their retention. A meeting was called by the "Right" but "hecklers sent there especially for this purpose, it is thought, succeeded in creating such a disorder. . . that it was rendered rather fruitless."[46]

The breach, if such there was, seems to have been eased by Wednesday, when the strikers came together at the Avenue Theatre to talk about the various options set before them. A show of hands revealed an apparent unanimity in refusing to go back to the camps "under any promise whatsoever." Oscar Salonin of the longshoremen took the stage to tell the men that if they stayed in Vancouver, his union, the VDWWA, would help financially unless it too went out on strike.

As the strikers filed out, they were each given two postcards addressed to Mayor McGeer and bearing this message:

> I have today furnished a meal (and/or) a bed to a relief camp striker. I protest your deliberate attempt to starve these boys back to camp. I furthermore demand continuance of relief and the opening of negotiations.[47]

The idea was that the strikers would peddle the cards in the streets.

General Ashton, of course, had kept the General Staff briefed on the Museum episode following which, he reported, Colonel Foster had phoned him at McGeer's request, with the suggestion that the Department of National Defence establish a camp at Point Grey, house the strikers there "while their cases were being considered." Ashton turned the proposal down firmly: the land belonged to the University of British Columbia; his office lacked enough canvas to erect tents for fifteen hundred men; once there, the men might determine not to leave; the Department of National Defence was not responsible for these men until they had been readmitted. On the other hand, Ashton signalled his conviction that "Situation breaking. If we keep firm over next 36 hours or so it would be all over."[48]

But when the General discovered at mid-week that "quite evident Communists have persuaded camp men remain in City to foment trouble and using promise longshoremen and seaman strike working towards general strike," he forwarded an inventory of the "civil force" held in readiness for immediate action in Vancouver: RCMP 111, Provincial Police 71, VCPD 218, Special Police 40.[49]

And then, seemingly, a profound silence fell across the city. Or so one might think. Ashton's messages to Ottawa from 24 to 28 May: "No reports received." The VCPD agent checked in on 24 May with this speculation regarding Evans: "No doubt he is singled out to take the rap...so if he is picked off alone a cry will go up for funds to defend him from all over the country." And then the agent confirmed that "everything will be quiet until Monday [the 28th]."[50]

But not everyone had taken a breather. No doubt still steaming from the rebukes heaped on him on the sixteenth just before the march to City Hall, Dr. Lyle Telford took to the radio on Friday evening, 24 May, and delivered a vitriolic address in which he attacked Evans and Taylor as communists who had taken control and who were using the strikers as means of stirring up strife.

> They are not camp workers; they are mainly occupied with the task of getting these boys to do something dangerous in the name of strike action.

Finally and nastily, Telford accused Evans of having ducked to safety after giving a fiery speech at Cambie Grounds, having run into a nearby building and up to the second floor from which he watched the crowd march off, presumably to the City Hall.[51]

Next, Mayor McGeer gave an interview to the *Sun*, published on the twenty-seventh, in which he too indulged in some sarcasm.

> *Now there has been a great deal said about "Our Boys," many of whom can barely speak English, many of whom came from other provinces and from other countries than our own. The communists have been busy creating mothers organizations to protest on behalf of "Our Boys," many of whom are old enough to be grandfathers.*

And on the subject of city constables injured by the several fights:

> *Our boys, so called, have at least arrived at the stage in life where they do not need their mothers to protect them against the police.*[52]

That same day, the Mayor received a letter from Foster in which the Chief Constable passed on information gleaned from intelligence reports. There was money enough left among the strikers for one more meal, and the men were angry about this, having been promised by their leaders that "they would look after them." Foster also confided to McGeer that many strikers were disgruntled because a meeting had never been called to discuss the Mayor's old idea of a return to the camps while their committee stayed in the city to negotiate. One division was supposed to have passed a motion calling for such a ballot.[53]

Over the next twenty-four hours, in fact, the Strike Committee met to debate a call for a vote on whether to stay, rejected the plan handed over by Kelly, Shaw and Walsh that a secret ballot be given out "to see who would want to return to camp" and accepted, instead, a ballot with the open question, "Do you wish to carry on the strike? Yes or No?"[54]

There were other signs that the strikers' ranks were yielding. Sands's platoons of pickets were removed from the yards.[55] The VCPD noted that 800 men had been allowed to request readmission to the camps though Ashton's office set this figure at 330, a more reasonable estimate.[56] By the thirty-first, Ashton could report that 516 had applied in the past four days.[57] The attacks continued. Smokey Cumber came to trial, charged with obtaining clothing and board in a relief camp under false pretences. The Crown prosecutor said of Cumber that he had been a professional hobo since his arrival in Canada in 1905. "It is not manual labour that Cumber is interested in but the job of general secretary of the relief camp workers of British Columbia."[58]

On 29 May, the *Sun* carried a full page advertisement signed by a group called "The Citizens' League" which described the threat "to the very life blood of this province" by "cunning and unprincipled organizations." The League promised to launch a series of exposés of "red activities" and urged every citizen to do his part. The League aligned itself with "The 500 Club" which itself sought to combat radical control of trade unions.[59]

The Citizens' League of Canada, created in April 1935, was an extended association of several dozen Vancouver business leaders brought together at the urging of the Shipping Federation to confront "the communist menace" which seemed about to overwhelm Vancouver labour, most specifically, the waterfront workers. The threat of a general strike in the city no doubt acted as further reason for such development.

> An aroused citizenry is determined that government, industry and commerce of this province shall not fall into the hands of a group, the avowed purpose of which is to reduce and revolutionize our whole economic and social structure in accordance with its own narrow and destructive interpretation.[60]

Prominent in the organization and administration of the League were K.A. MacLennan, a manager of Robin Hood Mills and a member of the Shipping Federation; Victor McLean, a wholesale merchant and one-time member of the Vancouver Welfare Federation Board; and Colonel C.E. Edgett, Chief Constable in Vancouver, 1931-33.[61] A special interest group if there ever was one, the League sought to warn the community of the encroachment by communists through media campaigns and private briefings with city, provincial and federal officers. On 28 May, for instance, General McNaughton met with two CPR executives, C.A. Cotterell, Assistant General Manager, British Columbia District, and J.O. Apps, General Executive Assistant, who told him about the menace of the WUL on the West Coast and about the League which "is remarkably representative of the business men of Vancouver." Cotterell asked McNaughton to release money from the relief fund for use by the League and to provide two hundred more RCMP for Vancouver. McNaughton could not provide Dominion funds for the League, and the assignment of the RCMP was the responsibility of the Attorney General. But he made it clear "that he is indeed glad to learn that the responsible citizens of Vancouver are alert and that they appreciate the fairness of the attitude adopted by the Dominion Government."[62]

Politically powerful, the League was prepared to stay the course and to provide whatever assistance it might during the period of labour unrest. While it did not make itself known publicly until the final hours of the relief camp strike, there is little doubt that its private support of McGeer aided that harassed official in maintaining his resolve. Once the waterfront strike began on 4 June, just as the Trekkers left the city, the link between the League and the Shipping Federation came more clearly into evidence, with the Federation even supplying automobiles for Foster's special police.

Undeterred by the League's notice, the relief camp men met on the afternoon of 30 May in the Avenue Theatre and, after several hours of discussion, a delegation went off to petition McGeer for a permit to hold a tag day on 1 June, the object being the solicitation of funds to support a march to Ottawa. McGeer, needless to say, declined to help.[63]

Then the results of the ballot carrying the crucial question "Do you wish to carry on the strike? Yes or No" were released. Six hundred and twenty-three men had voted to continue. Two hundred and seventy had voted to return to camp. Sixteen ballots were spoiled. The VCPD indicated that "fully 400 men did not vote and also about 200 or 300 have left town on freights."[64] The RCMP concurred: "Several hundred who are drawing provincial relief refused to vote and many have, individually, left the city for parts unknown."[65]

What now? Malcolm Bruce is supposed to have said to a comrade, who turned out to be an informant, that regardless of the vote, the strike was over, though Bruce claimed victory.[66] But it would be very difficult for the men to go back to the citizens of Vancouver and ask them for sustenance over the next weeks. And one could still see that there was a hard core intact, camp men committed to the extension of the strike.

So, before the Avenue Theatre meeting adjourned, perhaps even before the ballot had been disclosed, the decision to go to Ottawa was made. The actual source of the proposal may never be known. Liversedge writes of Evans jumping up and crying "Comrades, we've got to get militant." But the men replied with a "loud and collective groan." Nevertheless, one striker did rise, reminded the gathering that their objective had always been negotiations with the federal government... "so I say, let us go to them. I hereby move that we go to Ottawa to discuss work and wages with the federal cabinet."[67]

However it happened, and it may well have been the Strategy Committee which, in a last gasp, planted the idea before the meeting took place, the On-To-Ottawa Trek was quickly ratified.

The strikers, those who had pledged to go on the trip, were exultant. Other witnesses were not so sure. The RCMP: "The trek to Ottawa, it is intimated, is merely a last effort of the Strike Committee to secure further funds from the citizens of Vancouver. It is believed that the trek to Ottawa would be abandoned immediately the strikers got out of sight."[68]

Ashton to Ottawa: "Impression general that proposed march to Ottawa possibly announced to save faces of organizers and give excuse for breaking up strike."[69]

The VCPD agent never seemed to have doubted that the men were serious about getting across the country: "...the strike is being shifted from Vancouver to Ottawa with a hell of a lot of nuisance demonstrations on the way. The fact that half of them shall be arrested on the way does not bother them any...It will be one huge 'bumming' parade." In anticipation of their departure, and the close of the strike in Vancouver, the VCPD agent now began to file dozens of names with his superiors, along with financial records.[70]

Taylor, Evans and Bruce appeared at a rally on the evening of the thirtieth in reply to the earlier attacks by Telford and McGeer, but only Taylor seems to have come up with a phrase that caught the mood. Alluding to the arrests of Buck and his comrades in 1931, he cried: "I defy the authorities to lay their bloody hands on a single communist or camp striker in Vancouver!"[71]

Colonel Foster's men were not impressed. Although the strikers had been more or less careful after the Museum episode, the Chief Constable did report to McGeer on 1 June that strikers had been observed tagging without a permit and so about twenty-five had been arrested.[72]

And on 1 June, for that matter, *The Worker* in Toronto, apprised no doubt by telephone or cable of the trek, came out with this surprising comment:

> It is only while concentrated in large numbers in main centers that the strikers will be able to force the government to recognize the issues that have been raised by their strike...the fight of the B.C. camp workers is in Vancouver.[70]

We might imagine that on this last point the Communist Party of Canada and the Prime Minister were in complete accord.

One last social hour: a picnic for the strikers at Stanley Park on Sunday, 2 June. The ranks of the camp men were noticeably depleted now; nearly half the original force had left the city. But the picnic passed cheerfully enough. Ron Liversedge: "It was happily marked by an absence of speechmaking and propaganda." The sentiments ran strong. Families shared hampers of food with young men who were by now pretty hungry.

> There were staunch and lasting friendships made that day and right now...I know of two aging family men, in Vancouver, one of them a grandfather, who both met their wives for the first time at that memorable picnic.[74]

The relief camp strikers, call them Trekkers now, reorganized for the expedition. The four divisions were cut to three, committees trimmed or eliminated, though a first aid detachment was added. Men with noteworthy jail records were encouraged to stay behind though not all complied. The very old fellows, like Tin Pan Bill (who went on the Trek) were given the option of going or staying. Cooking equipment appeared, blankets, heavy jackets for the mountain chill, scrub boards. Friends who could not go gave their few dollars to those who would, but most Trekkers left Vancouver as broke as when they arrived, more so, in fact.

Twenty or more men had already gone ahead, advance parties, Bill Davis among them, pressing on to Calgary, Medicine Hat, Regina, to notify unemployed workers' associations and town authorities of the march. The former were to help with provisions and general support, the latter were to maintain order and see to lodgings.[75]

One last bit of business: an audit of funds taken in during the strike, $22,433.34. After $800 was wired to the Trek in Kamloops, there remained $134.

There was another audit of sorts published at this time. On 31 May, the MacDonald Commission signed its report, exactly two months after it had set to work, too late then to prevent the strike, too late now to appease the strikers. For the most part, the Commission was "generally" or "fairly" satisfied with the operation of the camps in the province. This, after visiting 46 camps and interviewing 277 "witnesses." The superintendants and foremen were acquitted, the food pronounced "good," blankets sufficient, sanitation "good," though at Point Grey the facilities were "disgraceful," the rise in tobacco prices such that quantities available had to be restricted. The absence of wages so prevented men from setting out on their own to look for work or for society that men "drifted into either an attitude of hopeless indifference or of studied rebellion."

The Commission, although prevented from making recommendations by its terms of reference, nonetheless called attention to the unrest caused by the absence of wages, the presence of youths who had no opportunity for schooling, the argument for a raise in the food allowance per man by three cents a day, a leave of absence for those with "continued service," canteens in the camps, camp truck transportation to sporting and entertainment events, more and improved recreational equipment. Although they found no evidence for it, the Commission still believed that the men were convinced that they are a "forgotten group."[97]

But the strikers, probably, could have cared less. Those who intended to make the Trek now began to pack and on 3 June, in the evening, they began to move from Cambie Street to Cordova and Hastings and the Cenotaph to the Canadian Pacific Railway yards.

Five
The Trek
"Hold the fort, for we are coming!"
— Traditional song

The On-To-Ottawa Trek began in this way: A crowd of two thousand spectators gathered near the idling 10:10 P.M. seaboard freight which was equipped with two dozen or so pieces of rolling stock: "the drag." They passed tobacco and food to the Trekkers as these men marched up, and then the citizens joined in sing-a-longs. And if these citizens, for some remarkable reason, had never heard the relief camp men yodel in the streets of Vancouver, then they thumped out the words of "Hold the Fort" inscribed on sheets passed around for the occasion. A pleasant scene, touched with the nervous energy of imminent departure; the Trekkers eager to be off, the townspeople friendly, pointing out those travellers who had chalked "On-To-Ottawa" on their coats.[1]

All of this was observed by a small group of city, federal and railway police who counted heads, took notes, but did not interfere.

A few minutes before 10:00, 831 Trekkers assembled beside the cars, more or less by divisions. (Another two hundred would leave at dawn and link up with the first group somewhere west of the mountains.) Jack Cosgrove, a World War I veteran from Calgary, designated Marshal of the Trek, stood before them. A tall, thin, blue-eyed man, Cosgrove dressed in khaki coveralls and a cap on which he perched a pair of goggles. He gave the order to mount, he would give many more over the next two weeks. In one motion, the Trekkers began to swing up the ladders, about thirty to a car. The food, the cooking gear, were stored below. The last goodbyes were called out; the songs died away, the citizens drew back. The train edged beneath bridges, women leaned over the railings and dropped parcels to the men as they passed under.[2]

Recalling the departure, Irven Schwartz:

I don't think anyone was fooled. I don't think there was even one in the group who thought that even if we did get to Ottawa that we would win our demands. But we would put them before Parliament anyway. We would fight as long as we could. There were no misconceptions among the men.

Most were quite certain that we would be met by a full brigade of RCMP or by the army and that we would never get to Ottawa. "How far do you think we'll get? We might get to Rogers Pass. They'll most likely stop us at Banff. They'll never let us get through the Rockies." We wondered later why they didn't stop us sooner. All we ever saw was a few Mounties watching us go by. I suppose they thought we would tire ourselves out. That we would just fall apart by ourselves.[3]

Others wondered, too, why the Trek had not been stopped, and in Vancouver! Learning of the expedition, Ottawa Mayor P.J. Nolan wired Mayor McGeer:

You ought to be fairminded enough to see that your troubles should not be forced on other communities. Ottawa as a city has absolutely nothing to do with a national problem and as far as I am concerned I shall refuse to deal with such a question.

McGeer replied:

Vancouver has suffered enough and you ought to be willing to bear your share of the national grief that the depression caused. Most of these men came from Eastern Canada and ought to return there.[4]

One wonders whether Nolan and McGeer ever met at a Mayors Conference later on. In any case, McGeer had no time for sympathy nor for rest. On 4 June, the long dreaded longshoremen's strike began in Vancouver.

Few of the Trekkers at this point knew that Arthur Evans would not be making the trip east. As WUL district organizer, Evans had necessarily neglected his original assignments while the camp men were in Vancouver. The very "success" of that strike had excited other unorganized groups of workers to action. Evans had to see to these, bring them into the League and so he could not be spared for the long haul.

Evans did win this concession from his district superiors: he would leave a day before the main body for Kamloops and Golden, prepare receptions for the Trekkers, see them into the mountains and then return to Vancouver. Before his own departure, Evans had wired Morris Rush in Kamloops and the Golden Workers' Protective Association of the impending arrival of one thousand men into their communities.[5]

But when Evans reached Kamloops on 2 June, he found to his dismay that his local contact had left the area on a personal errand. Moreover, Mayor W.J. Moffat then told Evans that there were no facilities for housing the men for two nights though they were welcome to sleep along the tracks. And tag days were not really welcome in his town. Evans replied to this last that a tag day "would be a democratic way of allowing the citizens to express their support, their approval or disapproval by donating or refusing to donate..." Evans had a point, of sorts, but he also knew and Moffat probably had heard that the relief camp men could be pretty persuasive when it came to waving tag cans in the faces of the citizenry. The mayor was adamant. A chagrined Arthur Evans left for Golden, arriving there on the fourth.[6]

Meanwhile, the seaboard freight glided out of Vancouver, past Coquitlam, north along the Fraser River, past Lytton and onto the banks of the Thompson, past Ashcroft, past Savona and into Kamloops. All through that first night, the train chugged along. The men on top of the cars, so large a company, held on to the slats of the roofs, clutched each other, braced themselves. Though it was June, the air chilled. Not all of the men wore gloves. Once in a while, the train paused long enough for a smoke and for bladders to be emptied downwind.

The Vancouver authorities thought the Trekkers would abandon the march as soon as they were out of sight of the city, but there is no evidence that men did scurry off and away in the darkness though it is possible that a few left.

The Trek pulled into Kamloops on the morning of the fourth and into Mayor Moffat's reluctant care. That fellow, as we know, had already refused a request for a tag day, but the men made a quick canvas of the small community anyway. Moffat is supposed to have offered the use of an empty hospital as a dormitory but his guests declined, preferring to sleep in boxcars and in Riverside Park, three or four to a blanket. While they waited for the second smaller detachment to join up, they lit campfires, cooked meals, held impromptu concerts where they alternated World War I songs with contemporary hits.[7]

One man who paid close attention to the Trekkers in Kamloops was a young reporter for the Toronto *Star*, James Kingsbury, who rode with the men from Vancouver to Regina, providing his readers with intimate details of the Trekkers.[8] He was not the only "outsider" to ride with the men. At least one professional burglar is said to have come aboard at Calgary. An RCMP constable joined up at Moose Jaw.

It was Kingsbury who spotted the O'Brien sisters, Yvon, aged nineteen, and Catherine, aged twenty-two, climbing up the ladder of a freight car in Kamloops. Just how far they travelled is not known for nothing was ever reported of them again, either by the *Star* or by Trekkers. The likelihood is that if the O'Briens set out, they soon quit, probably at Calgary.[9]

Unhappy with the reception in Kamloops, Cosgrove wired Evans in Golden that they would not linger another day as planned but would start off on the fifth. So they trooped to a freight conveniently poised to go east, mounted and resumed their journey.[10]

Somewhere between Kamloops and Revelstoke, one story goes, the train pulled into a siding for a few minutes and the men on top looked down and discovered a gang of relief camp workers labouring nearby. These innocents strolled over to say hello and then it became apparent that they had either rejected the strike in the first place or else had returned from the strike to await negotiations in Vancouver. While men on the train exchanged gossip with the camp workers, others dropped behind the cars and picked up stones which they passed to their buddies who then hurled them down on the heads and shoulders of their unsuspecting colleagues.[11]

In Revelstoke itself, where the train lingered for an hour, a crowd of Trekkers hurried to nearby cafés for coffee and sandwiches. A few pieces of crockery were broken in the stampede, apparently by two drunken travellers who were immediately dismissed from the march. But someone took notes and when the Trek reached Calgary, a money order for five dollars was sent to the restaurant owner.[12]

Well before dawn on 6 June, the On-To-Ottawa Trek rolled into the town of Golden, British Columbia, where it found a jubilant Arthur Evans very much in control. Evans had turned out the workers' protective association who "went among the farmers and collected butter and eggs and I wired for 800 loaves of bread from Calgary and ordered four cords of wood and borrowed every wash boiler in Golden." And then Evans and the others set out to make a stew.

When Evans had reached Golden the day before, he had been advised by the provincial police that the Trekkers ought to sleep in the local jungle. But there was an auto park about a mile from the yards and Evans pointed out that there was "no reason why the camp strikers should be known as — should be treated as any different than any other tourists around...."[13]

So when Red Walsh got down from the train and trudged to the park, this is what he saw:

> Here's an old lady standing up over a bath tub with a ladle about that long, stirring the bouillon in the bathtub. "Good morning, boys!" And the two washtubs nearby, all of them overflowing with dumplings as big as footballs and lamb stew.
> "Line up the boys over there and give them a hot meal!"[14]

That stew, Evans later exclaimed, "would go down in the history of Golden and Canada."[15]

After the meal, Evans called the Trekkers together and announced that he had to return to Vancouver, as directed. The men groaned;

"I pointed out to them that I was subject to the discipline and subject to the decisions of my district committee...."[16]

Well, then, who would lead them to Ottawa? Evans rose again and introduced George Black, a member of the Worker's Ex-Servicemen's League. "And who is Black?" called a few skeptics. "And Black stood up and gazed around the meeting and they accepted him as leader then." Black, a Glaswegian ten years in Canada, a one-time employee of a Saskatchewan power company, had been an enlisted man in the Scots Guards, which probably accounted for the gaze. Though single, Black had not received medical clearance for entry into the camps. From 1932 on, he had been on relief intermittently. During the strike in Vancouver, Black had served on the Action Committee where he won a reputation as a responsible advocate.[17]

All in all, the stay of twenty-four hours in Golden had been just fine, the locals competent and tender-hearted. Even the provincial police, a unit of three, had proven supportive although, at the end, their ranks were increased by a half-dozen constables from Revelstoke, among them a sergeant whom Evans had known for years.

Evans left for Vancouver, and around 3:00 A.M. on 7 June the Trekkers prepared to move on. One division spent a few minutes sweeping the auto park for trash and then trooped into town to await the arrival of another train and of a pusher engine which would be added so that the grades before them could be mounted. Once again, Jack Cosgrove came forward:

> He had them line up with division captains, who would watch
> him for signals whenever they were ready to go which was a
> signal of his arm, the captains would then pass the signal along
> and the men would then start to climb on the cars.[18]

Around 7:00 A.M., the train finally set off, reaching Field by 10:00 A.M. Outside that town, Willis Shaparla, sitting on top, minding his business, watching the scenery, was approached by an RCMP constable who swung up a ladder and proceeded to walk along the drag while a companion marked time with him on the road bed below. The officer paused beside Shaparla and said "How do you do, sir?" Shaparla thought he emphasized the "sir" rather heavily.[19]

These two constables, joined by a railwayman, briefed Black and Cosgrove about the perils of Spiral Tunnel. Though many of the men aboard had been on this route before, still they had not come in this fashion, so many clustered together. Irven Schwartz:

> Everybody was pretty worried. There were footpaths over the
> tunnels but you had to stay on board. Some of us put wet hand-

kerchiefs over out faces. It was hot in the tunnels. First there was a blast of cold and then a real blast of heat and finally the smoke came back. You think you're not going to live. We were afraid of panic. The guys might panic and try to jump off the train inside the tunnel. But we got through alright.

Anyway, the Rockies are a thrilling scene and, as Schwartz adds, jauntily, "You get a much better view from atop a freight train than you do from a passenger car...."[20]

Bill Hammill missed the good time in Golden. When he arrived with the Trek, Arthur Evans told him to go on to Calgary and help co-ordinate the local efforts to house and feed the expedition. Somewhat to his surprise, Hammill found the authorities there well disposed to assist however they could. Though permission to hold a tag day could not be given, Hammill claims that members of the city council told him they would still not stand in the way of such a manoeuvre. They also offered the Trekkers the use of the city's Exhibition Grounds for lodging, as long as it was understood that the marchers would leave after the weekend. Most prairie towns along the railways had some sort of exhibition facility for summer fairs and auctions. The Trek would visit more than one during its existence, for the grounds were a natural and convenient way of housing the men: the buildings, some of which were covered pavilions, were located on the edge of town adjacent to the yards.[21]

When the train arrived in mid-afternoon on Friday, the seventh, a committee of well-wishers appeared. CCFers, YCL kids, unemployed protective association veterans. Cosgrove dismounted, signalled the captains who brought the men down. Hammill greeted them and produced a photographer who took pictures. One shows the trekkers just climbing down, another observes them marching in a column to the Exhibition Grounds led by three men dressed in suits and ties, more than likely their hosts.

While the Trekkers gobbled sandwiches and coffee in the basement of the Grandstand, Black took the Strike Committee aside for a meeting. They had no food; there was no way that the citizens' support group could manage to feed them over the weekend. "In order to have this respite," Ron Liversedge recalls, "we must have food every day; therefore the first thing on the agenda was the winning of relief." And so a major demonstration was set in motion for Saturday: a tag day and a siege of the provincial relief office, "blitzkreig tactics," as Liversedge puts it.[22]

An audacious plan. How to walk a narrow line between a genuine appeal for support from the citizenry and intimidation of the authorities? How to restrain the hundreds of men in the ranks who had not yet dramatized their expedition to the nation? What if the besieged called in police and the army? And why jeopardize the Trek so early in its history?

That Friday night, the men rested in the Grandstand basement, but because it was drafty and because they lacked sufficient blankets, many ended up pacing here and there to keep warm. Meanwhile, their committees probed the city, met with newsmen, arranged radio interviews. Liversedge and Perry Hilton were assigned to speak at a rally of supporters of the Canadian League Against War and Fascism. The main event, however, was A.A. MacLeod, national secretary of the League, a one-time employee of the YMCA, a Communist party veteran who had, coincidentally, turned up in Calgary.

According to Liversedge, MacLeod turned down their request for a place on the agenda and instead ordered the piper to play "O Canada!" thus closing the meeting.

> I sprang up and howled out: "Mr. Chairman, I sent a note to you asking for a few minutes on the platform. Now I want to ask the people here if they wish to hear a delegate from the On-To-Ottawa Trek which landed in your city today."

Of course they did. Liversedge, nervous and dry-mouthed, took a glass of water from MacLeod and read his message. The Leaguers applauded and then appointed a delegation which included a somewhat sobered MacLeod.[23]

Back at the Exhibition Grounds, Black began to dispatch telegrams east to cities and towns along the intended route. And wires came in, "greeting us and wishing us well."[24] The Trekkers needed all the good wishes they could muster, for in Calgary they were about to be tested for the first time since leaving Vancouver.

The next morning, a thousand Trekkers, minus a few squads left to guard the Grandstand, locked arms and marched in column of four into city centre, in their lead, one "Comrade Marsh," a Trekker noted for his skill with the concertina which he carried with him constantly and shoved in front of his chest as if to ward off assault. At the provincial relief office, the men began a snake dance that wound around and around the block; several hundred citizens came up to the entrances of the building, up onto the stairs, up the fire escapes, to wait, cheer and jeer.

The stage was being set for a drama of considerable tension and conflict, not to say inadvertent humour. Because several participants later described the siege as it was carried on inside the relief office, including a clerk who took nearly verbatim notes of the interviews, it is possible to reconstruct those moments.[25]

Within waited the Chairman of the Relief Commission, A.A. MacKenzie and his associates, Edward Kolb and Angus Cochrane.

In their company, perhaps a chance visitor, was Colonel Gilbert Saunders, a retired North-West Mounted Police officer.

The initial Trekker delegation comprised George Black and Gerry Winters.

Before any real discussion of the marchers' demands could take place, Colonel Saunders launched into a harangue in which he denounced the expedition as "communists, hooligans and tramps." MacKenzie interrupted to assure Black that under no circumstances could his office issue relief funds to the men because those funds were reserved for Albertans.

Black, somewhat taken aback, left to search for witnesses who could corroborate the conversations about to ensue. He returned promptly with A.A. MacLeod of the League Against War and Fascism who brought with him three Calgary women who were also Leaguers. MacLeod asked to read the request for instructions which MacKenzie had just sent off to Ottawa:

To H. Hereford, Esq. Relief Commission, Ottawa.
One thousand single men from B.C. in Calgary defying authorities. Demand assistance. Immediate action necessary. Waiting instructions.

Macleod said, "No, that will not do. You will send a wire demanding that we be fed and sheltered. You send another wire and tell them that we demand assistance and that you will be prepared to give this at their approval. Until this is done, you might as well know that these men can go without food just as long as you can in this office." Not until then, recalled Edward Kolb later, did he and the other officials realize that they were being held prisoner.

Relief Commissioner MacKenzie reiterated his first remark that he had no authority to expend provincial funds in this manner. "I have no vote to provide for an invasion of other provinces when they leave the province where relief is available."

Black replied "We have the people outside who voted you in!"

MacKenzie stood by his instructions and then some:

If they want to vote me out, I will go out voluntarily. We have money for Alberta people but none for B.C. residents. These people outside are people who are trying to cause trouble and have got a bunch of young fellows to cause trouble. It is a revolutionary movement which is handled very cunningly. The only people who can do anything for you are the Dominion Government.

MacLeod returned to the offensive with his own revision of the cable to Ottawa: "Interviewed delegation British Columbia single men. Demand food until Monday. Some immediate action

necessary. Will distribute funds or food if you can make available.
A.A. MacKenzie.''

Edward Kolb picks up the story:

> *MacLeod said "Now I will send it." To this I said "Nothing*
> *doing. Any wire which leaves this office is to be sent by us and*
> *not by you. However, if it will do you any good, I will ring*
> *the telegraph and read it to them." MacLeod said "Alright,*
> *but make sure you ring the telegraph office." I might say that*
> *it was not so much what MacLeod said as it was the manner*
> *in which he said it. Very dictatorial. MacLeod said "I must*
> *have a copy of that wire so I can show it to these men." To*
> *this, Mr. MacKenzie objected. He said he was not permitted*
> *to allow government correspondence to leave the office. MacLeod*
> *said "There is no use of me going back to these men without*
> *something official to show that their demands were being taken*
> *care of." Shortly after, MacLeod left the building with a copy*
> *of the wire; loud cheering was very plainly heard...*

Very shortly thereafter, MacKenzie received word from the
provincial government in Edmonton authorizing two meals per day
per Trekker until the march moved along next Monday.

A second ''quarrel'' now broke out between Colonel Saunders
and two of the League delegates, Bertha Gusland and Elsie
Anderson. We have the women's side of the exchange:

Bertha Gusland:

> *Colonel Saunders said in a very gruff voice, ''Who are you?'';*
> *I said ''Gentlemen, I happen to be a Christian and today my*
> *mission is to come and see if my brothers, the boys, who are*
> *marching out there have food for today and tomorrow. Will you*
> *please give them two meals for Saturday and Sunday and they*
> *will be away on Monday morning...We want you to do the*
> *same for these boys as we would expect our boys to be treated*
> *in Vancouver.''*

Elsie Anderson:

> *Colonel Saunders...took quite a part in the discussion and he*
> *seemed more interested in the subject of communism and the*
> *red bogey in the camps than to see about conditions in the camps*
> *and the reasons these boys were on the march. He didn't say*
> *much about the necessity of them having food, but he said we*
> *were very badly misled women and so were the hundreds of other*
> *Calgary citizens who were on the streets at that time. He said*
> *that if we were sensible people, we would go out there and tell*
> *these boys to go back to camp. Well, this is not what we believed*
> *and naturally we refused to do that. We said we had come there*

for the purpose of seeing that these boys were fed. We believed that the country owed these boys, at least, their food. . .Well there was a good deal of conversation in that office. . .it was largely a philosophical discussion of communism.

Colonel Saunders, Bertha Gusland and Elsie Anderson withdrew from the office and walked into the street which was packed with spectators, Trekkers and citizen-pickets. Saunders got into his car but the crowd closed around and prevented his departure. Elsie Anderson perched on a fender in emphasis of his predicament. So Colonel Saunders and Elsie Anderson waited, chatted, while MacLeod and MacKenzie concluded their negotiations upstairs. Elsie Anderson thought that, after all, the Colonel may have seemed to have found some humour in the situation, and in fact, bought a tag from another woman who shoved a tin can in his face.

Black and MacLeod soon emerged and called the siege to a close. The pickets and the Trekkers moved along, the last group to carry on with the tagging which netted them about fifteen hundred dollars.

Never again would the Trekkers pass the days in such high spirits as they did that weekend in Calgary. Public sentiment came vigorously to their side. The grant of relief made hot meals possible. Saturday night the men relaxed in the comparative security of the Exhibition Grounds while their committees prepared for a rally and picnic on Sunday.

Word came that a team of Young Communist Leaguers who had gone off to Edmonton to recruit camp workers were about to arrive in Calgary with nearly three hundred strikers. This new element required the reconstitution of a fourth division led, it is believed, by Sven Uden. While recruits were sought at this stage, nevertheless, as Ron Liversedge points out

the material which was already flocking to our banners in large numbers was, to say the least, very raw. There is the possibility that we, the B.C. originals, had also started to regard ourselves as being a wee bit exclusive. Nevertheless, there can be no doubt that without the original "family," that hard core of class conscious, politically conscious relief camp workers of B.C., the trek could have been overwhelmed and defeated by the great influx of raw, crude unemployed recruits which joined us in Calgary. . .The newcomers had to be taught organization and discipline and there wasn't much time for a leisurely approach.[26]

Some organization and reassignment of the original Trekkers into the new division and Edmonton men into the old divisions did take place. Lectures on the origins and history of the relief camp strike and the objectives of the Trek proceeded. Liversedge is satisfied that the Edmonton faction "soon fitted in and became a new source of strength on the Trek." But the strain of induction and orientation would grow over the next three weeks as hundreds sought to join up in Medicine Hat, Moose Jaw and Regina, among them two RCMP constables and one Joseph St. Laurent who sidled up to a Calgary constable who had drifted briefly and anonymously amongst the Trekkers that weekend and who proposed that they travel together and share the receipts from burglarized homes in the towns and cities the Trek would visit.[27]

Sunday afternoon, the men marched to a rally and picnic sponsored by local supporters. Along the way, some started singing the *Internationale* but others in the ranks squelched the harmony. Red Walsh chaired the meeting, a pep rally as much for the Trekkers as for the citizenry. Anyone who applied could have a few minutes on the platform; dozens of congratulatory telegrams were read or acknowledged. At the close, Walsh introduced a message from a group of Calgary women who proposed to join the march. "One passage in the letter stated that the women realized how lonely the men must be and wished that there could be a woman for every man on the Trek."[28] In fact, according to James Kingsbury, the *Star* man, there were two divisions of unemployed women who sought admission. Recognition, not romance, was their intention.[29]

The O'Brien sisters notwithstanding, were there any women on the Trek? One marcher years later described a woman dressed in camp clothes huddled with a fellow who was later identified as an RCMP constable, the insinuation apparently being that the legitimate Trekkers were celibate while the police were promiscuous. The only constable who did board illicitly did so at Moose Jaw and so spent just a few hours on the train before it was halted at Regina; even if there had been a woman there, he would have had to have an unerring instinct to find her in the crowd.

The On-To-Ottawa Trek prepared to leave Calgary; early Monday morning, 10 June, the men marched to the yards. James Kingsbury, who had been given permission to continue with them, describes the occasion.

> *Sitting on the grass in their designated groups with their packs crowded about them, the lads chatted with the large crowd of citizens on hand to see them off. But they kept a watchful eye on the freight as it was being made up and at a sign from Black and Cosgrove leapt and swung out along the length of the train as the railway police kept back the curious. The whole contingent was packed on the fifty cars with every group shown to its place*

by a group leader. Only those with strike cards were allowed to board the train.[30]

So thick were the crowds of citizens that Division Three was momentarily thrown off its stride as it approached the train. The Edmonton boys who had been assigned to this unit marched in its rear "and started cutting up, leaving the ranks, rushing over to the sidewalk and hugging girls and generally whooping it up." Ron Liversedge, failing to bring the men to order, sent word to Doc Savage, his captain, who dispatched Paddy O'Neil to the rescue.

Paddy roared into the mob: "What the hell's going on here? Have you bastards gone mad? Get back into line there or get the hell off the Trek. Do you think we've spent years building our organization to have you come and wreck it? If we want clowns here, then we'll apply to the Ringling Brothers. Now get into line!"

O'Neil, who boasted an awesomely ugly face, then turned on Liversedge and chastised him "for being too much of an anarchist." An appeal to good sense won't work when the men lacked discipline. 'They are good boys; they'll learn with the right teachers, and we'll teach them.' And then with a wink at me, he says 'Our way.'"[31]

Spectators walked along the drag after the men had climbed up, throwing tobacco and food parcels to grinning faces. One mother hurried back and forth calling in vain for her boy. Jack Cosgrove's mother was there to wave goodbye to her son, the marshal. Cosgrove had said, in a chat with Kingsbury, that as a youth he had delivered R.B. Bennett's newspaper! A youngster came running up with a sweater and a suit of overalls which he swung up to his brother. Kingsbury counted eight cats and three dogs carried to the roofs of the cars. He talked with Fred MacDonald who, with his dog, Switch, had crossed the continent four times by freight.[32]

The Trekkers no doubt knew that Arthur Evans would soon rejoin their ranks. A telegram had been sent on Saturday to the WUL office in Vancouver requesting his return. The WUL complied and so on Sunday, Evans set out with the expectation of reaching the march at Medicine Hat. There is no evidence that the men had balked at George Black's leadership; more than likely, they simply realized, and Black with them, that Evans had a grasp of the situation and such a powerful personality that they could afford, at least, to make the appeal. In any case, it was their Trek.

The routine of departure had been more or less fixed; the co-operation of the train crew and of local railway superintendents became necessary and expected. The latter may very well have acted on their own initiative. Recalls Arthur Evans:

> *Cosgrove, Black and I got on board the tender of the engine...the place where the leaders and the marshal decided to travel so we would be facing the entire body of men on the roofs...that way we would be able to check up on discipline and see that everything was going along in the proper way. The Divisional Freight Superintendent came up alongside the engine and yelled up the the Engineer and he said ''In going away I want you to be very careful,...when you are starting or stopping [I want you] to give a loud blast of the whistle before you start up the train.''*[33]

James Kingsbury left Calgary riding on the tender. ''Someone produced a huge package of soda wafers and butter and the 'front line crew' had a welcome snack with a touch of cinder here and there.'' The men behind needn't have been envious. They carried with them some twenty-four hundred sandwiches prepared and delivered by supporters in Calgary.[34]

The courtesy of the train engineer became almost paternal. Medicine Hat is about 180 miles from Calgary; with stops along the way, the trip took eight hours. A considerable rain storm began to fall for a fifty-mile stretch and once through it, the train stopped for a spell. The men clambered off to stretch, smoke, wring shirts and jackets out, wipe the coal dust from their faces; the engineer called out to them cheerfully not to worry, that he would blow the whistle well in advance of departure so no one would be left behind.

And off they went again.

> *Then the sharp wind sweeping across the open prairie whipped up a fine coal dust in the faces of the reserved seat riders and hunks of it were whipped back off the top of the coal heap to make things more interesting.*

To escape it all, Jack Cosgrove rolled up in a sheet of canvas and went to sleep.[35]

Bill Davis and his friend, Con Shaw, left Calgary that Saturday to meet with Medicine Hat authorities and friends about a brief layover. As the negotiations proceeded, Davis had a telephone call from Calgary: ''Ask the mayor if he would accept a proposal that he give us $1,200 and we will pass up the town.'' Davis's surprise and chagrin at such an idea grew out of his belief that plans were all but completed for the stop. If the train did pass up Medicine Hat, then the Trekkers would have no real respite until they reached Swift Current. The anxious youth hopped a passenger train back to Calgary to make his protest only to find that the idea had been dropped. So Davis turned around and took a freight back to Medicine Hat and concluded the arrangements there.

Davis walked down to the yards to watch the arrival. Nearby stood a railway constable, "the one who always put off the freights when we got into Medicine Hat,

> so he was an old hand at watching trains come in with one or two boys but he's never seen the train come in completely loaded from one end to the other. The train had come to a stop. Nobody moved. Nobody got off that train except Cosgrove, the marshal. He gave the command for everybody to dismount and they all got off and then they all stood there, put their packs on their shoulders and right turn, quick march, and that's all there was to it. That old bugger who'd kicked us off the freights day in and day out, he was just overwhelmed. And they went to the ball park and ate, and I got on that same freight and went on to Swift Current.[36]

What was Ottawa officialdom doing all this time? The Trek was a week old and what Ottawa knew, by and large, was what it read in the newspapers and what its officers in Military District Eleven (Victoria) and Military District Thirteen (Edmonton) had relayed to the General Staff. In sum: once the Trek cleared Vancouver, "no known efforts being made by railway or other to prevent movement eastwards."[37] Relief camp foremen at Salmon Arm counted thirteen hundred on board as the train passed by, an exaggeration since the two sections had not yet joined up. The events in Calgary were described accurately with the added caution that "Lord Strathcona's Horse standing by but until formal requisition will not move."[38] Coming away from Calgary, the Trek now numbered fourteen hundred, an accurate estimate. In a lengthy cable to Ottawa, the commander of Military District Thirteen laid out the Trek itinerary and a bit more.

> Talk amongst men this is a revolutionary movement. Large numbers expected to join at Winnipeg and Toronto. Addressing gathering today. . . Hold relief commissioner and other hostages until provinces agrees feed men. Tag Day collection exceeds $1,500. Itinerary announced. Medicine Hat, Moosejaw, Regina, Brandon. One day each. Winnipeg, four days. Toronto, four days, then Ottawa. If sufficient food collected here, not stopping at Medicine Hat. Speakers said today public militant action will be taken anytime demands not acceded to. Attack camps and administration and said large number joining strikers enroute to Toronto.[39]

By the time the Trek reached Medicine Hat, Ottawa had received another assessment, this from A.A. MacKenzie who had been so humiliated by Black and MacLeod.

> *Regarding British Columbia single men. A dangerous revolutionary army intimidating and defying provincial and municipal governments by threats and actually holding officials as hostage until demands met. Their success having a far reaching effect that may be difficult to control. Single men relief is a racket and cannot be successfully handled until all males registered.*[40]

It is certainly unlikely that Prime Minister Bennett ever intended to let the Trek reach Ottawa. Nor did he have to be persuaded that this was "a dangerous revolutionary army." More than likely, the decision to stop the march at Regina had already been made by the time the men left Calgary. Why Regina?

The On-To-Ottawa Trek had not been halted previously because the railways had not complained to the national government nor had they asked for help in preventing the marchers from commandeering trains. Even if they had, it is not conceivable that Mr. Bennett would have made a move while the Trek was in Calgary, his own constituency. If he waited until the march reached Winnipeg, then he would have to deal with a Trek that would have doubled in size in a city which already had a volatile labour crisis.

Regina was the site of the Royal Canadian Mounted Police recruit training depot. It could be effectively sealed off once the railways refused to collaborate any longer. And Regina was in a province whose premier was a Liberal, the Honourable James Gardiner.

The first evidence of Ottawa's decision to bring the Trek to a close in Regina is contained in a telegram from RCMP Commissioner MacBrien to Assistant Commissioner S.T. Wood, commander of "F" Division, based in Regina. The message contained a plan for coping with the Trekkers once they found out the trains would not take them eastward: (1) the railway yards were to be patrolled to prevent the men from boarding; (2) troopers were to ride trains eastwards towards the Manitoba border to a point beyond zone in which men are likely to reboard train, this precaution obviously taken in case the Trekkers decided to walk to Winnipeg; (3) both the CNR and the CPR were prepared to cooperate and would provide forty police officers each to assist; (4) forty five additional RCMP were to be posted to Regina. "Arrange for all possible strength your own division also all available men in depot including training class"; (5) once in Regina, the Trekkers were to be briefed as to their "rights."[41]

Apparently not having anticipated such a barricade, the Trekkers left Medicine Hat as confident as ever. In their vanguard, Bill Davis and Con Shaw arrived in Swift Current, no longer confused, it would seem, about a gentle game of extortion. Mayor James Taylor later testified that the two youths approached him with news of the march and invited the town to give them a subsidy of $250 and one meal and that the Trek would be on its way within two hours. Mayor Taylor replied that the town was in the hands of its creditors and that no monies could be issued without their permission. A meal could be found though and thus when the train rolled in around noon on 12 June, the marchers lined up at the seven cafés and restaurants in Swift Current. The train engineer waited an extra fifteen minutes while the men gobbled their food and then hiked back to the yards. There were the inevitable spectators, among them a lady who spotted her husband trooping by. He had deserted her five years before, so she exclaimed, and she wanted the train halted until she could get her hands on him. But the knave skipped away.[42]

Moose Jaw's Chief Constable, John Fyvie, had prepared a carefully designed route of march to the city's Exhibition Grounds but when the Trekkers arrived at 8:00 P.M., they ignored the instructions and took an alternate path led by local friends. Fyvie's men spotted a few of the men begging about the town, but otherwise the men stayed together for a talk by Evans, an exhortation of sorts, in which he warned them against any ''hooliganism'' once they reached Regina. So they lounged and ate and rested all day on Thursday, the thirteenth, and then at midnight set out for the train. Enroute they were told that it would not be ready for another hour so they squatted or stood along Manitoba Street for several blocks, the damp chill air hinting at the rain expected that night. In their midst stood eighty recruits, among them Constable Henry Cooper of the RCMP detachment in Regina who had found easy access to the card committee and who carried as Number 295 his assignment to Group 25, Division 3.[43]

As they waited, more than likely the Trekkers passed along the rumour that a reporter had heard that the march would be halted in Regina. This fellow told a police officer who told Fyvie who told Evans.

The good will and patience expressed by the city of Moose Jaw can be appreciated in an interview which Mayor Harris Johnstone gave to the *Evening Times* on 14 June: "After giving tacit consent to the march across Canada to present their grievances to the Dominion Government, the strikers should have been received with the same courtesy."[44] This is not to say that some observers hadn't become anxious about the intent of the On-To-Ottawa Trek. Irven Schwartz spent some hours visiting relatives who lived in a hamlet near Moose Jaw and he came on the mayor of the village who cried: "Is this the revolution?"[45]

During the layover, Arthur Evans went by freight to Regina, met with local supporters and his own advance team, confirmed for himself that some sort of detention there appeared likely and then took a bus back to Moose Jaw.

And so the Trek edged along to Regina, Saskatchewan, "this sleepy prairie City," as Matt Shaw called it.[46]

Six
Regina
"They had better keep away from here..."
— Mayor Cornelius Rink

With its wheat economy and its topography, Saskatchewan had suffered as miserable a fate as any of the provinces during the years of the Great Depression. The drought across the Palliser Triangle seemed to be in some sort of malignant conspiracy with those other "unnatural forces" which broke the wheat market, ruined farms and businesses and homes and jobs. At one time 20 percent of the population of Regina were on relief; per capita income had dropped 72 percent in the first four years of the havoc. Unemployment became the chief, the abiding concern. Public works projects and direct relief made some difference but not nearly enough. Nearly $2 million went into the former by the time funds were exhausted in Regina in 1932. The "dole," cruel and humiliating as it was, still provided a family of four with a monthly food allowance of sixteen dollars, a bit more for coal, light and water and up to twenty dollars a month towards rent. Clothing might be obtained from private charities and the Lieutenant Governor's Emergency Distress Fund.

Regina may have been a prairie city but, by 1935, it was certainly not "sleepy." By a considerable act of will and courage, the citizenry had hosted the 1933 CCF convention and had organized the highly successful World Grain Exhibition and Conference at the city's exhibition grounds that same year. Present at the opening ceremonies were the Governor General, The Earl of Bessborough, Arthur Meighen, W.L. Mackenzie King, one thousand Indians, twenth-eight thousand "other visitors" who admired the murals and paintings adorning the new Grain Show Building and the "Made in Regina" exhibits. The two-week long festival included a New York cast production of *Aida* and a tent city for those who could not afford hotels and boarding houses.

Yet the troubles persisted. Stem rust ruined a sizeable portion of the 1935 wheat crop. An early frost and a persistence of drought damaged grain and vegetable fields. As farm values decreased, so did the farmers' ability to pay the interest on loans secured for relief and seed and implements. In 1935, the provincial government conceded $10 million worth of relief notes back to the farmers, thus lifting, at least for a time, the frightening prospect of bankruptcy and foreclosure.[1]

By that year, both Saskatchewan and Regina had new governments. James Gardiner, a veteran "pol" and a former premier, had returned to office after upsetting the Co-operative Government in 1934. Cornelius Rink, a colourful Dutchman, seemed visibly pleased to be Mayor of the Queen City. Both men had distinct liberal leanings, and their natural sympathies for the down-trodden and the homeless created a strain when they had to confront the On-To-Ottawa Trek and the fact that the Dominion Government chose to halt that march in their city and province. Whereas Gerry McGeer had taken the brunt of the confrontations with the men in Vancouver while Premier Pattullo stayed in the background, the Trekkers would find themselves, in the main, negotiating with Premier Gardiner while Mayor Rink waited in the wings, never, in fact, to make a notable appearance. It was Gardiner and not Rink who launched an angry series of cables to Ottawa regarding Prime Minister Bennett's decision and its consequences.

On 10 June, just as the Trekkers were leaving Calgary, Premier Gardiner discussed with his Labour and Public Welfare Commissioner, T.M. Molloy, the status of the men whilst they crossed (as it was assumed they would and must cross) Saskatchewan. The two men agreed that the Trekkers were "ordinary transients" and thus municipalities in the province, which might put the men up, could provide lodging and two meals a day and be reimbursed by the province at forty cents per man per day. This was a standard practice though never applied before to nearly fourteen hundred men at one instance. This discussion with his aide may well have been the last confident judgement the Premier would make for some time to come.[2]

Meanwhile, Colonel S.T. Wood, commanding Saskatchewan's "F" Division of the RCMP, wired Commissioner J.H. MacBrien for his instructions.

A transfer of surveillance and briefing responsibilities in the Department of National Defence also took place as British Columbia's District 11 gave way to Alberta's District 13 which gave way to Saskatchewan's District 12, commanded by Brigadier H.E. Boak. Unlike E.C. Ashton in Victoria, Brigadier Boak seems not to have figured in the negotiations and interviews about to ensue.

On 12 June, Colonel Wood informed Premier Gardiner that he had just been told by Commissioner MacBrien to implement a plan intended to prevent the Trekkers from passing east of Regina.[3] Gardiner turned to his telegrapher and poured out a set of cables that bristled with frustration and outrage. Implicit in Wood's announcement to Gardiner were the dismissal of the "ordinary transients" ruling which the Premier and Molloy had just concocted, as well as the shift from provincial to dominion authority of the RCMP posted there.

Gardiner protested to Bennett that the plan to halt the Trek in Saskatchewan had been conceived without his knowledge. Clearly, the 1928 Dominion-Provincial Agreement with respect to the Force placed the RCMP under his jurisdiction. "We object to police force which acts in matters of law enforcements under instructions of this government being used for any such purpose and will so instruct them."[4]

Bennett's reply was that "both railroads are forwarding request to you for assistance to stop unlawful travel by trespassers upon their lines eastward. Mounted Police have been asked to assist in this work. In my opinion continued unlawful use of railways should be stopped and assume that you will co-operate to this end."[5]

It was absolutely necessary, so far as Ottawa was concerned, that the railways request aid for once it had those requests, the national government could invoke the Railway Act and transfer the RCMP back into its embrace. In fact, by the time Gardiner first cabled the Prime Minister, he had already met with railway officers.

On 11 June, the Premier received a message from W.G. Mather, CPR superintendent for the Western Division, who implored him to help and co-operate so that the Trek could be stopped.[6] The next day, S.J. Hungerford of the CNR in Winnipeg cabled a similar plea to Regina.[7]

Gardiner's wrath fell first on Mather. How, he wanted to know, could either railway, after having carried these men across two provinces, in little more than a week, suddenly complain about trespassing? The premier had information that trains had been split in two, cars added and special stops arranged, never mind safety instructions from crews to the men. And yet, no protest until now![8]

Mather responded that no trains had been split nor cars added. Calgary officials had requested that the train stop on the western edge of the city so that the Trekkers could move more easily to the Exhibition Grounds. For that matter, Mather triumphantly added, so had your Mr. Molloy made the same request.[9]

Gardiner was not convinced. The railways had made accommodations and concessions. They had not protested before and so "your Company must at once assume its full share of the responsibility for any consequence that may develop as a result of any action...."[10]

In this exchange across 12 and 13 June, Mather may be said to have had the last word, and a rather smug word at that:

> ...these incidents were the result of the observance of usual operating rules and practices and would be recognized as such by one familiar with railroad operation.[11]

On 13 June, the nation learned of the plan to halt the Trekkers in Regina when Justice Minister Hugh Guthrie disclosed the reasoning and prescriptions of the government to the House of Commons. Guthrie announced that ''the government is satisfied that the present easterly march of the so-called camp strikers from British Columbia, which has now reached Regina, has been organized and is under the direction of certain Communist elements throughout Canada and is a deliberate attempt to disturb the peace, order and good government of Canada by unlawful means.''

The Trekkers had been trespassers since they left Vancouver but the two railways have ''intimated to the government that they are unable, through lack of sufficient railway police to clear their trains of these marchers. . . .'' Now that the call for help had been received and the Railway Act invoked, the Government has ''determined to utilize the forces at its disposal to assist in preventing further trespasses or other breaches of law by the marchers and to maintain law and order.''[12]

Once he had orders to implement the MacBrien plan, Colonel Wood circulated an elaborate table of organization with a general description of his troops' assignments and a final word or two of advice. From ''F'' Division in Regina, Wood took 240 constables whom he divided into Troops A-D under Inspectors Montizambert, Moorhead, Mortimer and Brunet. Each troop yielded three ''detachments'' and each detachment, three ''patrols.'' These constables ''would render every assistance to railroad authorities in an effort to prohibit movement eastward of some 1400 relief camp strikers due in Regina on June 14.'' The RCMP would furnish escorts for east-bound freights and patrol cars to towns this side of the Manitoba border. None of Wood's men was to carry loaded firearms or, for that matter, any ammunition at all.

Now the advice. The Communist leaders of the Trek ''will endeavour to manoeuvre and provoke the police into starting hostilities. . . At the moment, there is considerable public support for these strikers as the public does not realize the motive and revolutionary tactics behind the movement.'' The Force must be very careful ''. . . for the public and press will be inclined to be very critical of the actions of the police.'' Even so, ''It is not intended thereby that when occasion demands its members shall not act energetically and with determination.''[13]

Colonel Wood sent one more message to Ottawa with a copy to ''D'' Division in Winnipeg: ''There is more than a possibility that if the situation becomes critical the Premier [Gardiner] will call upon the citizens of Regina to provide cars and the Province to provide trucks with which to carry these relief camp strikers to the

Manitoba boundary.'' Wood later testified that, indeed, Premier Gardiner had informed him that he might take such action.[14]

Regina Chief Constable Martin Bruton, twenty years on the job after a career with law enforcement units in Dublin, Edmonton and Winnipeg, circulated this notice to his men on 14 June:

> *During the time that the British Columbia strikers are in Regina, all members of this department who are on Weekly Leave will remain on reserve either at their homes or at the Police Station, and they will be subject to call at any time.*
>
> *The motor cycle constables and officers will direct special attention to the Stadium, where those marchers are housed, and will keep this office advised of their intended movements.*
>
> *All members of the department will exercise the greatest possible forbearance in their dealing with those people, and where they are found committing what may be called minor offences such as obstructing sidewalks, etc., they will not be interfered with for the time being. But if any attempt is made to raid stores or commit any crime of such nature, the officer in charge will be immediately notified and will decide what action will be taken.*[15]

We must reconnoitre this crucial week one more time and pick up the arrival in Regina of a two-man advance party sent by Evans: Bill Hammill and Mike McCaulay. This pair slipped off a freight on 12 June and made their way to Unity Centre, a union and unemployed workers' hall just down the street from Market Square, east of city centre by about four or five blocks. There they met Peter Mikkelson, a local leader of the unemployed, who took them right off to a meeting with Gardiner and Rink. The discussion turned naturally to the maintenance of the Trekkers at the Exhibition Grounds on the western edge of town and to meals, tag days, rallies, picnics. Did they talk about an order to halt the march in Regina? Apparently not. Gardiner presumably knew of such a plan by this time. Hammill and McCaulay probably did not though by the next day they did.[16]

Mikkelson had already begun to recruit a committee of support from among the citizens of Regina and this group gathered for the first time on 13 June. Representatives of some two dozen organizations and a number of unattached but sympathetic residents showed up, much in the fashion of the Action Committee formed in Vancouver: the CCF, the CPC, the Trades and Labour Council, three area unemployed unions, the German Workers and Farmers, the Women's Labour League, the League Against War and Fascism, the CLDL, the Milk Drivers' Union of the AFL. In that initial group were two women, Margaret Hogg and Elizabeth

Cruickshank. The chairman of the first meeting was one D. Fisher. Eric Bee agreed to be permanent secretary.

From its minutes, we learn that the group decided to call itself the Citizens' Emergency Committee (CEC). In addition, the group resolved that the province should reimburse the city council for feeding and lodging the Trekkers; that the province should also feed the Trekkers at Broadview (the assumption being that the march would proceed eastward). The CEC agreed that its members would host a rally on Friday evening, 14 June, and speaker and publicity committees were formed to make arrangements for this event.

It was resolved also that a telegram be sent to Mr. Bennett:

> We demand withdrawal of special detachments of RCMP and Railway Police in order that marchers be allowed to continue on their way to Ottawa.[17]

On 14 June, 6:00 A.M.,[18] out of a rainstorm that had been falling for twenty-four hours, a CPR engine pulling fifty cars appeared, stopped at the Elphinstone Street crossing some distance west of the city station. About a hundred citizens had gathered there and they cheered over the noise of the steam and creaking metal. The Trekkers nearest them cheered back and then fell silent. For the last time, although he did not know it, Jack Cosgrove dropped from the tender and walked to the middle of the drag. A few men, Moose Jaw recruits most likely, jumped down as well but scuttled back up when Cosgrove growled at them.

Cosgrove now gave the command, and the wet, coal-dust streaked, sleepy Trekkers descended, formed into their four ranks and turned to face the marshal. Another order, the column right-turned and set out west along Tenth Avenue. Reporters from the Regina *Leader-Post* and the *Regina Daily Star* took up positions alongside Cosgrove.

Leader-Post: *Are you in charge?*

Cosgrove: *No one is in charge. There is a committee of seventy-seven men. Would you step aside? We don't allow anyone not belonging to the march to walk with us. Would you step aside?*

The *Leader-Post* reporter dropped back and started talking with a loquacious young Trekker who chattered on about Ottawa and how no one would stop them. "A man two ranks ahead turned and spoke to the talker with a sharp glance of the eyes. That talker stopped conversation at once."

The *Leader-Post* reporter stood away from the column and watched the men pass by; he marked their wardrobe. Overalls, coveralls, suits, shirts of every colour, felt hats, cloth caps, here a pith helmet, there a straw hat. Many of the men wore goggles. They carried an infinite variety of packs and bedrolls, cardboard boxes wrapped with string. Many wore ribbons, streamers with "On-To-Ottawa" printed on them.

In a few minutes, the men had arrived at the Exhibition Grounds where they were directed to a large permanent pavilion. City police inspector Fred Toop greeted them, the first sign of any municipal authority. Still in four ranks, the column passed by into the building, walked across the straw-covered hall and then began to ease down into the bedding. Cosgrove stood before them and several times said, "No smoking, absolutely no smoking." Citizens' Emergency Committee members appeared and with great earnestness described the location of water faucets and laundry tubs, coffee and sandwiches. Cheers now broke out from the Trekkers along with a few hearty "moo-oo-oos and baa-aa-aas" just in case no one appreciated the fact that they were housed in a livestock arena.

While the men ate or wandered about stretching legs and arms, a twenty-five-member Regina choral society serenaded them with its version of the *Internationale*. Again, loud cheers. Cosgrove reappeared and announced that they would have a meal downtown later that morning. Again, "No smoking!"

The good-natured poise of the Trekkers was infectious. The local press and the CEC all thrived on the discipline, the efficiency, the quiet decorum. Observers sought out Jack Cosgrove, not appreciating still that while he was the marshal, he was by no means the leader of the expedition. More than once in the days to come, Cosgrove would be called "Commander" and "No. 1 Striker." His performance as a drillmaster would delight witnesses.

There were broad grins all around as Fred Stanicky of the Parkdale Dairy near Pilot Butte appeared with sixteen gallons of milk, a gift which caused many of the men to hurry over and begin to wrestle for cups and a place in line. Others wandered off to wash, launder clothes, take a smoke away from the building.

There was time for a nap which they most craved and then around 10:00 A.M., Cosgrove brought them to attention and led them off in a light rain downtown, along Tenth Avenue to Unity Centre. As they walked along, the men began to chant "Where are we going? Ottawa! Who's going to stop us? Nobody!" Naturally, the streets were quickly lined with Reginans, kids among them, quite a few pleasant expressions on their faces. One Trekker trooped along with a small dog perched on his shoulder.

Near Tenth and McIntyre, a Trekker suddenly stiffened and fell to the pavement. The column eased around him, a few men stopped to carry the fellow off the street and on to the verandah of Madame Morency's beauty parlour. His friends later explained that the man was a epileptic.

At Unity Centre, no doubt recognized by those who had spent time in Regina on previous trips across the prairies, Cosgrove and Mikkelson handed out meal tickets and, for the first time, the men were allowed to disperse and to find their own ways to one or another of the cafés nearby. These would do a good business over the next two weeks.

The Citizens' Emergency Committee met that day, its ranks now including thirty-one affiliates excepting the Regina Liberal Association which declined to furnish a delegate though it wished the Trek "a safe and peaceful journey to Ottawa." The Regina Conservative Association later protested that it was never even approached about joining up.[19]

The rally that evening sponsored by the Committee would go forward, rain or not. There was a full slate of speakers. Special streetcars would be available. Plans for a Sunday picnic were confirmed though a site had not been picked. One wag proposed that they use the RCMP barracks grounds to which a colleague replied that the Mounties might want to play games with the boys. M.J. Coldwell gently recommended that they use Wascana Park but this was eventually vetoed in favour of the Grain Show Building at the Exhibition Grounds. The Committee was reminded that the picnic was not just entertainment for the Trekkers. It was also meant to provide the citizenry a chance to fraternize with the men and thus to hear directly of their interests and ambitions.[20]

Still later that day, Mayor Rink received a deputation of four Trekkers, the only one known to Rink being a Regina youth named Billy Neuert. The mayor was told that the marchers needed clothing.

Rink: "We had too many of our own [people]."

[Trekkers as paraphrased by Rink]: "...everything would be nice and peaceful provided they got what they wanted; if not, if they had to stage three feet of blood on the streets of the City of Regina, they were going to have it. I said, "Boy, you are at the wrong address. Don't try to start out that way."

And did the four need clothing? Rink: "No. Well now, I don't know what you mean. They didn't. If they wanted to be dressed up to go to the Saskatchewan Hotel I would say yes, they needed it badly. But if you are talking about needing clothes, if a man is hard up, they didn't need it at all!"[21]

This threatening overture so early in the visit to Regina remains a mystery. Certainly no such intimidation of city officials at this

Richard Bedford Bennett (left) was Prime Minister of Canada from 1930 to 1935. His term was characterized by his inflexibility towards organized protest movements such as the On-to-Ottawa Trek. Grote Stirling (right), a civil engineer and politician, was Minister of Defence in the Bennett government. *(Public Archives Canada C7731, PA47576)*.

The relief camp for single unemployed men at Salmo, British Columbia, was typical of many across Canada. Men there cleared stumps from an area which eventually became Salmo airport. *(Glenbow Archives NA 2279 2)*.

"Hut News" (above) was a news sheet published by the Relief Camp Workers' Union (RCWU), one of several associations founded by the Workers' Unity League (WUL), a trade union organization created by the Executive Committee of the Communist Party of Canada. Jacob Penner (top right) and Annie Buller (centre right) were among the WUL's Executive members. *(Vancouver Public Library 8833; Public Archives Canada PA125066, PA124362).*

The decision to strike and have the camp workers meet in Vancouver was made at a meeting of the RCWU in Kamloops, 10 March 1935. The set of demands eventually presented to Bennett in June 1935 were adopted at this meeting. *(Vancouver Public Library 13316).*

Thomas Dufferin Pattullo (left), Premier of British Columbia from 1933 to 1941. *(Public Archives Canada PA 53714).*

Arthur H. Evans (right), labour organizer and one of the leaders of the On-to-Ottawa Trek. *(Glenbow Archives NA 3634 7).*

Arthur Evans was jailed in September 1933 following his efforts to establish a local of the Mine Worker's Union of Canada at Princeton, British Columbia. Subsequent foreclosure on Evans's home in Vancouver was protested by family, friends, and members of the RCWU. *(Glenbow Archives NA 3634 6).*

Rally of RCWU strikers in Vancouver, British Columbia, in spring of 1935. *(Glenbow Archives NA 3634 3).*

Gerald McGeer was Mayor of Vancouver at the time RCWU strikers were making their demands known in that city. *(Vancouver Sun).*

On 23 April 1935, a peaceful march involving 1,400 strikers became disorderly, the strikers entered the Hudson's Bay Company store with a request that their demands be considered by the authorities. Violence erupted after a verbal exchange between the men and Deputy Chief Constable Alfred Grundy. Upon their removal from the store, the strikers converged on Victory Square, where Mayor McGeer read the Riot Act. *(City Archives, Vancouver).*

The strikers formed into columns following the reading of the Riot Act and marched away from Victory Square down Pender Street. *(City Archives, Vancouver).*

On 1 May, a group of 7,500 strikers and their friends marched from the Cambie Street Grounds to the Malkin Memorial Shell to hear speeches by Arthur Evans and the leaders of the numerous unions represented by the crowd. *(Vancouver Public Library 8814).*

At Stanley Park three hundred women formed an enormous heart encircling the 1,400 strikers who participated in the Mother's Day Parade.
(Glenbow Museum NA 3634 10).

To create a diversion and deflect police attention from the efforts to occupy the Vancouver City Library and Museum, Division Two was sent to Woodward's Department Store (above) to attempt entry there. *(City Archives, Vancouver).*

Local bake shops and delicatessens sent food to the strikers occupying the Vancouver City Library and Museum. Supplies were hauled to the men in baskets, pails and cream cans. By the evening of Saturday, 15 May 1935, the strikers' demands for relief funds for that weekend were conceded by Mayor McGeer. *(City Archives, Vancouver).*

A zig-zag parade, such as this, was held on 15 May in support of the occupation of the Vancouver City Library and Museum. *(Vancouver Sun).*

ON TO OTTAWA!

Place Your Donation in Can № 125

The strikers solicited donations and distributed paper tags bearing the slogan ''when do we eat?'' in Vancouver and at stops along the route of the Trek. *(Saskatchewan Archives Board R A7864).*

Upon their arrival in Calgary on Friday, 7 June 1935, the Trekkers marched in column formation to the Exhibition Grounds, led by a welcoming committee of sympathetic citizens. *(Saskatchewan Archives Board R B3484).*

On 8 June, one thousand Trekkers marched to the Provincial Relief Office in Calgary to demand food and shelter over the weekend. Among them was "Comrade Marsh," a Trekker noted for his skill with the concertina. *(Saskatchewan Archives Board R A21, 749 (1)).*

The strikers' ranks were augmented with new recruits in Calgary. Following induction, and orientation on the strike's objectives, the newcomers were expected to maintain the orderly arrangement demanded by Trek Marshal Jack Cosgrove. In spite of disorderly boarding in Calgary, the evidence of this photograph, taken at Medicine Hat the same day, indicates that the recruits were quickly initiated into Trek discipline. *(Public Archives of Alberta A5149).*

The fifty-car Canadian Pacific Railway train carrying the Trekkers approached Regina from the west on 14 June 1935. *(Royal Canadian Mounted Police Museum).*

NOTICE

In the absence of the leader of the Marchers at the Stadium Friday morning, the following notice was handed by the Railway Companies' representatives to Bert Canaven, who stated that he was qualified to receive it and would undertake to see that it got to the leader of the Relief Camp Strikers:

REGINA, 14th JUNE, 1935.

To Whom It It May Concern:

We are instructed to inform you that no person or persons will be permitted to further ride on the trains of the Canadian National Railways or on the trains of the Canadian Pacific Railway without authority or without holding proper transportation entitling such person or persons to do so.

It is requested that you will accept this notice and refrain from unlawfully boarding or riding on the trains of either Railway Company, and that you will notify and instruct those that may be associated with you or under your directions not to unlawfully board or ride on any train of either Railway Company.

We are further instructed to inform you that if you or those associated with you further persist in unlawfully riding on the trains of either Railway Company, the proper authorities will give every assistance and use every means available to ensure that the law in this respect is observed.

You are requested to disperse and return to your respective homes. If you will do this the Railway Companies will take up with the Dominion authorities the question of providing some means by which you can so return.

THE CANADIAN NATIONAL RAILWAYS.
THE CANADIAN PACIFIC RAILWAY.

This announcement, printed on the day the Trek arrived in Regina, gave notice that the railway companies were no longer willing to countenance the use of their trains by Trekkers. The companies' requests for aid encouraged the government to invoke the Railway Act. *(Saskatchewan Archives Board R A9413).*

O ON TO OTTAWA

The Relief Camp Strikers will leave Regina via C.P.R. Freight

Monday, June 17th
at approx. 10 p.m.

The Federal Government have declared an embargo on our leaving Regina by the same means by which we came.

Only the mass support of Regina Citizens will force the Authorities to keep their hands off us on our way to Ottawa.

We call upon every citizen who supports us in our fight against Forced Slave Labor to assemble at the C.P.R. freight yards between Albert and Broad Street

Monday, June 17th from 10 p.m. until we leave

We extend to Regina Citizens our heartiest thanks for their splendid support in this vital issue.

Publicity Committee.
Relief Camp Strikers.

This poster was circulated as a counter-resolution to the statement issued by the CPR and the CNR, which refused to permit the Trekkers to ride past Regina on their cars. *(Saskatchewan Archives Board R A7866).*

Liberal Premier of Saskatchewan James Garfield Gardiner was infuriated by the decision of the federal government to halt the Trek in his province. *(Public Archives Canada PA88440).*

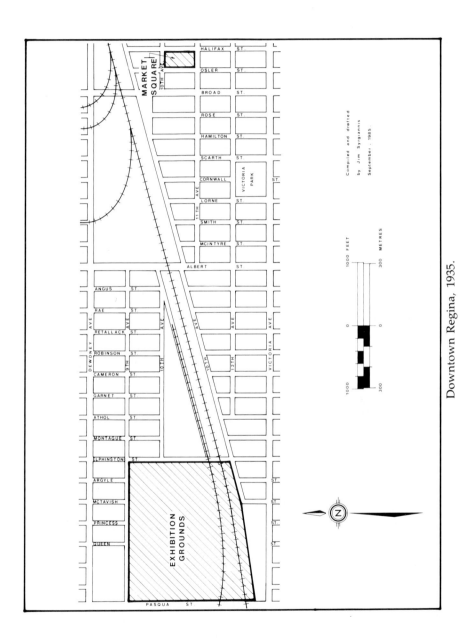

Downtown Regina, 1935.

One hundred well-wishers met the Trekkers with cheers as they disembarked at the Elphinstone Street crossing. *(Public Archives Canada C24840).*

Under the guidance of Jack Cosgrove, the men marched in their columns to Regina's Exhibition Grounds. Evans appears in the front rank, having rejoined the Trek in **Medicine Hat.** *(Glenbow Archives NA 3634 15).*

Spirits were high during the first few days the Trek halted in Regina. The strikers were housed in pavilions at the Exhibition Grounds and were joined by members of the Citizens' Emergency Committee and interested Reginans for a rally and, later, for a picnic at the Grain Show Building. *(Saskatchewan Archives Board R A21, 749C2).*

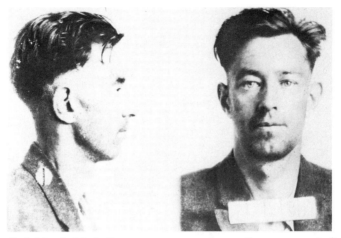

Trek Marshal Jack Cosgrove was one of a small group arrested on 27 June 1935, when an attempt was made to drive east of Regina following the establishment of police cordons to prevent the Trek from proceeding. *(Saskatchewan Archives Board R A 7868).*

Hear the Reply of the authorities to Strikers' Delegation requesting immediate Relief and opening of negotiations on counter-proposals to Bennett Government's offer of Concentration Camps

MASS MEETING
TONIGHT
Market Square 8 p.m.

(If wet will be held in Stadium)

Several Speakers representing local organizations will address the crowd

Winnipeg Strike Camp situation will be outlined. Latest developments will be given

Strikers' Funds are Completely Depleted

Support the Strikers and Force the authorities to grant immediate Relief

Negotiations continued between Evans and RCMP Commissioner MacBrien regarding the dispersal of the Trekkers, but government meal subsidies had ceased. A rally was called for 1 July 1935 to help maintain citizen support for the strike and to augment the depleted treasury. *(Saskatchewan Archives Board R A7865).*

On 1 July 1935, a combined force of Regina City Police and Royal Canadian Mounted Police interrupted the Market Square Rally in an effort to arrest strike leaders. The riot which resulted from this action left one policeman dead and hundreds of police, citizens and strikers injured. *(Saskatchewan Archives Board R B171(3), R B171(2), R B 171(1).*

Constable Archie Apps (left) was on duty on foot patrol in the city centre when he was ordered to join police at Market Square. . . . Inspector Duncan McDougall (centre) and his column of twenty-nine constables were stationed inside the police garage. . . . Plainsclothes Detective Charles Millar (right) died from a fatal blow to the head. *(Regina City Police).*

RCMP Inspector Arthur Stafford Cooper (left) led two troops of mounted officers the evening of the riot. . . . Inspector John Tapson Jones (centre) led the second unit of RCMP into the fight on Market Square. . . . Inspector Albert George Marson (right) led the third RCMP troop onto the Market Square from Osler Street. *(Royal Canadian Mounted Police Museum).*

Men who were arrested during the Regina Riot were identified on the Barracks Square, Depot Division, Royal Canadian Mounted Police. *(Royal Canadian Mounted Police Museum).*

The Honourable William M. Martin (left), the Honourable J.T. Brown (centre) and
Judge A.E. Doak (right) were appointed to the Regina Riot Inquiry Commission.
(Saskatchewan Archives Board R B2800).

The *Canadian Tribune*, a weekly newspaper founded in 1921 to report on the
Canadian labour scene, assembled this group photograph of ''On-to-Ottawa
Trekkers arrested on July 1, 1935.'' *(Public Archives Canada PA93922).*

juncture would have been countenanced by Evans. There was simply no need for it since merchants were already beginning to donate clothes and boots, maybe not enough to outfit the entire Trek but sufficient for those who were in bad shape. The Toronto *Star* reported the delivery of 250 pairs of socks and 50 pairs of boots that same weekend.[22] No doubt, there were other private contributions from time to time.

The relief camp men had staged and witnessed many rallies on their behalf and perhaps they had heard all that could be said about their expedition. But they turned out, nonetheless, for the meeting held in the Exhibition Stadium that Friday evening, along with four thousand or so Reginans.[23] The Trekkers sat in the front and led the cheering. George Black chaired the assembly, described the history of their strike, acknowledged their intention to depart for the east on Monday, 17 June. Then Black "called upon the citizens present to see that Bennett does not use his forces when we go on board on Monday or Tuesday." While Black may have only meant the use of public opinion, it was a remark like this that worried the authorities. Would the Trekkers, in fact, let the townspeople literally stand between them and the police so that they could resume their seats atop a freight?

The speeches continued. The Reverend John Mutch of the United Church urged the Trekkers to accept a hearing in Regina with the Prime Minister or his deputies. In that way, they could introduce their demands to the government and not have to go on to Ottawa. Not surprisingly, the Reverend Mr. Mutch's remarks met with a long silence, though at the end, after having advised the gathering to "cling to Christ for the sympathy we all need," he received a polite round of applause.

M.J. Coldwell appeared next. The provincial CCF leader had, on 13 June, wired the national leader, J.S. Woodsworth, with a description of his estimate of the Trek. Inquiries had led him to believe that the marchers "are a very fine bunch of young men who are not showing any connections of a Communist sort." Granted there were bound to be a number of Communists in their ranks, "but as far as we are able to discover, a large percentage of them are British Columbia CCF supporters."

> *While our stand regarding Communist affiliations is undoubtedly the only one we can pursue, yet in dealing with this problem of unemployment and youth, we should, I think, be playing into the hands of the Communists if because of the presence of Communist organizers, we did other than give them our sympathetic support.[24]*

At the rally, Mr. Coldwell exclaimed: "If you continue, no power will be permitted to stop your onward march." This was an exuberant endorsement which he might later regret.

By now, Arthur Evans surely knew how to gauge the audience before him and so he dramatically brought the rally to a close.

> *There are not enough Cossacks in the Dominion to stop us if*
> *the workers throughout the Dominion unite in saying: "Hands*
> *off the relief camp strikers!"*

It had been a good programme, a fitting end to a long and busy day. And $126.14 had been collected.

Brigadier Boak of Military District Twelve wired the General Staff that the rally had been conducted "in an orderly manner." Boak had been interviewed earlier by the *Leader-Post* because some of its readers had noticed that the 60th and 77th Battalions were on the move! Boak made it clear that these were militia units on summer manoeuvres. "We don't want to be drawn into it. We don't want them to think that we're all ready to bash these fellows on their heads!"

Finally, the Trekkers could sink into their straw beds for the first night of uninterrupted sleep since the previous weekend in Calgary. Pickets drifted here and there, watching for the over-curious citizen who might try to slip in or for the forgetful friend who lit up a cigarette. Evans, Hammill, Mikkelson and their immediate associates huddled in Unity Centre planning the Saturday tag day and the departure on Monday. Since Evans knew that the trains would not pull out, he must have approached this meeting with considerable anxiety.

Rain fell through the weekend, so the Trekkers turned out in one hundred man shifts to tag on Saturday, netting over fourteen hundred dollars. Brigadier Boak noted that "many responsible citizens contributing." It was possible for the majority of the men always to be back at the Exhibition Grounds, out of the rain, snug, catching up on sleep, laundry and gossip. That night, the Olympic Boxing and Wrestling Club provided them with an hour's diversion.[25]

The Citizens' Emergency Committee pulled out all stops for the Sunday picnic in the Grain Show Building. To be exact, the crowd consumed 4,000 gallons of lemonade, 96 gallons of coffee, 48 gallons of tea and 3,000 sandwiches. The Trekkers dutifully mingled with the townspeople, giving out autographs at that. The Regina Citizens' Boys' Band tootled in the background. The din of chatter and music grew so loud that the CEC gave up on the mandatory speeches and instead circulated a flyer urging everyone to turn out on Monday evening to send the boys on to Ottawa. One of the most popular sights that afternoon was a Trekker, thought to be an Indian, who wandered about with a small white mouse in one shirt pocket and a kitten in the other.[26]

Elsewhere that day, a number of Regina ministers took up the matter of the Trek in their sermons. The Reverend John Mutch, who happened to be the current chairman of the Regina Ministerial Association, was quoted at great length by the newspapers the next day. A compassionate man, a sympathetic man, the Reverend Mr. Mutch called for a public airing of the issues described by the Trekkers. Federal deputies were known to be arriving on Monday and so that meeting with the local authorities and the march leaders should be opened to the public. A "decent settlement of the issues" must be forthcoming.

Although the Reverend Mr. Mutch believed that the Trekkers "have a real basis for arbitration in their demands," nonetheless he felt obliged to raise a warning. Some of the Trek leaders were "irreconcilables" and "dangerous." One in particular had a "bad record" and was a "dangerous guide," a reference presumably to Arthur Evans and a judgement which the minister might well have obtained from the police or from Vancouver newspapers. But the Reverend Mr. Mutch claimed that he found this out at the Friday rally when he heard "this man" make "vicious" remarks. Subsequently he had discovered that the Trekkers had put it about that the local ministerial association supported the marchers although no such official endorsement had been granted.

The popularity and influence of the Reverend Mr. Mutch probably explains the overflow audience in his church that night. But two women were seen to pick up and leave during his talk, conspicuously displeased although at which theme it was not clear.[27]

Picnics and sermons aside, what was in the minds of citizens and Trekkers that weekend was the threat of a physical clash between the police and the marchers with the townspeople literally caught in the middle. The railways had posted their refusal to transport the men east and the Trekkers had circulated their counter-resolution that they would indeed go on, although how they expected to commandeer trains whose crews had fled and whose boilers were cool they did not explain.

The Reverend Mr. Mutch had placed some hope in the arrival of federal ministers on Monday and indeed, that morning, two of Mr. Bennett's deputies and surrogates did alight from a westbound train. R.J. Manion, Minister of Railways and Canals, and Robert Weir, Minister of Agriculture, produced credentials authorizing them to negotiate with Evans and "try and settle their claims if possible." The two men admitted that they did not know what they would offer Evans until they heard his demands. Nor did they know whether, should the talks collapse, the order to halt the march would be carried out. "We cannot say about that. We are not giving orders."[28]

For the rest of the morning, Manion and Weir met in their rooms at the Hotel Saskatchewan with Premier Gardiner and his Attorney General, T.C. Davis, all in an effort to secure as much information as possible. Word came from Evans that if the ministers wanted to see him, they could reach him at Unity Centre. Manion called there and after a lengthy conversation persuaded Evans to come to the hotel at 3:30 that afternoon and to bring his associates with him.

Returning to his interview with Gardiner, Manion made it clear that his government looked upon the Trek as "an attempt subversive to government in general...the beginning of a revolution, peaceful so far but one which would gradually lead to bloodshed." The railways had now asked for help. And despite Gardiner's attitude, "the Ottawa government was responsible for whatever trouble might arise here in Saskatchewan." The Saskatchewan government "should at least give passive assistance to us in curbing this movement" which could result in ten or twenty thousand men moving on the capital.

Though "apparently quite friendly" through most of the conversation, near its close Gardiner became "very resentful" of the actions of Ottawa in losing authority over the RCMP and in not being briefed. And then, according to Manion, Gardiner

> very emphatically said that if tonight when the men were threatening to board the train at 10 o'clock there should be riots, so far as he and his government were concerned, they would order their police to deal with the rioters who they considered were not only those men who were threatening to board the train but more emphatically the CPR police who were interfering with them and he said that he would instruct his police to deal as severely with the CPR police as with the Trekkers because he said that both were equally guilty; in fact, he considered the CPR more guilty because they had permitted these men or even aided them to come thus far without interference.

Manion was naturally surprised by this threat and replied that Gardiner "would be taking a very great reponsibility if he aided and abetted revolution in any such manner." Manion acknowledged that he had no quarrel with those who charged that Ottawa should accept responsibility for the men being halted in Regina, "while at the same time I admitted nothing in this regard." Manion once again asked for "passive co-operation" from Gardiner "but his whole attitude was one of antagonism to anything that the Ottawa government had done and he took the position of not co-operating to any extent whatsoever."[29]

One might suppose that Gardiner's threat against the CPR police was made in anger. It was certainly a rash remark and one he did not allude to when he spoke before the commission of inquiry weeks later. [30] It bears the same sort of recklessness about it as did his statement to Colonel Wood a few days before that he might organize a caravan of trucks and take the marchers to the Manitoba border.

Mid-afternoon, Evans appeared in his familiar overalls, accompanied by Red Walsh, Doc Savage, Mike McCaulay, Jack Cosgrove, Paddy O'Neil, Tony Martin and Pete Neilson, an inner sanctum of strike leaders by any definition. Across from them sat Manion and Weir, nearby, Mayor Rink, Premier Gardiner's delegates, representatives from the Board of Trade, the Regina public school board, the Canadian Legion, the Canadian Manufacturers' Association, the CPR, the CNR, the Exhibition Board, the separate school board, in all about fifty, plus two or three reporters.

Evans opened with a recital of the origins and history of the strike, the Vancouver episode, the demands, the MacDonald Commission, case histories of injured camp workers. Manion commented here and there, sympathetic, more often than not, with a question or two about details.

Shortly Manion began his response, noting first "The fact that the government at Ottawa sent us out shows a desire to be reasonable and to avoid trouble between groups of men." As the minister sought to place the immediate predicament in the context of a world-wide crisis of unemployment, Evans interrupted:

> I object to a political discussion. I object to discussing politics like this, taking in the entire world. The whole question is this: are we to trek to Ottawa to discuss the six demands?

Manion replied that he was not "making propaganda...you have not the right to prevent my statement being made" and so he continued, focussing on the first of the demands which dealt with work, wages and hours. Manion was pretty sure that this request, if met, would cost the nation about $1 million a day, a sum clearly beyond its means.

Then Manion made his proposal: Would the Trekkers send a deputation to Ottawa at Dominion expense to meet with the Prime Minister while the rest of the marchers waited at the Regina Exhibition Grounds, fed and housed at government expense?[31]

Evans and his men may have been expecting such an invitation but they did not let on at the time, saying only that they would bring this matter before a meeting of the strikers that evening. The unspoken warning was that if they turned down the invitation, they would go to the trains. Shortly after the room cleared, Manion sent a telegram to Bennett in which he briefly recounted the major features of the interview and the substance of the proposal, the extent of public sympathy for the Trekkers, the prospect of illegal departure.

> The position is quite delicate but so far I feel very well satisfied with the situation but am not at all sure that they will accept our proposition; in fact, I am inclined to think they will not as our best information is that their leaders are radicals of the most extreme type. . . .

But on the other hand, Manion closed, although they occasionally became "heated," Evans's committee had not been "too extreme" after all. The real difficulty that day had come from another source: "So far as Gardiner and Provincial Government are concerned, their attitude very ugly and anything but helpful."[32]

According to Red Walsh, the subsequent discussion of the invitation to go to Ottawa found Evans initially against any sort of compliance.

> Most of us were against it too. Art got up and walked away — he said, "Whatever you decide, I will go along with it." Well, we discovered we couldn't turn it down; the newspapers would come out against us. But no one thought we would get anything out of them. I was positive that we would end up in handcuffs.[33]

When the matter was put before the strikers, the major objection to the whole plan that emerged was that it was a ruse that would enable the government to gain time to bring in large numbers of police to Regina. Walsh chaired this assembly and by now he and Evans and the Strike Committee must have been convinced that they had to go in any case. When the matter was put to a vote, the Trekkers accepted Manion's offer. A second vote affirmed that the original negotiation committee would make the trip. In the end, it would appear that the real fear of a bad press dictated the decision.

Although this meant that there would be no departure that evening, there was no reason to cancel the parade to the city centre and so it went forward, if only to let off steam, if only to rally support, if only to tease the authorities for another hour. Several hundred townspeople had been gathering at the entrance to the Exhibition Grounds, anxious for news and orders. More than one saw a truck backed up to a gate, presumably making ready to carry packs and equipment to freight yards.

It was after 8:00 P.M. when the Trekkers emerged from their meeting and swooped up their friends who moved out in the lead towards Victoria Park. It was a high time. Word spread quickly that the departure was cancelled and the relief and the sense of triumph excited the throngs that now flooded downtown, ten thousand in all, Colonel Wood thought.[34] Jack Cosgrove moved his men in expert fashion, hup-trupping, swinging the column neatly around a corner. Once he "columned right" so suddenly that the townspeople up front went one way and the Trekkers another. There was much singing and chanting: "We want relief — we want work and wages."[35]

Finally, the column of Trekkers arrived at the Hotel Saskatchewan, Evans and a few others, pushing forward and then trooping into the basement room where they had spent the afternoon. Manion and Weir soon joined them.

Bearing in mind that the invitation had only described the trip to Ottawa and the maintenance of the remainder of the men in Regina, Evans now began to barter for added conditions, given their acceptance of the principle: (1) the men staying in Regina would be fed in restaurants and not by food kitchens at the [Exhibition] Grounds; (2) quarters and sanitary facilities would be expanded; (3) the government would make no attempt, even inadvertently through press releases, to disrupt the contingent in Regina; (4) the deputation would leave within 36 hours and not 24 as requested by Manion; (5) after 300 relief camp strikers due in from Dundurn camp were absorbed, no encouragment would be given for more recruits while in Saskatchewan; (6) the contingent in Regina would obey the law and not trespass on railway property.[36]

Evans asked about meals for the delegation enroute to Ottawa and Manion replied: "Couldn't you take care of that yourselves? I have heard that you fellows have more money than you know what to do with." It can be presumed that Evans was not amused.[37]

The minister wired Ottawa of this contract: "The whole arrangement has been accepted here with very great satisfaction on all sides."[38]

Evans left the hotel, telling Cosgrove to draw the men together so that he could pass the word. A block away, he jumped on the bumper of a car and gave his report.

Probably no one was more relieved than Colonel Wood who cabled Commissioner MacBrien that "From a police standpoint, it would have been a very difficult task to have prevented the strikers and their supporters from entering upon railway property.''[39]

The next day, 18 June, the Strike Committee of the Trek met to reorganize for the duration of their stay in Regina. Division officers were shifted about in light of the departure of Savage and Walsh who had been prominent captains thus far. A final general meeting in the afternoon, a parade to the station, a rally where Matt Shaw spoke of the need of the men to maintain their ranks, keep the discipline and wait for the delegation to return. Off the squad went, in the early evening, riding the cushions, Ministers Manion and Weir on board as well, though presumably not sitting cheek by jowl with the likes of Paddy O'Neil or Red Walsh who may just have carried the aromas of the stock pavilion with them.

The pressure removed, at least for the time being, Colonel Wood sat down and drafted a lengthy report to Commissioner MacBrien. A bit after the fact, Wood described the plan for coping with the marchers should they have tried to move towards the Manitoba border. Though it was hypothetical, Wood felt that his plan might yet be implemented if the talks in Ottawa collapsed, as he believed they would. First the evening freights would be shunted aside, with the men being allowed to board a morning forty-car train, which would be heavily guarded, and which would be stopped at Pilot Butte, a few miles away. The Trekkers would then be searched and then forced to walk back to Regina where they would be given the option of turning in to a temporary relief camp set up in the Exhibition Grounds.

Colonel Wood had no doubts about his ability to stop the Trek. Hold the trains, harass the marchers every time they make a move to leave. ''I think we can tire them out.''[40]

What if the men refused to board that morning train? What if they refused to dismount at Pilot Butte? What if they refused to march back to Regina? What if they absolutely refused to enter a relief camp again? Colonel Wood did not speculate.

Premier Gardiner had no doubt whatsoever about what was going on. On 19 June, he wrote William Lyon Mackenzie King about a conspiracy.

> The further this movement went here, the more I'm convinced that it was all planned between the railroads and the Government. The CPR, fearing a strike at the coast, planned to move these strikers out to the prairies and divide the forces. . . Both the government and the CPR representatives told the same well rehearsed story of a communistic movement across Canada which was to break all at the same time.[41]

The Citizens' Emergency Committee in Regina went about its business, nearly all of it that homely, often tedious parliamentary procedure that seems to have been invented to take the edge off of any impulsive activity. The Picnic Committee gave its report on 18 June: the surplus food and a small amount of cash had been turned over to the Trekkers. A resolution thanking local merchants, business houses and citizens for their assistance was passed. The entire body voted to remain intact at least until the delegation returned from Ottawa.[42]

Most of a 19 June meeting was given over to the idea that another picnic for the boys would be held the next Sunday, the twenty-third. Nominees were invited for positions on the new picnic committee but, as is often the case, there was an insufficiency of volunteers because the duties of this task force were not made clear. Peter Mikkelson finally got up and explained that, no, one did not have to canvass and, no, one did not have to prepare the food. One could offer general assistance, run errands, and so forth, and with that Mikkelson put his own name down and then others came forward.

It was next moved, seconded and agreed that all bona fide members of the CEC should wear a ribbon with the word ''Committee'' inscribed on it.[43]

There being no pressing business, the CEC did not meet again until Friday, 21 June. At that time, the group took up the matter of a fee for a local band which would play at the picnic on Sunday. Since that fee was usually twenty-five dollars and since the Committee could not afford this, the band's director, one K. Shan, proposed that his musicians be allowed to take a collection. Permission was granted.

Bill Hammill, still the Trekker liaison, indicated that free publicity was becoming more difficult to secure but that a radio broadcast on the occasion of the return of the Evans delegation was available. A fifteen to twenty minute spot would cost ten dollars. This expenditure was approved. Finally, a suggestion that a lapel pin be devised and sold in behalf of the Trekkers was accepted and a committee struck to take charge.

Committee minutes are determined to be dry. ''Much discussion'' can obscure the most vexatious quarrels, as well as long technical deliberation. On 24 June, when the CEC next met, someone moved that a subcommittee be formed to draft a statement to the effect that the CEC ''is working in a constitutional manner to bring about a peaceful and satisfactory settlement of the strike dispute.'' An amendment sought to substitute ''peaceful'' for ''constitutional'' and to add the clause: ''we will assist in every possible way to see that the strikers continue their way eastward." Still more discussion followed after which "the whole thing" was deleted. And then: "Cowan and McKenzie tendered their resignations and left the room."

Since Cowan and McKenzie figured in the final deliberations of this meeting, were, indeed, present, they must have been prevailed upon to return to their seats. And so they had been. Local Methodist Church pastor, the Reverend Samuel B. East had scurried after them, had persuaded them to continue participation. Their reason for quitting has not been made clear: did they object to the original motion or to its amendment or to the dismissal of "the whole thing?"[44]

In the front ranks of the 17 June parade downtown and in the foreground of the events of the next two weeks was the Reverend Samuel B. East, eight years resident in Regina, born in Hertfordshire, moved to Canada in 1904, now aged sixty-two, exuberant, energetic, loquacious, committed to the social gospel. Of the relationship between the Reverend Mr. East and the Trekkers, his colleague on the CEC, K.C. Fraser later remarked: "East provided for their spiritual needs. I think he went a bit beyond that perhaps...."[45]

When East learned of the approach of the Trekkers to Regina, he began to make inquiries about their motives and ambitions. He called associates in Vancouver who told him of the support of the women of that city. Because he had learned as a boy to admire his mother's instinct for trusting or distrusting vagabonds who came to the back door, and because he had seen a photograph taken at the Stanley Park Mother's Day picnic of mothers framed in a heart around a group of strikers, East decided to work for the CEC. "I persuaded myself to a rightness of a cause, and then took the chance of championing it, and I think every man worthy of the name ought to."[46] When his appeal for assistance from the Regina Ministerial Association went unheeded, East joined the Committee as a private citizen.

The fact is that East did not depend only on mothers' sentiments for his sense of the "rightness of a cause." He readily admitted that he was an advocate of communism. "...Communism is not a devil's doctrine, it is one divine far-off event towards which all creation moves." His defence of labour had made him, by his own admission, unpopular with the district hierarchy of his Church. East's research into the origins of the relief camp strike "showed me that if they had remained quiescent in the camps they would have lost their manhood, they would have ceased to be men; they would have lost their souls, their personalities. . . . '' Their right to demonstrate ''has been unquestioned.''[47]

At a meeting earlier in Toronto that year, East had said, quoting John Dougall, editor of the *Montreal Witness:* '' . . . for God's sake, let's keep a united front, and if you can't keep it for God's sake, keep it for Lenin's sake.''[48] On the other hand, East professed not to be sure what the Comintern was.

East is one of the few Reginans remembered afterward by Trekkers. Whether or not his notions about communism or the Soviet Union were informed, there is no doubt that East could act as well as talk. When a handful of Trekkers and citizens attempted to break out of Regina on 28 June, it was East who led the expedition; it was East who was arrested.

What did the Trekkers do in Regina while they waited for Evans to return? For one thing, they took into their ranks another three hundred recruits, two-thirds of whom came from the relief camp at Dundurn, near Saskatoon, the balance being unemployed men from the area. These men were placed into a new division, numbered Five, and forthwith drilled in the history, routine and discipline of the march. George Black saw to this. Evans had agreed not to accept any more men after this lot had been approved. It's likely that no more were wanted anyway, for the time being. Quality rather than quantity was foremost in the judgement of the Strike Committee. In any case, Winnipeg must be given its chance to join up.[49]

Despite the hard times of the Depression, that summer of 1935, there were literally dozens of cafés and tea shops in Regina. Walking from the Exhibition Grounds, on the northwest corner of the city, a fellow would encounter the Mickey Mouse Cafe, the Greenaway Cafe, the Sandwich Shelfe next door to the Opal Cafe and, as he neared Unity Centre, the Europe Cafe, the Austrian Kitchen, the Silver Gray Cafe, the Sunlight Cafe. With their meal tickets issued each day, the Trekkers trooped in and out of these small diners, sitting for hours over cups of coffee, talking with townspeople, with the owners.

Victoria Park became a natural and central gathering place. Men sat in small groups, taking in the pedestrian and automobile traffic, accepting the stares of curious citizens, snoozing in the sun. Perhaps it was at this time that some tunesmith sought to immortalize the Trek with this song which was intended, no doubt, to supplement the noble ''Hold the Fort.'' It was sung to the tune of ''Home on the Range'':

And we're on the tramp
From Bennett's slave camp,

Our demands before him we will place
We will soon be there
And we want no hot air
And he won't get no thirty days grace.[50]

Chief Bruton told his men to refrain from making arrests for loitering or innocuous disturbance of the peace.[51] There had been a flurry of burglaries the first few days the men were in town, but these had subsided. In any case, Trekker police details, wearing armbands with "P" inscribed on them, along with first aid squads, who wore red cross emblems, made routine circuits of the city centre. Frank Bobby, a Trekker, joined a police detail. One evening, he was called to Wascana Park to investigate an alleged child molestation by one of the marchers. The man was apprehended and when searched and questioned, turned over a number of relief camp strike cards with a variety of groups and divisons already set down. The implication was certainly that he either planned to drift here and there across the Trek or else turn the cards in to the authorities for use by the city police.[52]

As we have seen, it was relatively easy for Constable Henry Cooper of the Regina RCMP depot to join the march in Moose Jaw, but a few days later, Cooper was recognized by Reginans as he strolled through the streets and these folks told Mikkelson. On 19 June, Cooper's place was taken by Constable Donald Taylor who received Card Number 141, Group 12 of Division 5.

Taylor's witness of the daily movements at the Exhibition Grounds and on the streets was less than shrewd. For instance, he later admitted that he had never bothered to learn, much less to report, the names of the men in his Group 12. Taylor also confessed that he scarcely spoke with the strikers during the week he lived with them. Each night, the officer would meet with a contact and deliver his notes compiled from the day's observations. Much of this was undigested gossip — eleven hundred dollars had been collected on the Trek so far but that as much as two-thirds of this amount had been spent on reimbursement for damages caused by the marchers, though what damage was not ascertained. Taylor recorded the daily assemblies of the Trekkers where, he said, the men more or less passively accepted the resolutions or orders proclaimed by the Strike Committee. On one occasion, the sighting of two carloads of RCMP officers driving near the stadium provoked a few men to panic and to begin making clubs which shortly disappeared, Taylor believed, into their packs and bedrolls once the crisis passed.[53]

There is some indication, vague at that, though plausible, that Chief Bruton inserted one or more of his constables into the ranks of the marchers though no real evidence of their identities or achievements has been uncovered.

With the introduction of federal supervision and maintenance of the Trekkers at the Exhibition Grounds, one C.P. Burgess, a civil servant in the Dominion Department of Finance, based in Regina, came forward with orders to implement the agreement among the Province, Ottawa and Evans, having to do with the general care of the men, hospitalization for any who became ill, supplies and straw bedding, and meal tickets, the first of which was issued on the morning of 18 June.[54]

In the meantime, the Evans delegation went to Ottawa. Red Walsh:

> *We had first class passage on the train. We were sat at a table and the waiter would come with the three knives and four forks and three spoons. They opened a hotel in Ottawa for us that had been closed. I had a room to myself. I wanted a bathtub. I hadn't seen a thing like that in five years. Everybody came there: MacInnis, Woodsworth, Tom McEwen.[55]*

On Saturday morning, 22 June, at 11:30 A.M., the Trekkers met in the Prime Minister's office in the East Block with Mr. Bennett and his cabinet. The two groups of men settled into rows of chairs facing one another, the one dressed, presumably, in business suits and morning coats, the other in Trek uniforms, though if they shared Walsh's passion for a bathtub, their faces were scrubbed, hair slicked back. All in all, an unsmiling lot, on either side.

Bennett opened the proceedings by asking the delegation to introduce themselves and to produce a spokesman. Evans stepped up and launched into a history of the strike and the march, punctuating this with references to specific cases of camp worker ordeals. In his description of a man arrested while distributing ''class literature,'' Evans noted that he had been charged with resisting a police officer.

Bennett: ''In other words, he got into a fight with a policeman.''

Evans: ''In other words, he was dragged out of bed at two o'clock [in the morning].''

Bennett: ''Before he went to bed he got into a fight with a policeman?''

Evans: ''That is not correct.''

Bennett: ''What is it, then? He got into a fight with the provincial police?''

Evans: ''He did not; he was lying in his bed.''

Bennett: ''His wounds were before he went to bed at all.''

Evans:	"I say that you do not know what you are talking about."
Bennett:	"Let us finish this while we are at it."

Evans went on with a list of demands: work and wages; coverage by workmen's compensation; adequate first aid; camp committees; removal of the Department of National Defence jurisdiction; a workers' social and unemployment insurance bill; the franchise. He brought this phase of the interview to a close with a charge that he had read just that day that sixty RCMP officers had been dispatched to Regina, an action which he thought violated the agreement with Manion and Weir. Manion countered that Evans had already broken the agreement by inflammatory remarks given out at the station at Fort William on the way out.

Bennett stepped in and queried each of the Trekkers as to his age and place of birth. Only Evans had been born in Canada. "We have been in this country something like 112 years." As for the rest, Cosgrove was from Scotland, Neilson from Denmark, Martin, Savage and McCaulay from England, Walsh from Ireland, O'Neil from Newfoundland.

Bennett then began his reply. There is a world-wide depression. The food, shelter, and clothing in the relief camps are adequate. There is no compulsion to sign on and no discipline in the camps. The twenty cents a day is a gratuity. Nonetheless, agitators have come into these camps "representing a form of government that we will not tolerate in Canada. . . . representing Communism which we will stamp out in this country with the help of the people of Canada."

> When you talk of Soviet committees, when you talk of Communistic boards, I only say to you gentlemen that this government represents a form of government that will be maintained by us as long as we are here, and by our successors. Let there be no misunderstanding with respect to that. Let us have no misunderstanding.

Bennett continued to probe the matter of agitators both in the camps and on the outside, the Workers' Unity League in particular. "They endeavour by force, if necessary, to destroy the institutions of this country and substitute for them others." The police have been brought in to protect life and property. The Trekkers have won the support of the citizenry by persuading them that the relief camp men have been treated shabbily.

> You have not shown much anxiety to get work. . . . It is the one thing you do not want. What you want is this adventure in the hope that the organization which you are promoting in

Canada may be able to over-awe [the] government and break down the forces that represent law and order.

The police have moved west; they have moved east; they will move in increasing numbers wherever it is necessary to maintain law. Take that down. Tell Mr. Cosgrove to take it down, Mr. Evans.

When Bennett asked the Trekkers what their purpose was, Evans replied that their purpose was to secure a work and wages programme.

Bennett: "And we have made it perfectly clear so far as we are concerned that these camps were not established for that purpose."

Evans: "That is passing the buck. We want work and wages."

Bennett: "Just a moment...."

Evans: "You referred to us as not wanting work. Give any of us work and see whether we will work. This is an insidious attempt to propagandize the press on your part, and any body who professes to be Premier and uses such despicable tactics is not fit to be premier of a Hottentot village."

Bennett: "I come from Alberta. I remember when you embezzled the funds of your union and were sent to penitentiary."

Evans: "You are a liar...I have stated I used the funds for hungry people instead of sending them to Indianapolis to a bunch of pot-bellied business agents."

Cosgrove jumped to his feet: "I take exception to any personal attack on this delegation and will not...."

Bennett: "Sit down, Mr. Cosgrove."

Cosgrove: "I will not."

Bennett: "Then you will be removed."

Evans: "Then the entire delegation will be removed."

Bennett: "Sit down, Mr. Cosgrove."

The outbursts subsided as Bennett turned to the demands which he proceeded to appraise and dismiss:

1. The camps were never intended to provide work and wages. Such a programme was beyond the capacity of the nation although such projects as the Trans Canada Highway did recruit relief camp men.

2. At present, compensation acts were provincial concerns, not Dominion. They "are not Acts over which we have any control, remote or near, direct or indirect."

3. A man can make any complaint to a camp foreman that he wants to make but the idea of "...setting up Soviets, we will not tolerate...."

4. The authority of the DND will remain in place. They have the equipment and the personnel available. There is no military control or training in the camps.

5. The government will have nothing to do with a non-contributory system of unemployment insurance.

6. Every worker has the right to vote if he comes within the provisions of the Franchise Act. If he does not, he has not.

Bennett: "That is all that can be said. I want to warn you once more, if you persist in violating the laws of Canada you must accept full responsibility for your conduct."

Evans: "And you also."

Bennett: "I am prepared for that."

Evans: "So are we."

Bennett closed with a warning against further trespassing on the railways but also assured them that opportunities for work were forthcoming.

Evans closed by rededicating himself and his men to their responsibility since the Dominion wouldn't deal with their demands. "In place of that they attempt to raise the red bogey and it appears that the Prime Minister has the red horrors of this government. Our responsibility is we must take this back to the workers and see that the hunger programme of Bennett is stopped."[56]

As he left the room, Red Walsh turned to look back and what he says he saw became one of the legends of the Trek: Mountie boots peeking out from under the drapes hanging across the windows of the Prime Minister's office.[57]

Evans and his associates spent the balance of the weekend huddled with relief camp men from the east and with Tom McEwen of the WUL. On Sunday evening, Evans spoke to a rally at the Rialto Theatre and then they left Ottawa, on the cushions, having wired ahead to friends in Sudbury, Port Arthur, Fort William, Winnipeg and Brandon of the times of their arrival so that speeches could be made.[58] What Evans did not know was that Bennett would go before the House of Commons on that Monday to describe the meeting, affirm his government's capacity to meet the challenge and to announce the creation of a temporary relief camp at Lumsden, Saskatchewan, where the Trekkers would be sent.[59]

In Sudbury, apparently, Evans drew up on the platform and gave himself over to a powerful oration in which he imagined blood running in the streets of Regina. At Winnipeg, he was told that the press had quoted him as saying that unless the government backed off, blood would be spilled. Evans maintained that he had really proposed that government interference would cause blood to run.[60]

Tim Buck had been in Winnipeg and he appeared with Evans before a huge crowd near the station for a quick summary of the Bennett interview. At Brandon, Evans read a wire from George Black telling him of the Lumsden project. It was a grim, scowling Arthur Evans who arrived in Regina at 7:00 A.M. on the twenty-sixth.

While the Evans delegation was making its way back to Regina, in that city Colonel Wood filed a two-part report to Commissioner MacBrien in which he reviewed the events of the past ten days. Certain details of that message are worth identifying:

> If the police can ''handle the situation'' outside the city limits, this will effectively eliminate local supporters.
>
> The provincial government has grown so lenient in dealing with transients arrested within its borders over the past two years, the cost of feeding these men once they were in jail being considerable, it is advised that the Dominion should prosecute and retain these vagrants.
>
> No signs of defection in the Trek but many men dislike being labelled ''Reds.''
>
> Fifty-five railway police from both companies are stationed at Union Depot and will monitor the yards.
>
> The Trekkers will still not ''antagonize the public support they already have'' by ''making themselves obnoxious in the City.'' Should they, however, Wood prefers a plan of seizing the Exhibition Grounds and the mens' packs while they are away at a meal ''thereby forcing them to negotiate with us for the return of their packs and admittance to the buildings.''
>
> All truck and bus companies in town have agreed to co-operate and let his office know of any application for use of equipment by Trekkers.
>
> One hundred and thirteen men from ''F'' Division due in Wednesday night, making RCMP strength 340 all ranks.[61]

Commissioner MacBrien replied to Wood that steps must now be taken to prepare the installation at Lumsden; C.P. Burgess would be placed in charge although the responsible department in Ottawa would be Labour. Wood, that weekend, had sent one of his men along with a Department of National Defence officer to scout the region and they shortly came up with the Muir farm, south of Highway Twenty and north of the Qu'Appelle River, a beautiful site, really. Now, 120 relief camp men from Dundurn, not all had struck for Regina obviously, were sent to erect tents, mess halls, and the like, dig latrines, install four large ranges, load two granaries with beef, butter, flour. There was a spring nearby for water. Though the area was more or less between Lumsden and Craven, after a day or so, it became simply "Lumsden," a word with all sorts of connotations for just about everybody watching this crisis.[62]

As the Lumsden camp went up, C.P. Burgess established a registration office for would-be inmates at the Grain Show Building, first having asked for a bodyguard. The RCMP obliged. A Royal Canadian Army heliograph operator waited there as well. In case of disturbance, this fellow would apparently move to a window and flash a signal to a unit of constables stationed a block away. A few Trekkers eventually drifted in though the cat-calls from their former friends standing nearby must have proved distressing.[63]

Back in Regina, Evans and his associates found some breakfast and then set off to talk with Premier Gardiner, who was himself joined by Colonel Wood, Mayor Rink and Chief Bruton. Evans was quick off the mark: would the Province supply the relief that the Dominion had withdrawn that morning? Would the Province secure the Trekkers against police interference? Would the Province provide money for transport of the Trek to Winnipeg?

Gardiner's answer to these questions was legalistic, realistic and, if you like, statesmanlike.

> From the time of the Manion-Weir agreement, the Trekkers had left their status as transients in Saskatchewan, subject to the Province's care and maintenance. If they want to regain this status, apply to the city of Regina.
>
> The Province has no jurisdiction in Regina vis-à-vis police unless summoned. The RCMP still answer to Ottawa.
>
> The Province will not assist the men to the Manitoba boundary. Why do to others what has been done to you?[64]

If Gardiner had ever entertained the idea of transporting the men to Manitoba, as Wood once suggested, he had now changed his mind.

With the assurance from Rink and Bruton that his men could remain at the Exhibition Grounds until the Dominion said otherwise, Evans stalked off to the Olympia Cafe where he met the Reverend Mr. East for lunch. East found a telephone and called the CPR ticket office to ascertain the cost of leasing a passenger train as far as Winnipeg. Not above a little white lie, East told the clerk he had a church excursion in mind! For the next two or three days, the Reverend Mr. East would be at Evans's side as he was that afternoon when the two men walked to Mayor Rink's office to talk about an application to return the Trekkers to transient status. But Rink had yet to receive instructions from Gardiner on this matter, so East and Evans drove out to the Legislative Building where Gardiner told them to go back to city hall and tell Rink to feed the men and send the bill to Gardiner. But Rink said "no" once more; the order had to be in writing. Evans went back to Gardiner who now said he would have to wire Ottawa. Whereupon Evans said ". . . you know just as well as we do what Mr. Bennett will say: there is the Lumsden Camp, you can take that. . . . " Evans was furious by this time so he turned away from the fruitless search and began to prepare for the rally that evening at the Exhibition Stadium where he would report on the Bennett interview.[65]

Though the rally was not the last of the Trek, it was the best attended of those held in Regina and, in a real sense, the most profane in the invective hurled at Bennett. The taunts ranged from CCFer George Williams's remark that "It is rather obvious that if the general public in Canada can be made to believe the unemployed are enemies of the people as well as of capitalism, it will weaken the attack on the present economic system" to Communist Party spokesman William Stokes's insinuation that Bennett belonged up there with Hitler and Mussolini who were also "political hooligans" to the Reverend Mr. East's "Bennett sees a chance to usher in a fascist regime. He wants to be Mussolini of Canada. Shall we let him?" The crowd loved it.[66]

From the day the Trek arrived in Regina to discover that its route eastward on trains had been blocked, the prospect of a mighty motor convoy into Manitoba seemed a real alternative. Premier Gardiner, in the early throes of frustration, apparently spoke of his government underwriting such a scheme.[67] By the time Evans came forward to speak to the rally, the search was already underway for money and vehicles to undertake the manoeuvre. Evans exclaimed that the convoy was feasible and "that we want to avoid trouble and we're not going to allow Bennett to turn his Cossacks loose on us." Once in Winnipeg, he said, the Trek, reinforced by another one thousand or more men, would return to the trains for the remainder of the march.

Then Evans reviewed the meeting in Ottawa, boasting that "It surprises me when I think of it that I didn't go up and punch him in his ugly mug!" And he closed the evening with the cry: "The Prime Minister asks the people to aid law and order but have the people of Regina ever seen a group so orderly as the strikers?'' And of course the crowd roared ''No!''[68]

By radio appeals and personal messages across the immediate area, the Strike Committee spent that evening and the next morning calling for trucks, cars and drivers. The response was discouraging. Thursday, 27 June, the day the convoy was supposed to depart, was unusually hot and dry. As the police cars wheeled in and out of the Exhibition Grounds, great swirls of dust were thrown up so that at times, the trains passing nearby could hardly be seen. Evans and East visited Gardiner's office on three occasions in an effort to secure special licenses for the convoy so that they could carry passengers. All to no avail. The Trekkers lolled about the Exhibition Grounds, sunbathing, watching a softball game. Someone hung an effigy of Bennett from a power pole. As noon passed and the men ate one last meal of milk and sandwiches, it became apparent that there would be no convoy of any real dimension because there were no trucks and cars forthcoming.

Colonel Wood really believed that a sizeable group intended to set out in a first attempt. It was his understanding that at 2:30 P.M. on Thursday, Division One was to muster at the Stadium, pick up sandwiches and board trucks.[69] What he seems not to have anticipated is just how diminished the spirit of volunteerism had become. Most certainly this was the result of Wood's proclamation that anyone aiding the Trekkers in their effort either to break east or to move into their own encampment would be liable to arrest. This became distorted within a few hours so that citizens believed that it was a threat to arrest anyone for helping in *any way* whatsoever. The Citizens' Emergency Committee bore the burden of this rumour as it carried on its meetings in the Labour Temple at the invitation of the Trades and Labour Council (TLC). The TLC told the Committee it would have to find new quarters otherwise their hosts might get into trouble.[70]

So the Trekkers waited through the afternoon and slowly it dawned on them that they were not about to leave Regina in a convoy. The only vehicles that appeared were a lone truck and two automobiles. When Evans's application at 5:00 P.M. to the CPR to *hire* boxcars was refused, the decision was made to test the reflexes of the authorities by sending the truck and the cars out to the highway. John Cosgrove agreed to go along as did Trekkers Ivan Bell and John Edwards. A citizen named James Lennox drove one car, Cosgrove another and the truck was driven by John Halaburd, who was accompanied by his wife and the peripatetic Reverend Samuel B. East.[71]

The caravan crept off at 9:30 P.M., bound for the junction of Winnipeg Street and Highway One; a crowd of Trekkers and citizens walked behind. At the intersection, the vehicles were stopped by RCMP officers dressed, as East puts it, "in pie pan helmets, crinkled top sombreros and old sleuth-type slouch chapeaux." East flourished a permit, such as it was, before a constable who simply waved it aside. Mrs. Halaburd burst into tears. And then the occupants of the truck and the cars were arrested, taken first to the RCMP town station and then out to the training depot where they were held in a large stable used for riding drill. But there was water standing on the floor of the stable so when East protested, the group was moved to the post library. If Mrs. Halaburd was stricken, East was jubilant. Two guards brought straw mattresses for the prisoners and chairs for themselves. East: "One stopped to light a cigarette before he sat down and I was able to beat him to the chair and spent the night very comfortably."

There is a photograph of the arrest: a helmeted officer taking notes, Mrs. Halaburd wiping her nose and the Reverend Mr. East, his head held erect, light reflected off his glasses, a grin on his lips. Perhaps East has just proclaimed to the officer the call which became a bit of lore that week: "We're headed east with East!"

The next day, believing that arrests of the Trek leaders were imminent, Colonel Wood wired associates in British Columbia and Alberta for any documentation of criminal activities during the strike and the Trek by a certain twelve Trekkers, among them Evans, O'Neil, Shaw, Black and Cosgrove. At his side, Wood now had two crown attorneys, F.B. Bagshaw and E.C. Leslie, who advised him that unlawful association — Section 98 of the Criminal Code — was the crime that seemed to be in evidence. Wood also learned that RCMP Sergeant John Leopold was on his way to Regina with more evidence and would arrive on 1 July. Leopold, everyone knew, was the constable who had infiltrated the Communist Party of Canada in the 1920s and then had testified against Buck in the 1931 trial.[72]

The replies to Wood's cables to Edmonton and Victoria now arrived. Edmonton was trying to help but their information was "very slight." On the other hand, Victoria was forwarding its files and would seek a search warrant in order to go into the RCWU office in Vancouver. On 29 June, Wood found it necessary to wire MacBrien to the effect that there was not enough local evidence to arrest Evans and the others.[73]

The pressure on the Trekkers to move to Lumsden mounted although few of the men gave in. Because Evans had begun arguing that the camp was surrounded by barbed wire, the Regina press proposed a citizens' committee go out there and investigate.[74] Premier Gardiner told Evans on the twenty-eighth that if he would take his men to Lumsden, then he, Gardiner, would see to it that there was no militarism applied except for discipline and that he, Gardiner, would take their case to Ottawa. Evans said that he opposed the offer and would tell his men so. Evans then stated that the Trek would leave Regina and establish its own camp in the vicinity![75]

Whether a real plan or a spur of the moment idea, the prospect of all those men trying to set up camp provoked Gardiner to reply that he did not want his province put in the position of adopting eighteen hundred men. On the other hand, if, somehow, the Trekkers did leave for the east, he would see to it that they were fed at Broadview, as he had promised two weeks before.[76]

The Dominion Day weekend came and with it the assurance on the part of the Trekkers that with the issue of forty cents apiece on Saturday for food, their treasury was exhausted. Despite the intimidating glares, twenty-five men had checked in with C.P. Burgess for transport to Lumsden. Colonel Wood watched and listened and then wired Ottawa: "Strikers acknowledge hopelessness of their intention to proceed. Dissention [sic] in ranks and prospects of disintegration shortly."[77]

On Sunday, the thirtieth, the Citizens' Emergency Committee hosted one last picnic at Wascana Park (though they did not know this was to be the last). Either the invitation did not circulate far or else the men were too weary and apprehensive. Only three hundred or so appeared and these drifted about, scarcely grateful for the food or the hospitality.[78]

On Sunday, the thirtieth, Premier Gardiner had retreated to his farm for a rest.

On Sunday, the thirtieth, Colonel Wood rested in his quarters, having done all he could for the time being to assure the Trekkers that Lumsden was not a penal colony and to make clear to Ottawa that he still waited for sufficient documentation to effect the arrest of Evans and his associates.

On Sunday, the thirtieth, the Reverend Samuel B. East, released from the RCMP arrest, was on his way with Matt Shaw to Toronto where they would speak at rallies about their cause.

On Sunday, the thirtieth, Bill Davis finished off a speaking engagement at a nearby village.

1 July 1935. Dominion Day. A long day. Before it is over, a police officer will be killed, dozens of Trekkers, police and Reginans shot, bruised, broken-limbed, and the centre of the city shaken and wrecked by riot.

The day opened with a telephone conversation between Colonel Wood and Commissioner MacBrien regarding Wood's new plan that the Trekkers should be allowed to disperse from the Exhibition Grounds. Although MacBrien said, go ahead, C.P. Burgess refused to co-operate, insisting that the men must first go either to Lumsden or Dundurn. Evans, up and about in his relentless search for compromise, sought to bring Burgess together with Gardiner but the Dominion agent turned him down. Evans did reach Gardiner at his farm and persuaded him to drive into town that afternoon for a meeting with a Trek committee at 4:00. Before the morning passed, Evans did secure an interview with Burgess and Wood, the high point of which was Wood's accusation that Evans wanted to take his men back to the west coast to help with the longshoremen's strike! Evans, of course, denied that such a move was on his mind. With no visible means of support or transportation, the Trekkers would have had a long, hungry walk back to Vancouver.[79]

When Gardiner arrived, Evans proposed that the men be allowed to disperse under their own organization or if not in that way, then by provincial support. Presumably, provincial assistance and charity were infinitely to be preferred over federal discipline. Evans also spoke for the exemption of his men from any prosecution though he would hold himself aloof from this condition. Gardiner agreed to meet with his cabinet that evening and hoped to have a reply early the next morning.[80]

Colonel Wood returned to his office at 5:00 P.M. to find Bagshaw and Leslie ready and waiting with warrants for the arrest of seven Trek leaders. The documentation for those warrants may well have been brought west by Sergeant Leopold, although no trace of his presence in Regina that day has been disclosed. As for Wood, who was still waiting for information from Edmonton and Victoria, "it came somewhat as a surprise...I still had some doubt in my mind, whether there was sufficient evidence to justify issuing warrants."[81]

Nonetheless, accepting the advice of his counsel, Wood summoned his aides and called in Chief Bruton and CPR and CNR constables for a briefing. Where and when to serve the warrants? The Trekkers had called a rally of townspeople for that same evening at 8:00 on Market Square, just down the street from Unity Centre and adjacent to the Regina police station and fire hall. These two buildings sat on the edge of the Square. The plan that evolved was simple and dangerous. Inquiries would be made at Unity Centre at 7:00 P.M. and if this failed or was incomplete, then the police would attend the rally and make arrests there. There was discussion of the risk in making the arrests at the Exhibition Grounds and of scouring the streets for the suspects but it was thought that the Trekkers had assembled an armoury of home-made clubs with which they might defend their premises. And it was believed that Evans and the others now walked about with bodyguards. So, that left the Centre and the Square.

Though dubious about the extent or calibre of the evidence needed to make arrests, Wood was prepared to move. He believed that public support had declined so greatly in the past two days that the Trekkers had very likely come to accept that their own conduct did not have to be predicated any longer on winning and keeping the sympathy of the citizenry and so they were growing increasingly mischievous. Out of money and food, the Trekkers might soon take some sort of action: invading and holding the Hotel Saskatchewan, for instance. On the other hand, their discipline and commitment might have sagged so much that most might not even come to the rally.[82]

At 7:00 P.M., a police detail appeared at Unity Centre and finding none of the seven leaders there, it retired to the station. Whether or not this inquiry prompted an alarm among the Trekkers is not known. The majority were back at the Exhibition Grounds, allegedly watching a softball game. At Market Square, townspeople began to gather in the clear summer evening, strolling here and there, pausing to watch electricians set up a public address system. Arthur Evans sat in the Quality Tea Room, some distance from this activity, finishing his supper.

Seven
Market Square
"Why do you keep pounding him?"

— *Jacob Brunner*

City Constable Archie Apps is near the end of his foot patrol in and around the city centre at 7:45 P.M., 1 July, when he overhears a conversation between two pairs of Trekkers, one walking east along Eleventh Avenue, the other moving west. The conversation ends: "You damned fool, you better come with us and get some rocks. There is going to be some trouble on Market Square tonight."[1]

A few minutes later, Apps crosses to the United Cigar Store on Cornwall Street and calls the station; his sergeant tells him to come on in so the young officer begins to saunter east. He has not reported the conversation he has overheard and will not think to do so for some days to come.

At the Regina police station on the southeast corner of Market Square, Chief Constable Martin Bruton waits for the rally to begin and for the team of city and RCMP constables who will make the arrest of the speakers to find their way to the centre of the Square. They are in plainclothes, of course. Bruton's men have checked Unity Centre at 7:00 but find no one there for whom warrants have been prepared. Thus, the decision is made to carry out arrests at the rally although it is not known which of the Trek leaders will appear there.[2]

In support of the officers who will rush the platform, three troops of RCMP constables will draw up in moving vans on the north, west and east boundaries of the Square. A fourth troop of RCMP on horseback stand at Twelfth and Osler, a block south.

Inside the city station garage, whose north door opens on the Square, Inspector Duncan McDougall waits with his column of twenty-nine city constables, formed in four ranks. These troops are dressed in blue uniforms and "bobby" helmets which are lined with cardboard. Whenever a Regina City Police Department (RCPD) officer is on duty, he is armed with a pistol and ammunition, although the gun is unloaded. In addition, he always carries an 8½-inch billy, leaded at one end, and weighing nine ounces. On 1 July, McDougall's men carry a third weapon, a "baton" which is actually an 18-by-1½-inch sawed-off Woolworth baseball bat weighing eleven ounces. These have been acquired four years before and have not been used until this evening. The batons retain

135

their natural wood colour and can be seen easily from a distance. No doubt because these batons are particularly lethal, the officers are instructed to use them only in defence and then only to apply them to arms and legs and never to the head.[3]

Bruton has just briefed McDougall's men to this effect: There are many innocent citizens out there. Be careful. Remember that the extra baton is for defence. And then Bruton tells his men that when the whistle is blown for the plainclothesmen to make their move, McDougall's column will go onto the Square. At least that is what Bruton believes they are to do for that is what he understands his orders from Wood to have been. Wood, on the other hand, believes the plan is that the city force will come on only when summoned or if they perceive that the arresting team is in trouble. Moreover, Bruton, if his later testimony can be said to recollect his judgement that evening, has doubts about the whole manoeuvre: "Then I mentioned to him, did he consider it advisable to make the arrests at the Market Square."[4]

Nonetheless, Bruton, McDougall and City Detective Charles Millar, in plainclothes and standing in reserve, peer through the windows of the garage door at the gathering crowd.

This is Market Square that evening: the police station in the southeast corner, beside it, the city fire hall. A few yards in front of the fire hall is a drill tower and in front of the drill tower, a thirty-foot long train of street repair equipment, a roller and carts containing brooms and shovels. On the west central edge of the Square are the city scales to which are hooked two pairs of loudspeakers, their wires stretched in the air to a small flat-bed truck north and east towards the centre of the square. With the permission of the fire department, Ben Keefe, a local electrician and a friend of the CEC, has come out earlier to set the speakers in place. The flat-bed of the truck faces north.[5]

The crowd assembles, perhaps fifteen hundred in all, the majority are citizens of Regina. Steve Fustas is there with his wife and two children, one an infant in his arms. Fustas takes his family to the speakers' truck and sets the older girl on the edge of the flat-bed. Somehow a chair is produced for Fustas who sits down with the baby.[6]

John Cheers is drifting around. On his way downtown to a movie with Mrs. Cheers, he has stopped off at the Square because "the wife had never seen these strikers in a body before and she said she would like to see the boys."[7]

Wesley Krainicheck is all the way north, across Tenth Avenue, standing in the doorway of the beer parlour of the Metropole Hotel. John and Christina Lynch are also in the northwest corner. And

William Arnold who has just come from an afternoon's fishing at Wascana Lake. And Frank Swinnerton who stands on Tenth Avenue; because he is short, he has trouble seeing the speakers. Jacob Brunner waits to the northeast, at the intersection of Tenth and Halifax; his garage with its huge sign BRUNNER is just behind him.[8] The Reverend J.F. Stewart of Carmichael United Church has come on an errand to the Police Station. But when he sees McDougall's troop assembled in the garage, he says: "Perhaps I had better come back tomorrow." And a constable agrees, replying: "We are very busy." Stewart walks out onto the Square where he joins his colleague, the Reverend Harry Upton, pastor of First Baptist Church. Together they go into the crowd.[9]

Ernest Doran, a telephone company employee, is strolling down Eleventh Avenue from the west and towards the rally. With him is his eight-year-old son.[10]

And many more, one thousand or more Reginans, out for a holiday walk, on the way downtown to the movies, or else on the Square to hear from the Trekkers.

There are about three hundred Trekkers on Market Square that evening. It will be claimed later, though without sufficient evidence, that most of these fellows are from Division Three, the unit in the relief camp strike which has been said to contain the hard core of the blacklisted veterans from British Columbia. Caspar Blum, from Calgary, is a Division Three man. He walks on the square after taking supper at the Austrian Kitchen nearby. Gordon Phillips is also from Division Three and has also come from supper. He has ridden all the way from Vancouver but has never been on the blacklist. Phillips stands near the Metropole Hotel. Clarence Mason is originally from New Westminster, British Columbia, but he has joined the Trek in Regina when Division Five was formed at Unity Centre; Mason stands quite near the truck. Sidney Stevens who travelled all the way from Dundurn to Calgary, to Edmonton, back to Calgary and on to Medicine Hat and finally Regina, in pursuit of the On-To-Ottawa Trek, is glad to be there in Division Five. He stands six feet north of the truck. Kenneth Forsythe of Division One is there as well.[11]

The whole point of the subsequent allegation that Division Three is on the Square is that these tough, dedicated men are responsible for the vicious nature of the riot. Perhaps so. Perhaps not. The ranks of the divisions have never remained "pure" once the Trek reached Calgary, as over eight hundred recruits come forward there and on the prairies. Another point of the allegation: that these Division Three men came downtown to start trouble, as Constable Apps suggests. The Trekkers had been told already by Evans to anticipate problems, that they might be driven out of the Exhibition Grounds, for instance. But if trouble is planned by the Trekkers, why are most of them, fifteen hundred or more, back at the Exhibition Grounds watching a baseball game between a local squad and, reputedly, those travelling All-Stars and hirsute eccentrics, the House of David, and listening to the tootling of a Regina boys' band?

Bill Davis is standing near the truck, dressed in a suit which someone has loaned him so that he can look proper when he travels to towns like Estevan and Melville to make speeches. Davis has just returned to Regina after a tour.[12]

And Arthur Evans, just back from supper himself, strolls in the crowd, clearly visible to so many who have seen him in the past two weeks, conspicuous, without the bodyguard he is supposed to move with since his return from Ottawa.[13]

Evans is now approached by George Black, his deputy, by Gerry (Tellier) Winters and by John Toothill of the CEC. These four climb on the flatbed, set some chairs down. The crowd is quiet now as Toothill begins to talk, making introductions, explaining the purposes of this meeting. As he chats away, Black and Evans spot vans drawing up nearby, the same sort of vans which appeared at the roadblock the night of the twenty-seventh.[14] J.B. Preece, a local office clerk, hears a Trekker in the crowd pass the word around that the vans have arrived.[15] One truck eases up Osler, near the centre line of the Square, a second stops near the Metropole Hotel on Tenth Avenue and a third parks on Halifax, south near the Police Station.

Toothill goes on and then Winters steps forward and begins to make an appeal for donations. The Reverend J.F. Stewart hears him speak out in a jocular tone: "They were in need of funds and any person in the audience who had any money they did not know what to do with, if they would send it up, the Trekkers would treat it kindly."[16]

It is 8:17 P.M.. Deep in the crowd, Inspector Walter Mortimer raises a whistle, blows a piercing signal, whereupon RCMP constables Percy Lovock and W. Bailey jump to the truck and intercept Black and Evans who are in mid-air as they attempt to flee. Regina officers Ewen MacDonald and Robert Bruce are there as well and the four men begin to hustle Black and Evans away. On the way out, Bruce grabs and arrests Clarence Mason, from Division Five, who tries to snatch Black free and in so doing, lashes out at Inspector Mortimer. Black and Evans are off the Square in seconds.[17]

At the cry of the whistle, spectators begin to yell "Police, Police!" for before the echoes of the signal have died away, the police garage doors blow open and out come McDougall's troop, the baseball batons held vertically from waist to shoulder. They come at a quick march towards the truck, "slammed bang into the crowd" as citizen Allan Miller sees them, McDougall in front calling "One side please." McDougall's men are premature in their advance. They have not waited to see whether Black and Evans have been arrested and removed, most likely they don't even know whether the arrests have been made or, for that matter, who has been arrested. But here they come.[18]

The crowd, startled by the whistle and seeing the batons held up, divides, breaks and runs, the major part scurrying west onto Osler and across that street into the vacant lots, onto the curbs, against the walls of the B-A Gas Station, the Regina Hotel and north to the Metropole. Once away they drift back into the street to watch. A second group, mostly strikers but some citizens, hurries to the northeast corner and across Halifax.

McDougall and his men will later testify that their run to the truck is unimpeded, that the crowd moves so quickly away that no one is within five feet of the flying column. They reach the truck in formation and then break rank to stand in a group.[19]

At the whistle, the rear doors of the three vans open and out come the three troops of RCMP. They are all dressed alike in boots, breeches, brown serge jackets, .45 colt revolvers in holsters, empty ammunition pouches, steel helmets and twenty-one-inch long leather batons. They line up in single files facing the Square.[20]

Except for normal parades and the regular muster at the RCMP training barracks, these men have not had to come together in such numbers in Regina in quite a while. A few have been at the road block on the twenty-seventh, others have been at the city centre on the night of 17 June. Among them are constables who remember the Royal North-West Mounted Police: Sergeant Fred Camm who joined in 1914 and who holds the Distinguished Conduct Medal, with three years in Europe; Sergeant Bertie Stangroon who enlisted in 1913, went abroad with the Princess Patricia's Canadian Light Infantry and won the Military Medal; Inspector John Jones enlisted in 1914, ten years with the Alberta Provincial Police; Inspector Joseph Brunet who joined in 1923; Inspector Albert Marson who transferred from the Alberta Provincial Police in 1932 and who has just been posted to Regina from Edmonton on 21 June.[21]

If most of the crowd have run off the Square, John McCarthy stays put. McCarthy has come to Regina "in '83 or '84" and now lives in the Regina Hotel on Osler Street. McCarthy goes over to McDougall's troop. He knows many of the constables. "I had a shilalleigh [sic] in my hand, a good cane, and

I walked alongside of them...I said something to them. Of course, they never seemed interested...I took a look north. I saw a picture there that I never expected to see in the City. There was a small man with his two hands raised above his head on his knees and someone in a uniform with a club which seemed to be playing over his head...I followed him for a few steps and struck at him with this cane and he grabbed it and went off...there were about six inches of it broke off before...I went a little bit East through the centre of the square and was kind of looking to see if there was any sign of the part of my cane on the ground. Because it was a souvenir from Ireland...And in the mean time I had felt some blood on my face and my eye-glass here seemed kind of dim...So I walked down there and up to one of the policemen, Sergeant MacFee. he looked at me and said, ''You had better get that looked after. You might get infection.

When I got to Osler, I met a small man there, an Irishman that I knew. He had blood on his face and he looked at me and said, ''We're mutual...'' [22]

Now the bad part begins on the Square. All of this is happening simultaneously. McDougall and his troop, their pause finished, are suddenly hit by stones and bricks thrown from the northeast corner, Tenth and Halifax. They reassemble and run to that place which is now churning with two hundred or more men who have raced off at the whistle and are now returning from the nearby alleys and lanes with the débris which they hurl forward. [23]

The Halifax Street RCMP troop, under Inspector Joseph Brunet, marches onto the Square past the police garage, bound for the speakers' truck. They are punished badly by the barrage thrown at McDougall and from behind them. Brunet had thought to support McDougall but this is not possible. [24]

McDougall's troop break formation and fall into individual clashes as they dart in and out of the throng descending from the north. Constable George Splitt takes a rioter under arrest and starts with him towards the station, joined quickly by Constable Tom Hogan. A group of men cuts in front of them. Splitt:

They ran right around in front of us and one of them demanded that we release this prisoner, saying, ''He is not doing any more than any of the rest, you had better let him go.'' Just then Constable Hogan said something...and I turned around and saw him fall down, and something had hit him on the back of his head, the blood just seemed to spurt out. [25]

Hogan has heard the insulted inspector call out to them. Splitt stops to tussle with this man, Hogan presses on, is struck down.

Splitt falls next and both officers are out for a few seconds, long enough for their prisoner to escape.[26]

Brunet's men pass this scene, coming under fire. A brick strikes Constable D.P.D. Shaw in the mouth; as Shaw stumbles under the impact, another brick hits him in the back of the head. Nonetheless, Shaw runs on, clear across the Square, struck again and then a fourth time, as he goes to help a constable who is down and out. And so it goes on the east side of Market Square, the riot beginning there, perhaps because of the arrests of Black and Evans, probably because of the appearance of McDougall's column.[27]

If the crowd around the truck runs for the sidelines at the whistle, they do not all escape easily. Agatha Sentes, there with her husband, sitting in a chair near the flatbed, is hit on the back by a baton. As she falls, she sees another woman, an older lady, trampled. It is Mrs. Hungle, who is picked up, whisked west to Osler, her leg broken, finally heard to cry, "Holy Mother of God."[28]

Steve Fustas, in the front row, baby in his lap, hears "Steve, here is the police, I says, what police? She says, look up, I turned my face towards the city police station and I saw the policemen come out waving their clubs and starting to holler clear up the Market Square, get out of here" Fustas runs off with the baby, then stops, realizing that his wife and daughter are not following

I started to cry and I asked a policeman, a Mounted Policeman,
I says, say, you look very sharp and you get my girl. He says,
no, I haven't time, I am busy, I am not looking after your girl.

Fustas sees a man down, so he calls out "Help, ladies and gentlemen, there is a man there badly hurt..." And then Fustas finds his wife who has taken the daughter to Osler and everything for them is all right.[29] Except that Stanley MacKinnon has seen Fustas: "...a foreign fellow, who did not speak very good English, came up to me and he said — he had a baby in his arms — ...and he showed me his wrist where it was black and blue. He said he had tried to protect the baby's head from being hit...."[30]

One of the legends of the riot on Market Square is about overturned baby carriages, the sight of these easily elevated into enduring symbols of innocence beaten down. Chris Kostichuk, there with his own kids, assists a woman with a carriage into a side street. Metro Bokla sees two carriages pitched over, the infants sprawled on the ground, howling, but immediately retrieved by their mothers. Bokla saunters around for a while, spies a few women's hats on the Square, takes these up and drops them in back of the speakers' truck[31]

John Cheers, whose wife wanted to see the strikers, grabs her hand and heads for Osler, only to get there, look back and find the hand belongs to someone else. Shortly, Mrs. Cheers emerges from the riot.[32]

McDougall's troop in the northeast corner makes two charges on their assailants. In one of these, Jacob Brunner sees three officers pounding on a man

> *Just wherever they could hit him, they were hitting him on the head, and anywhere they could — arms and everything, and, well he was kind of smothered there with blood, you couldn't tell who he was. . .you could see it was a man. . .And I walked towards them. . .and I saw one of them that I knew, . . .a sergeant, Tommy Logan, and I said to him, "What are you doing here, are you trying to kill him. If you are trying to kill him, why don't you shoot him and be done with it, and if you are going to arrest him, why don't you take him in, he is on the ground there, you could take him in," and I asked him, "Why do you keep pounding him?"* [33]

A dramatic scene. A terrible scene. The officer identified, the cries of the outraged witness perfectly recalled. Sergeant Logan will say later that he struck no one on the Square and that, in fact, after pushing the rioters back across Halifax and Tenth for the second time, they dispersed and his corner became quiet. Brunner, meanwhile, goes to his shop and watches from the window, "to take in the sights."

Such contradictions will occur again and again as participants and witnesses recall their movements and experiences that evening. And no wonder. Behind and within each "reality," the "truth" of each witness, lies a lifetime of bias, discipline, intelligence, ideology. Brunner may believe, forever after, that he saw Logan and two other officers maul the man. He may believe that he said what he said to them. And Logan will claim that he struck no one on the Square. It is possible that Brunner was mistaken and did not see Logan at that moment. He is very specific, however, and since he works just across the street from the Police Station, he must know many constables, if only by name and slight acquaintance. Logan, on the other hand, never mentions Brunner. There will be many, differing versions of the events of the riot that night.[34]

A second unit of RCMP enters the fray. Led by Inspector John T. Jones, these leave the van on Tenth Avenue. It is Jones who spoke with the three troops assigned to the vans at RCMP barracks scarcely half an hour earlier. "I warned them if they were called upon to do anything, to keep together, to keep calm and cool, that they would probably be subjected to considerable abuse. People would call them a lot of unpleasant names. . .They were to take no notice of it!'' And so Jones marches south towards the station where he comes on Brunet, under fire. Several of his men step over to assist Sergeant Harold Fleming who has been struck down by a brick in the face. But suddenly Jones's men are hit by rocks thrown from their rear, perhaps by the very men who ran through their ranks as they came on the Square. Jones calls ''Sections about — Charge!'' and the constables run back north to skirmish.[35]

Gas grenades have already been thrown at the rioters and the fumes drift, linger, stifling citizens, strikers and police alike.

A third troop of RCMP under Inspector Albert Marson come on Market Square from Osler at the whistle, encountering the greater number of spectators who are fleeing west. Its ranks adjusted, this detail pivots northwest where it too comes under a storm and, like the other formations, is momentarily dispersed. Constable David Parsons is surrounded by rioters and beaten to the dirt.

And immediately some of these men grabbed me and pulled me down on the street and proceeded to do considerable clubbing, and kicking, and throwing rocks and such like...And I remained perfectly quiet until they got through and left, and I got up and went back to my troop.[36]

By keeping still, Parsons probably escapes severe injury though his unloaded revolver, snug in its holster, is ruined, the trigger guard bent by the kicks and clubs and rocks ''and suchlike.''

Constable A.W. Francis, rushing ahead to break up a group gathered at Osler and Tenth, outdistances his troop.

Well I finally got into the thick of them and everyone seemed to come out of their [sic] from nowhere. The baton knocked out of my hand. I used my left hand to protect my face, and it wasn't very long before though, before the forearm was useless...I attempted to grasp some of these clubs that were falling around me. One of the flung stones caught me in the stomach and as I bent forward I received a blow on the back of the head.

Francis falls: ''I felt the crowd, you see, pressing on me.''[38]

Constable K.J. McLean runs in and finds a man sitting on Francis's chest, beating on his face and two others standing alongside, kicking at Francis's ribs. Brunet's trooper, Gordon Ridge, is there as well and chases the chest-sitter, one Mottle, who, when caught, begins bragging ''about how the Communist Party would bestow recognition on him for his part in the riot.'' John Guenther, a Marson man, goes up to Francis but is attacked by a youth, aged fifteen or sixteen, who whisks Guenther's helmet off with a three-foot long fence post. But Francis is finally lifted up and carried to safety by his colleagues.[38]

Busy as they are in that northwest corner, several of the officers catch sight of a lemon-coloured truck drawn up at the intersection. Again, the contradictions. Rioters are observed going to it, removing a container from the back (it is a pick-up truck), dumping rocks out and hurling these at the police. There is a name on the cab: Southern Motors. But later, its driver, David Parker, will sheepishly admit that he borrowed the truck without permission, drove to the Square and at the intersection saw a man reach into the bed of the truck and steal a five-gallon gas can which he then proceeded to pound on the pavement. A mystery. If Parker is telling the truth, and given his profound embarrassment, surely he is, then he is not an accomplice of the strikers and he has not come bearing ammunition as the police witnesses supposed.[39]

McDougall, Brunet, Jones and Marson all come on Market Square at the whistle. The Square is emptied of spectators immediately and filled again, as it were, by the police and by the rioters who bull their way onto the block, are driven off, and who either run back on or else stand in the adjacent streets and lanes hurling rocks and curses.

Ken Liddell, a *Leader-Post* photographer is there, perched on the drill tower, snapping pictures that will be reprinted again and again over the next decades. Men saunter about the Square, hands in pockets, hands tucked behind, one fellow chatting with another. A moment before or after, Constable David Brims, one of Marson's men, who has already been denounced by one rioter as a ''yellow son of a bitch,'' approaches two women strolling arm-in-arm near the fire hall. ''You better get out of here, ladies.'' To which advice, one replies, ''You go to hell.'' K.J. McLean, who has just brought Francis in from that deadly northwest corner, sees a woman with a baby also near the fire hall and suggests that she clear the field. ''I have as much right as any other person to be here,'' she retorts but McLean takes her off, nonetheless.[40]

Just west of the train of street maintenance gear, half-a-dozen men stand, frozen, looking east down the line of carts to a sight, a man going down, dying. Detective Charles Millar.

Millar has been in the police garage as a reserve but when rioters make for the gear in the carts, he goes out, past Bruton and Wood who have been watching from the doorway recently cleared by McDougall. (They have been knocked around a bit themselves by débris hurled at Brunet.) As Millar runs onto the Square, he bumps into Ernest Doran and his eight-year-old son, who have been walking along Eleventh Avenue. When the boy hears the uproar, he skips ahead between the fire and police stations and is suddenly in danger. Millar deflects a collision with the youth by grabbing his shoulders and swinging him aside and then passes on.[41]

As Millar comes to the nearest cart, he is set on by one, two, perhaps three men, who beat him to the ground, the blows fracturing his skull (already damaged by a World War I wound), setting off massive damage, ruining his brain. Doran sees this:

> a gentleman coming over from the Market Square, from the north, he ran down and enroute he picked up a piece of cordwood...three feet long...and he arrived just at that moment and came right over, very close behind Millar, and lifted the piece of wood over his head and struck Millar on the head.[42]

City Constable Alex Hill, who has just hustled a rioter into the garage, returns, sees Millar

> in a sort of kneeling, bowing position, like kneeling with his head bent over, on his knees...I ran towards Millar, and these people were around him. They backed away. I thought he had been knocked out, and I reached over and caught him underneath the armpits...I spoke to him. I said something to him, and I went to lift him up, and that is my last recollection...[43]

Hill's fellow constable, C.A. Anderson, in the garage, sees Millar fall and Hill slumped at his side. He goes out and assists Hill in raising the detective to his feet and the two men begin to walk Millar inside. Hill is struck and "just kind of fell away." Anderson trots Millar inside, sets him down, goes back for Hill, is himself smashed down, recovers quickly as does Hill, and the two officers go back onto the Square. Behind them, Millar is slumped against a wall until he is picked up, put into an ambulance which sets off for the hospital; on its way, the ambulance is struck by a bullet, the only time that evening when someone other than a constable fires a gun.[44]

Meanwhile, two additional contingents of RCMP have arrived. One is a twenty-man detail from the RCMP Town Station on Cornwall, to the west, and is led by Sergeant Charles Clarke who has received a call from Wood at 8:30 P.M. Clarke crosses Osler and is quickly absorbed in the storm of rocks, although he too has time to glance at Parker's notorious lemon truck. Constable John Gibbons quickly subdues Carl Whitney who is observed throwing the shock absorber spring of a car at an officer. Gibbons is struck by John Weden; an iron pipe cuts the constable's elbow to the bone. Weden trips, falls, resists arrest by squirming on his back, kicking out with his arms and legs like a child, until he is hauled up and away.[45]

The last police force on the scene consists of two troops of thirty-eight mounted officers under Inspector A.S. Cooper. The horsemen have been waiting at Twelfth and Osler from the outset and now they move north on Osler, break into two squads and proceed to trot up and down the street. Frank Swinnerton watches a trooper chase a man into a lane between the Regina Hotel and Gaetz's Garage, thunk him on the head, lay him out, whereupon a woman darts from a side door of the hotel and drags the rioter to safety. John Lynch, a citizen, nearly trampled, grabs a horse's reins and is dragged along the sidewalk until he falls away. Raymond Reed, another local, has been hit on the head and arm, has staggered to Tenth Avenue where he finds a friend, Carl Richards, who sits with him in front of the "B C Rooms" where Richards lives, until they are driven inside by a horse which is ridden right into the doorway. William Rochon, south on Osler by the B-A Station, crowds against the wall before the horses and escapes finally, bitten on the head by an irate stallion. Wesley Krainicheck, taking his ease outside the door to the Metropole beer parlour, finds himself scrambling inside along with a hysterical elderly woman and a dozen other refugees.[46]

It is now 9:00 P.M. A score of constables of both forces have been sufficiently injured to require hospitalization. Most who have come on the Market Square have been struck again and again. McDougall, one of the first out, has been hit by a horseshoe; he will come down with blood poisoning. But for a moment, the officers gather in the middle of the Square, smoking, resting, waiting.

McDougall's detail has come into the struggle carrying unloaded pistols and ammunition. The RCMP have not been issued ammunition previously but now they are, as the result of telephone calls from the Town Station announcing the arrival of rioters near that block and from Wilfrid McCubbin whose hardware store, on the corner of Eleventh Avenue and Smith Street, seven blocks to the west, has apparently come under siege. Constable Robert Welliver, advancing with Brunet, carries five fifty-round boxes of bullets in a haversack, a burden which has not prevented him from using his baton on the shoulders of a rock-thrower. Welliver is told to issue twelve rounds to each man though these are not to be loaded.[47]

The pause over, the police begin to move on. Jones's troop walks down Tenth to Unity Centre and without incident removes papers and pamphlets of no particular value. No arrests are made here. McDougall is briefed on the McCubbin incident and sets out with the remnants of his column, about half the original number, for the west side of the city; RCMP Constable Walter Hutchinson drives the officers over in a van. Marson's men are also transported by van to the Town Station where they will pass the evening escorting arrested rioters to the RCMP barracks. Clarke's contingent, which has come from the Town Station, now returns on foot along South Railway Street. Cooper has dispatched a section of mounted RCMP under Sergeant George Griffin to give support to Jones at Unity Centre; once this raid is over, around 9:15, Griffin crosses Market Square and proceeds west along Eleventh Avenue. Brunet follows on foot. The remaining section of horsemen under Cooper, and Jones's detachment, remain on or near Market Square.[48]

McDougall in the vanguard, Clarke, Griffin and Brunet are all in pursuit of approximately 250 Trekkers and an unknown but considerable body of townspeople who have set off from the Square, bound west. The Square itself is strewn with enough rocks, bottles, bricks and half-bricks, cordwood, broken concrete and simple junk to fill five trucks when the area is cleaned up the next day. They leave assorted injured police, rioters and citizens, among the last the Reverend Harry Upton who, on running off, has been hit on the thumb by a baton swung, more than likely, in the air and not at the preacher. Though the blow hurts.[59]

They leave behind John McCarthy who still has not recovered his shillelegh but who has returned to his room in the Regina Hotel to have his lacerated face repaired. McCarthy thinks it undignified for a man his age to go to the doctor's office so he calls his friend, Dr. Sweeney, who comes down and looks him over. As this is in progress, in comes a large RCMP constable who is looking for rioters-in-hiding.

> "Why, did somebody hit you? Did you get wounded?" "Well,"
> I told him, "Apparently I have a bandage on, anyway." As
> soon as he spoke I said, "You are from Kerry?" He said, "No,
> I am from Clare," and I said, "You must have come from the
> same place as De Valera when he was being run down at
> Oglesford?"

And then the constable departs, Dr. Sweeney departs, and John McCarthy sits in his room that evening writing a poem about the riot. Being an honest man, when he comes to tell of his own injury, McCarthy puts it right that in fact he has not been struck by that officer on the Square whose baton "was just like the baseball clubs that Walter Scott and ourselves use to play with 40 years ago." McCarthy has hit himself in the face when he raised his shillelegh to defend the little man on his knees.[50]

On his way west from Market Square is one J.E. Bartz, who has been riding around town that evening on his bike, sees and hears the disturbance on the Square, thinks at first it is a sports day in progress, leaves his bike at Brunner's Garage, walks around, goes back to his bike and heads for the Exhibition Grounds, hot on the trail of the Trekkers: ''Well, I thought now I am going to see if they get there.'' [51]

Eight
Downtown

"Come on, boys, let's smash every bloody window in this town!"

— Overheard by Leslie Hainsworth

City Constable Archie Apps has finished his tour, has called in to his sergeant who tells him to return to the Police Station but does not allude to a riot in progress. Thus, when Apps comes along Eleventh Avenue, he sees a crowd marching towards him just east of Rose Street; Apps first thinks this is another demonstration. As he comes near, he hears a man call out: "Come on, lads, show these buggers. Let's break some of these windows!" Then Apps is spotted. "There is one of the sons of bitches! Let him have it!" Apps dodges the first rock which explodes behind him into a window of William Haddrill's store: "I then tried to get out of there in quite a hurry," and he almost makes it. But as he starts to cross Broad Street, he is knocked to his knees by a brick in the face. Now the crowd is on him, stones and bricks bouncing off his back and shoulders. Apps has to jump around a car which has just come into the intersection and that gives one pursuer a sudden advantage and he springs on Apps who ducks down and away so that the assailant goes flying over his head. Off Apps goes, struck once more "by something real sharp on the back and I went down on one knee. It lost me the use of my leg for a minute." But Apps staggers on and finally clears Osler and arrives at the Station. There his sergeant tells him to change his white summer-issue helmet for the blue helmet so Apps obliges and then goes onto the Square.[1]

The Regina Riot is about neighbourhoods in a modest city which become battlegrounds across which run men and women bent on escape, on mutual injury, on fun. Market Square is one neighbourhood. Here is another: Eleventh Avenue and the several streets which intersect with it west from the Square: Osler, Broad, Rose, Hamilton, Scarth, Cornwall, Lorne, Smith, McIntyre, Albert, all of these running north and south. Eleventh Avenue and these side streets are lined with homes and with shops, theatres, office buildings, banks, government buildings. Their names are homely but also familiar in western Canada. A string of United Cigar Stores on every other corner seemingly, Foodland, the Metropolitan Theatre, the Army and Navy Store, Kresge's, the Rex Theatre, the City Hall, the Post Office, the Public Drug Store, Ryan's Cafe, the Unique Cafe, the Mickey Mouse Cafe, the Bank of Montreal. And more. And through, around and over these buildings and blocks and streets, the riot spreads.

When Mortimer's whistle calls out, and the major part of the spectators charge off onto Osler Street, a hundred or more Trekkers and townspeople keep right on going along Eleventh Avenue, running into Archie Apps almost immediately. Minutes later, another group of about the same size, having fought with McDougall on the northeast corner of Market Square, breaks away and runs west on Tenth to Broad, turns north to South Railway Street, then west again to Rose and down Rose to Eleventh Avenue where it joins up with the first contingent which has now finished with Apps. That rock which Apps has dodged and which has gone into Haddrill's has struck Haddrill's daughter in the head, so that she becomes the first casualty of the riot downtown.[2]

This exodus is underway at the same time that Millar is dying, that Francis is being jumped, that McLean is being cursed, that Liddell is taking his photographs.

As the procession moves west along Eleventh Avenue, townspeople living or working along the route go to the door or window to watch. Leslie Hainsworth, a clerk in the United Cigar Store at Broad Street sees the crowd chasing Apps and hears someone yell out: "Come on boys. Let's smash every window in this bloody town!" They stand outside Hainsworth's store, talking, organizing, then they go on by. Physician Emil Sauer comes to the window of his second-floor office on the corner of Rose and gazes down on rioters plundering scantlings and other construction materials which are laid out in front of the Army and Navy Store which is undergoing renovation. Gerald Burchill watches as the crowd goes by the United Cigar Store on Hamilton where he works. A few men break off and go up Hamilton to the Western Cycle store where they smash windows but fail to gain entry. Burchill thinks they may be looking for rifles.[3]

Robert Scott, William Reader and Frank Varro, citizens who have been drifting with the crowd although more out of curiosity than ideology, all hear a man call the Trekkers to form fours and head for the Exhibition Grounds. This man is not identified. A formation is briefly conceived, but it does not last long. For one thing, the crowd is walking along city street car tracks and the street cars are running that evening. One has halted just down the way in front of the City Hall. George Roberts is the driver, and he has been stopped by a six-foot tall fellow wearing cowboy boots and a huge ten-gallon hat. No "dude" apparently, this man climbs up and pulls the pole connector away from the electric wire overhead, to no particular purpose, as it turns out, for then he climbs up again and reattaches the connector. Roberts goes on east. Very shortly, two other streetcars will be stalled just west of Scarth by the struggles between police and rioters and by the hordes of spectators.[4]

At the City Hall, the marchers disperse, most of them running here and there across the grounds in front, a few hammering in vain on the locked entrance. The City Hall will remain an outpost of sorts throughout the evening though rioters will probe further west and even south. For the moment, though, they throw up the first of numerous barricades of automobiles, this one across Eleventh Avenue, west of Hamilton Street. Robert Scott sees a car stopped, its driver told: "...You better move out of here, we are going to have a blockade. The gentleman in the car said: "Whereabouts" and the striker said "Right here." Whereupon the driver parks his car in the street as a contribution, pockets the keys and walks away.[5]

McDougall's squad has been the first to leave the Square, bound for Wilfrid McCubbin's hardware store at Eleventh Avenue and Smith Street. This will prove to be a false alarm though McCubbin, himself, has had a nervous moment or two. Apparently called to the scene by the neighbours, he finds "a motley group of excited men" huddled around the entrance. McCubbin calls, "...now boys, look here, I am the proprietor of this store, there are no guns in there..." to which he then is told: "...we are going in anyway...it will be all the worse for you if we find some guns in there." But the threat is only a bluff for quickly the strangers depart, some time before McDougall arrives.[6]

What is noteworthy about this encounter is that rioters, most if not all of whom are Trekkers, have walked or run so far away from Market Square. They are already well on their way to the Exhibition Grounds, if that is their destination.

North of Eleventh Avenue on Cornwall is the RCMP Town Station which contains cells in which Evans and other rioters taken at the Square have been lodged. Clarke's troop has left the Station by 8:30 P.M. at Wood's command but is quickly replaced by a detachment commanded by Sergeant Roberts who arrives fifteen minutes later from the RCMP barracks. Roberts discovers that the Station is already about to be compromised by some seventy rioters who have appeared at the south corner. Given the time and the fact that the larger group is still around the Post Office or approaching it, the likelihood is that the men threatening the Town Station have come there by various routes from the east and from the foremost ranks of the marchers who have drawn up at the Post Office.

Roberts's men climb from their van under fire as rioters edge towards them, hiding behind cars, pitching the now familiar (though not to Roberts) junk. Roberts lines his men across the street near the Town Station, facing south. They are hit again and again, in ranks and singly, as constables run forward to seize a man. Roberts has come with gas grenades and finally he hurls these at the crowd, eighteen grenades in all, one of which comes flying back. Then, pressed, Roberts draws his revolver and fires in the air, driving the crowd away. The street momentarily secured, Roberts goes into the Town Station and calls Wood, requesting mounted reinforcements.[7]

Watching this struggle, and in fact describing it to the Queen City, is a crew of broadcasters from radio station CJRM who have reconnoitred the terrain three days before in anticipation of just such disorder, and who have just climbed onto the roof of the Saskatchewan Life Building which is actually an annex of the Bank of Montreal, right on the corner. The view is superb, although when Wilfrid Woodhill starts describing the sights into this microphone, he has to shout above the noise. Rioters on the street below hear him praising the police and, righteously angry, yell that they will come up and separate Woodhill from his microphone. After this, one of the technicians hangs onto a utility pole, by which they have climbed to the roof, brandishing a length of pipe.[8]

Roberts's call to Wood bears fruit, for Cooper sends Sergeant Griffin and some twenty troopers on their way, to be followed by Brunet. When these officers reach City Hall, they are assaulted from the grounds and the adjacent street by débris picked up in alleys, from the Army and Navy Store or carried from the Market Square. Neither Griffin nor Brunet chooses to engage but instead each goes on to Cornwall Street where they find their fight.[9]

The rioters at that corner, driven back by Roberts's fire, and reinforced by two or three dozen men who have fled before Griffin, form into a column and start west, quite possibly bound for the Exhibition Grounds. As they come up to the Grand Theatre, whose patrons have already emptied into the street, they halt at the cry: ''Hold the ranks. Here they come!'' Another barricade of cars is forced into position as Griffin and Brunet arrive and with Roberts's men take on the rioters in a general, loud, brutal quarrel, constables rushing here and there to grab an assailant, rocks careening off buildings, off cars, off horses, through windows, onto bodies of men and women.

Edward Powell, an employee of the Saskatchewan Wheat Pool, is watching the rioters:

They had absolutely no chance, they were unmercifully beaten off the streets by the men on horseback with clubs, and they disappeared into the lanes, all that any human beings could do.[10]

There are other witnesses, for there are dozens and dozens of townspeople strung out along the streets and sidewalks, standing across the way in Victoria Park. Many, no doubt, have come from Market Square ahead of, in the midst of, and in the wake of the two main bodies of rioters. Others have walked or driven in from other points of the city, drawn downtown on errands, on their way to the movies. Perhaps they have heard Wilfrid Woodhill's broadcast which has begun at 8:50. For whatever reasons, these citizens are there, they are in the way. Many will go home weeping from tear gas fumes, some will be shot down. As dark descends, as the street lights go on though dimmed by the wafting gas fumes, the spectators run here and there, idle in small crowds, cheer, yell.

Mrs. Clara Beaton is driving around town that night with six children, family and their friends, mostly adolescents. Not until they turn on Eleventh Avenue and approach Cornwall Street do they realize what is happening. A rioter yells: ''Stop, Goddam you,'' but the Beaton boy who is driving goes on into the hail of stones which smash the car windows and strike his brother in the face.[11]

William Cummings, a barrister, is watching from the corner of Scarth and Eleventh:

There was a cry went out, they were starting to throw gas bombs and the crowd surged back toward the Bank of Montreal corner, giggling and laughing, some of them, as though it was quite a joke.[12]

Cooper now comes along with the second section of mounted constables and is also bombarded from the area around the City Hall. He retaliates, however, jumping his horses over the low fence onto the lawn, driving the rioters away though they reassemble as soon as Cooper leaves. Next, beyond Cornwall, Cooper is attacked from the roofs of the Donahue and Reinhold Buildings on the north side and from the sidewalks to the south. Cooper goes after the rioters on the sidewalks, scatters them west and south into Lorne and Smith Streets, and then he trots on west to Albert and the subway there. Wheeling his men about, he returns to Cornwall where, finding the gas fumes so strong as to bother the horses, he goes south towards Twelfth Avenue.[13]

In any case, the fight at Eleventh and Cornwall has all but come to a close although the scene is frightful. Shards of glass littered about. Street cars stalled, cars thrust this way and that. And in the memories of onlookers, vivid moments.

Elgin McIlroy, a grain buyer, near the Town Station, glances at another man, John Smith, standing with his hands in his pockets. Suddenly Smith is jumped by police who lay into him with batons and drag him inside. As it turns out, Smith is thought to have been Millar's killer although this charge is soon dismissed.[14]

If one rioter can curse Mrs. Beaton and her kids, others are not so vindictive. Carl Corbett, a clothier, is standing on the roof of the Reinhold Building watching two rioters who are wearing Red Cross bands on their arms, and who are undoubtedly Trekkers, run to two little girls, pick them up and thrust them in the doorway of an apartment block, out of the way.[15]

Samuel Stinson has walked downtown after the rioters in time to see a mounted officer careen into a utility pole and his horse stumble to the pavement. A rioter shrieks, "Kill him. Kill the bastard!" but the man and his mount are up and away.[16]

Victor Olson has also been at the Square and now is down by the Town Station and he overhears

> a lot of ladies with very decided English accents almost in hysteria talking about their British rights and British justice being taken away by "Yellow-legged Bastards."[17]

Ryan's Cafe on Scarth Street north of Eleventh is a popular sanctuary for Trekkers, a few of whom are sitting with proprietor Frances Ryan. Through the evening, Trekkers stagger into her cafe or are carried in by buddies, there to have wounds bound with strips of tablecloth. Once Mrs. Ryan goes outside.

> That boy was standing holding himself by the wall, and when this gas started, whatever it is, I don't know what it was, it was something horrid I know that, people started to rush east, and this poor boy was in danger of being knocked down and trampled, and I stayed with him and helped him.[18]

Florence Dean and her friend, Mrs. McMann, have been visiting with a sick acquaintance who lives on Scarth Street, but shortly they hear a commotion and go outside and meet Mr. Greenaway, a neighbour, who says "You had better hurry on home. There is things going on down at the east end." Mrs. Dean rushes west along Eleventh to her home around the corner on Lorne. Her small children are there alone. Soon after she is inside, she hears a noise at the rear door, goes there, finds men hiding in a small alley, piling stones which young boys and girls bring to them. Some of the men come up her backsteps and try to barge in but Mrs. Dean throws herself against the door and holds firm. Once that threat is past, she walks into her front yard to find two men carrying 2x4s punching them randomly through car windows. "Why do you want to do that? But they just laughed at me." Not until 1:00 P.M.

do the strangers leave her grounds. The next day, not to her surprise, Mrs. Dean finds garden and lawn trampled, ruined.[19]

If Eleventh Avenue is quiet, comparatively (and momentarily), with Griffin and Brunet on patrol, Twelfth Avenue is about to become a violent thoroughfare. Two hundred or more rioters have flooded south from the Cornwall struggle and have gathered on the corner of Twelfth and Scarth where they wheel one barricade into place across Twelfth and another across Scarth.

Ray Johnstone works in still another United Cigar Store on the corner. Some strikers tell him he should close up. He does and walks off: "I was all for peace at that moment." More durable is Colonel J.A. Cross, barrister and a former provincial attorney general. Colonel Cross has come downtown to inspect and perhaps defend his office. He parks, walks through the crowd, among whom are many local residents. A Trekker directs traffic. Cross is not threatened and once in his suite, he finds a splendid view of the intersection.[20]

Now the police begin to arrive. First, McDougall who has turned back from McCubbin's Hardware, runs into a barrage of rocks from atop the Donahue Building, turns south to Twelfth and proceeds east past Victoria Park to the barricade on the corner of Scarth. Over they go. John Deewold, a citizen, has gone up on the roof of the Capitol Theatre a few door away and watches rioters heave missiles much like medieval archers: "They were not thrown directly at the police. They were thrown in the air. There was a shower of rock, a shower. You might say it obliterated the view of the trees pretty well." For McDougall: "It was the worst bombardment we got all night." Not one of his constables escapes injury. And for the second time that night, the police open fire. The command is to shoot high and they do, except for one, perhaps two officers. Whether deliberately or by ricochet, three rioters fall wounded, two of whom are carried away by friends; the third is taken into the McCallum-Hill Building. Andrew McDermott of the *Daily Star* tries to follow this last victim, but he is shoved out of the building lobby.[21]

In the midst of this insanity, W.H.A. Hill, a patron of the Capitol Theatre, emerges, finds his car being used as a barricade, asks and receives permission to remove it, gets in, starts up, drives west on Twelfth, sees a troop of Mounted Police looming out of the dark, turns, darts up Cornwall, parks and walks back, hears the shots, waits in a doorway until that noise ceases. He has seen Cooper's patrol, trying to flank the tear gas on Eleventh, now trotting up behind McDougall. On the way over the barricade, one horse falls and is struck in the head by a rock as it gets up.[22]

McDougall's fire has dispersed the rioters so he goes into a store and calls the Police Station for more ammunition. Cooper swings his men north on Scarth and rides to Eleventh where he joins Griffin who has been holding nearby. It is now 9:45 P.M.

Now, a curious sight is reported by several Regina citizens who are on Eleventh Avenue near the City Hall. Fred Boor and James Wilcox both observe a black sedan speeding east and as it goes by, shots are fired from its windows. Both men see the flashes, hear the reports. No one is injured however; the car presses on. Around this same time, however, James Allin, who is standing by the Foodland Store near Broad, sees a car racing *west*, also shooting into the crowd near City Hall. Harold Dunn, at Hamilton, swears up and down that he sees a car filled with five RCMP officers race west also shooting. It is quite a mystery to these witnesses who may never know that they have respectively seen a car driven by RCMP Constable Walter Hutchinson who has taken McDougall to McCubbin's store and then, a bit later, is directed to carry Constable R. Wilson to the city police station for ammunition, presumably at McDougall's request. As the car wheels past City Hall, Wilson fires over the crowd. On they go, pick up the ammunition and back they come over the same route, Wilson to fire again as they cross Rose. Hutchinson, the driver, is as surprised as the rioters in the streets.[23]

Just as it is possible that the rioters who attacked Roberts's men outside the Town Station were attempting to break in and rescue Evans, so it is possible that the occupation by force of the Hotel Saskatchewan, south of Victoria Park, is the reason for the large concentration of rioters at Twelfth and Scarth. Several citizens are in that vicinity, some by design, as the Reverend J.F. Stewart who has been at Market Square, others by chance. John Deewold, who has driven west on Twelfth, or Charles Zetterstrand who is eastbound on Twelfth, encounter pickets who tell them ''You had better get away from here. There's going to be trouble.''[24]

In fact there is a brief probe against the Hotel just after the assembly on that corner. George Lowry, a CPR policeman, has earlier been dispatched with eight men to guard the Hotel and at about 9:20, as they stand in the lobby, a group of rioters runs towards the front door. Lowry takes his squad outside, charging into the street, driving the attack away, although they are stoned as they come and go. But no other movement against the Hotel occurs that night, McDougall's fire having dispersed the crowd.[25]

The climax of the Regina Riot approaches. His call for ammunition put through, and Hutchinson dispatched to the Square, McDougall forms his sixteen officers into a column of fours and marches them up Scarth, the sound of breaking glass in front of them. Near Eleventh, in front of the Monaco Cafe, they are hit again by rioters crouching behind stalled streetcars and by a second throng, presumably refugees from Twelfth Avenue who turn around in their flight, pick up more stones, the streets are thoroughly awash in them by now, and hurl away at McDougall. "I considered that every man I had was liable to be killed...There was no question in my mind what these men intended to do with us." So once again, McDougall's men fire on the rioters, and when this fails to drive them back, the officers fire again.[26]

A dozen or more men fall wounded, rioters and spectators, Trekkers and townspeople. One fellow crawls under a streetcar so McDougall runs to him and bends down calling "What is the trouble?" "I've been shot" yells Tony Tomachuck. "Well, come on out." Out comes Tomachuck, hit in the leg. Immediately, ambulances drift up and receive the injured, two men who have staggered to Ryan's Cafe, another who is in the lobby of the King's Hotel. More at the intersection. George Foley, Trekker, is down with a bullet in the foot; Alf Waalerud, Trekker, shot in the leg, as are Tom McMurray and Jack Johnson, both Trekkers. Robertson Clarkson has a bullet in the back, Griffiths Jones, one in the knee, David Lyon, a bullet in the stomach, M. MacDonald, a bullet in the face, W. Clarkson, a bullet in the shoulder, all Trekkers.

Down too are Jimmie Cross and Ephraim Delmadge, both citizens, both standing in the front ranks of the spectators at the intersection. Cross is struck through the right hip by a bullet which comes out his lower back, a ricochet no doubt, since Cross is facing away from the police when he is shot.[27]

William Rogers, citizen, is clear up Scarth near South Railway Street, on his way to the Apostolic Mission to check on the safety of a friend. He is hit in the chest.

Joe Rothecker has been in the King's Hotel beer parlour having a glass with his brother and his father-in-law, Victor Putz. Through the riot, they have been walking here and there, ending up in front of Foodland, over three blocks to the east. Rothecker hears a "ping" and goes down, not feeling anything at first, but sure enough, shot in the shoulder.

And here comes Joe Slabick, a section foreman, on Scarth, near South Railway: "We were just going to take a little walk and go down to the corner and George Davis, he says, here is the city police coming. I says, let's get away from here. We might get hurt. Just at that time, I was shot. I started to walk. I never said a word to George until I went a little way. I examined my hand on both sides and I said, I was shot!"[28]

Hospital records list twelve relief camp strikers and five Regina citizens down with gunshot wounds that night. Nearly all fall at or near Eleventh and Scarth. An exception is Trekker George Phillips who is shot in the legs while hiding in a nearby lane by a constable whom Phillips claims wore yellow boots — obviously an RCMP officer. Though one or two mounted police may have fired one or two shots that night in that neighbourhood, it is still not clear whether one of these fired at Phillips.[29]

It is equally unclear whether the men who fell at Twelfth and Scarth before McDougall's first volley made it to hospital. And it is possible that other rioters — citizens or Trekkers — were hit but fled the area rather than risk arrest along with medical care.

McDougall, Cooper, Griffin and Brunet continue active patrol throughout the city centre, flushing rioters from lanes and alleys, sending townspeople on their way. Jones's troop is finally released from duties at Market Square and he brings his men along the now battered Eleventh Avenue to City Hall where he too passes through a sort of initiation. It is a bit after 10:00 P.M. and there are still two hundred and more people gathered there, and from the crowd come the usual rocks and bricks. Jones leads his men among them, repels, falls back, is attacked again, repels, and then goes on west.[30]

J.E. Bartz, he of the peripatetic bicycle, has taken a northern route to the Exhibition Grounds where he waits for the Trekkers to return. He is met at the gates by tight-lipped pickets who finally begin to chat with him after he hangs around for a while.[31]

On hearing of the riot downtown, Colonel Norman Edgar, a militia officer, jumps in his car and drives to the Exhibition Grounds where he is accosted outside by a man brandishing a four-foot club, "and this fellow shouted: 'drive me down town' and jumped on the running board. I yelled to him to get off. . .he said: 'do you know I could bash your bloody brains in with this." Colonel Edgar wisely stomps on the gas and shoots ahead, leaving the angry man in his dust.[32]

The pickets whom Bartz has met are there primarily to keep the rest of the Trekkers inside, no easy job once "Extras," published by the *Leader-Post* and the *Daily Star* while the riot is underway, appear in the hands of fleeing rioters. Sebastian Haberlach and Kallan Shaw are in the Stadium with a local boys' band who play during the ball games, and these men are firmly told by the Trekkers not to take the kids away because there is shooting downtown. There are several hundred townspeople in the Stadium as well and gradually these file out and away.[33]

Trekkers who have been at Market Square have been drifting in for an hour and a half, although the main force does not arrive until after 10:00 P.M. Between that time and 2:00 P.M. on 2 July, seven or eight hundred Trekkers apparently leave the Exhibition Grounds and Regina and maybe even Saskatchewan, slipping off in the dark, putting behind them the Trek, Regina, the possibility of Lumsden Camp or arrest.

Colonel Wood has sent word to Cooper, Brunet and Jones to proceed to the RCMP barracks, turn in the horses, straighten themselves, pick up rifles and ammunition and hasten to the Exhibition Grounds, where they finally begin to appear at 2:00 A.M., a cordon thrown around the entire area.

City police continue to move about the city centre, checking damage, searching for hidden rioters. At dawn they find Caspar Blum, who has travelled around quite a bit that night, starting at Market Square, coming on downtown. It has been a long, exciting, dangerous night and Blum is exhausted so he crawls under a bush across the street from the Regina Courthouse and takes a nap, awakening at dawn to the curt command of a police officer who places him under arrest.[34]

Nine
After the Riot
"Don't weaken! Don't compromise! That's the thing!"
— Letter to R.B. Bennett

The centre of Regina was a shambles. Automobiles thrown here and there. Streetcars stalled for want of drivers. Lawns and sidewalks littered with bricks, stones, sticks, ruptured curbing. Tear gas fumes caught in the shrubbery across Victoria Park. By noon on Wednesday, 3 July, 180 panes of glass had been replaced, most of these in buildings along Eleventh Avenue. The Barnes Building at 2134 required $837.94 worth of labour and materials; the Crescent Furniture Store at 2238, $575.56; Walter B. Booker Ltd. at 2239, $263.12, and so it went. Most of these shops and offices were insured with additional policies shortly before the Trek arrived. The *Leader-Post* calculated that between $4 million to $5 million in riot coverage had been taken out by 70 percent of the Regina business firms, the rates being 300 percent higher for this service.[1]

Over a hundred citizens, Trekkers, RCMP and city constables had been injured sufficiently to require admission to a hospital although most were quickly released. Injuries ranged from contusions to rib bruises to gunshot wounds to skull fractures. One mounted RCMP officer suffered a broken collar bone from a missile hurled from a roof top. Mrs. Sebastian Hungle was run over by the crowd leaving the Square and had a broken leg. Presumably, many more who had been bumped or scraped or bruised did not need medical attention.[2]

Over a hundred rioters had been arrested that night although half of these were soon released, having been first charged with vagrancy and then having had those charges dismissed.

Ordered back to the RCMP training depot for repairs and rifles, Colonel Wood's men finally arrived at the Exhibition Grounds about 2:00 A.M. on 2 July, at least two hours after the melee down town had ended. During this interim, apparently, there were no police in evidence at the Exhibition Grounds. But there was a sizeable rank of Trekker pickets there and when those who had remained behind sought to rush into town either as reinforcements or to look for friends, they were prevented from doing so. The *Daily Star* heard that a pitched battle took place among the Trekkers because of this restraint although no details are provided and nowhere else is the story confirmed.[3] What did take place, however, was the hurried construction of about two hundred clubs made of chair legs, 2x4s, and heavy insulated wire. There seems to have been considerable fear on the part of many of the men that police were about to raid the Exhibition Grounds.

But when Wood's men arrived, they simply cordoned off the area. Wood later denied that he had brought in machine guns for this purpose although the Trekkers would always contend that he had.[4]

Mid-morning on 2 July, the RCMP took a count of the men inside the Exhibition Grounds and found 1,104 present. Since there were nearly 2,000 Trekkers on hand prior to the riot, and 1,358 were counted leaving on passenger trains on 5 July, and with about 50 lodged in jail, it can be concluded that as many as 500 Trekkers left Regina that night or otherwise went into hiding during the following days.[5]

Premier Gardiner learned of the riot when a friend called him at his office during the struggle. Here is his telegram to the Prime Minister:

> *You have no doubt been advised of latest developments. We wish to state that men had interviewed us at five o'clock. They stated they had advised your Government through your representative they were prepared to disband and go back to their camps or homes provided they were allowed to go under their own organization. They state this was denied them. They asked our government to take responsibility for disbanding them to their own camps or homes. While we were meeting to consider their proposals and any suggestions we might make to you trouble started down town between the police and strikers without notification to us of police intentions which has resulted in at least one death in the police force and scores of citizens strikers and police wounded. We are nevertheless prepared to undertake this work of disbanding the men without sending them to Lumsden. Will you consider negotiations on basis of this proposal.[6]*

It was, all in all, a restrained appeal. But it might be assumed that Mr. Gardiner had Mr. Bennett where he wanted him. This is the Prime Minister's reply:

> *Large number of so called strike marchers now at Regina have never been in relief camps and being homeless cannot be sent to any definite locality as being their homes. The Federal government is ready and willing to feed these marchers at Lumsden and transport them to that point. Apparently leaders demand transportation to Vancouver as organized bands which we are not willing to do in view of the illegal character of their organization and avowed purposes of their leaders. Of course*

we have no intention of interfering with any action you may decide to take that does not involve these men in violation of the laws of the country.[7]

With that, the Prime Minister capitulated. He might as well have left out the first three sentences of the message for all the good his stand on Lumsden and "organized bands" would do him. Saskatchewan Attorney General T.C. Davis later put it that from 2 July forward, "everything was done through us." What was most important (and revealing) was that jurisdiction over the RCMP had been returned to the province. Said Davis: "I don't know who got the instructions...it just happened." Presumably Commissioner MacBrien notified Colonel Wood of his new allegiance.[8]

Premier Gardiner quickly met with a Trekker delegation led by Mike McCaulay who had assumed charge of the men after the arrest of Evans and Black. McCaulay, of course, refused to take his people to Lumsden. Gardiner agreed that they could stay at the Exhibition Grounds and that the province would feed them and arrange for transportation away from the city. The Trekkers agreed to release into police custody any men for whom there were warrants. These were guaranteed a fair trial. Finally, McCaulay was told that a registration office would soon open to facilitate their departure.[9]

Around 4:00 P.M. on 2 July, a van carrying coffee and sandwiches moved into the Exhibition Grounds to provide the first food the men had eaten since the evening before. And they continued to subsist on this menu for two days until Colonel Wood removed his cordon and the Trekkers were allowed to board streetcars and go downtown for hot meals in cafés, the cost of these assumed by the province.

Gardiner and Davis were already at work on a plan for the dispersal of their visitors: one CPR passenger train would take men by the southern route to Vancouver, stopping at Moose Jaw and Calgary; one CNR passenger train would take men by the northern line, through Saskatoon where men from Dundurn would be dropped off, and then to Edmonton and Vancouver. Once in British Columbia, the men would be deposited at junctions nearest to the relief camps to which they would be returned.[10]

Attorney General Davis spoke with Brigadier Boak about the locations of these camps. According to Boak, Davis asked "that any camps closed as a result of walk out by strikers be immediately opened; that he be informed of detraining points for camps; that issue of clothing be made at Regina in cases of urgent necessity." Davis later claimed that Boak, after checking with Ottawa, reported back that he had been instructed not to have anything to do with the Attorney General of Saskatchewan! Even so, the Dominion

Government did intend to halt the trains in Kamloops and from there, send the Trekkers into camps.[11]

Gardiner and Davis were naturally anxious to send the men on their way. Rumours moved around quickly; they would leave on the evening of 3 July, then on 4 July. But then Mike McCaulay came forward to insist that they have another twenty-four hours so that they could conclude their search for missing comrades.

Until the men were released for a meal in town, they stood, sat, squatted and dozed in the summer sun. Those few who tried to slip away were quickly caught and returned. Occasionally, a Trekker wearing a Red Cross armband would exit and then return with supplies. Some of the men climbed onto the roof of the Stadium and from time to time raised a chorus of 'Hold the Fort.' From that vantage point they could see across to the Grey Nuns Hospital on whose roof sat members of the press, staring into the Exhibition Grounds.[12]

One provincial official who was to see a lot of the Trekkers that week was Thomas Molloy, Commissioner of Labour. Molloy had been at Gardiner's side since word of the Trek's departure from Calgary reached Regina. It was he who had arranged for meals at Swift Current and Moose Jaw. After the riot, Molloy took charge of the provision of food at the Exhibition Grounds. Asked about the mood of the men during this time, Molloy observed that their principal grievance was that they were out of smokes ''and when a man wants a smoke and can't get it, he is liable to be irritable.'' Otherwise, there were no disturbances.[13]

On the evening of Thursday, 4 July, after their first meal in town, the Trekkers returned to the Exhibition Grounds where they formed lines before tables at which sat Molloy and his associates who were to register each man for a train ticket and, where necessary, for a small stipend, both of which were to be picked up the next morning, before the trains left for the west. Those men who were going east would ride on regularly scheduled ''cushions.'' This task lasted for most of the night.

> . . . we registered a man as to his name, the camp he came from or his home address and the point to which he preferred to go. We sorted these into groups; Kamloops, Calgary, or where ever they were going, and turned it over to the railways who divided the tickets as equally as we could for the railway. The railways issued tickets and pinned it to their card. The men came in the morning, came in about 6 o'clock Friday morning to pick up the tickets. Naturally they had to pick them up by name, but a lot of names of tickets were not picked up, whether the men had forgotten the names they had given, or what happened I

do not know. . . . Those who left by special trains food was put on the train for them, those who left on regular trains as individuals we drafted a rough schedule, a man going to any point in Manitoba, we allowed 50¢, for food on the way, those going to Western Ontario $2.00, $1.50 I think to Forth [sic] William and Port Arthur, two to $2.50 for a man travelling to Toronto, as far as that and $2.50 to Quebec. . . . and then a schedule as high as $4.00 to persons going to Nova Scotia, depending on train connections and Branch Lines and necessary delays.[14]

Colonel Wood was deeply suspicious of the Trekkers returning to Vancouver who, he felt sure, were going there to join the waterfront strike. Wood had heard that men who had joined the Trek on the prairies were being recruited by the British Columbia camp men to identify themselves as having come from the coast so that they could go to join the demonstrations there.[15]

There are two legends about Molloy's registration procedure. One is that many men, noticing that the clerks seldom looked up from their work, simply went through the lines several times and secured several tickets. Of course, the one problem with this story is that the tickets were all issued from Regina. Unless a man came back again and again to Regina and started out again and again, the tickets wouldn't be of much use. The meal subsidies would have been, however. The other legend is that Trekkers formed a shadow division, the Fifth Division, and somehow managed to con tickets and funds from Molloy. In fact, there really was a Fifth Division, established in Regina when the Dundurn men arrived.

Brigadier Boak relayed a count to Ottawa that may be taken as definitive: 857 men had chosen British Columbia, 172 Alberta, 151 Saskatchewan, 54 Manitoba, 71 Ontario, 38 Quebec, 8 New Brunswick, 6 Nova Scotia, 1 Prince Edward Island, 1,358 passengers in all.[16] Those going on the special trains to the west took with them, at provincial expense (and later, federal expense):

2,400 loaves of bread
2,400 cans of fruit
6 cases of milk
100 pounds of coffee
2 rolls of snuff
3,000 cans of sardines
200 pounds of cheese
10 pounds of tea
1,500 packs of tobacco[17]

Mid-morning on Friday, 5 July, the Trekkers bound for the west trooped to the rail yards where they had detrained three weeks before. One of them carried an effigy of Prime Minister Bennett which was promptly hung from a window. Other cars bore huge Red Cross banners, put there by the government. As the food stores were being loaded, it was discovered that there were no butcher knives nor can openers so messengers were dispatched for these items.[18]

Colonel Wood had not wanted the Trekkers to keep their divisional organization for this trip, but there is no evidence that his wishes were followed. Presumably Macaulay, Walsh (who had not been arrested) and other senior members of the Strike Committee rode together. A number of railway police also made the trip.

So the men came to the trains, singing 'Hold the Fort,' and chanting "Are we downhearted? No!" Hundreds of citizens stood by cheering. James Litterick, an unemployed leader just in from Winnipeg, spoke to the Trekkers, telling them to "Go back as emissaries."[19]

Attorney General Davis waited nearby, chatting with Fred Griffin of the *Leader-Post*:

Davis: "You can't beat them as a bunch of boys. I wouldn't want to meet better."

Griffin: "Are they hoodlums and foreigners, as has been alleged?"

Davis: "I have not spoken to more than four or five. I should say that five per cent foreign-born would be the height of it. The majority are clean-cut Canadian boys, predominantly of Anglo-Saxon stock. There are quite a few Irish."[20]

Just about the time the trains pulled out, a funeral cortège carrying the body of Detective Millar made its way to First Presbyterian Church. In attendance was Millar's eight-year-old daughter, who was now an orphan and who was given over into the care of Elizabeth Cruickshank of Regina. That gracious woman had been a busy member of the Citizens' Emergency Committee. Gerry Winters, who had been on the speakers' stand that riot day, but had not been arrested, also came to the funeral. A sympathetic and perceptive Fred Griffin saw between those two processions, the trains west and the funeral, "a link that can never be broken."[21]

No account or record survives that brings that trip to British Columbia into focus. One can assume that the men ate well, sardines and canned fruit, topped off with a smoke, that they slept, that they sauntered up and down the aisles, chatting, reminiscing. One can assume that McCaulay and Walsh were hard at work figuring out what to do next. As the trains passed through Kamloops, Saskatoon, Calgary and Edmonton, the men about to depart shook hands for one last time, stuffed food into packs, and then went off with cheers and back onto the streets or into camps or right across the tracks to pick up a freight.

Well aware of what had happened in Regina on Dominion Day and then also aware that Premier Gardiner had sent the Trekkers back to Vancouver, Chief Constable Foster met with Mayor McGeer and then with a trio of officers to prepare for their return. In that trio was Major General Victor Odlum, a member of the Citizens' Committee who agreed to create a force of 750 men "immediately the funds are made available to him." Presumably these would have been vigilantes. Present also was Lieutenant Colonel Cadiz of the RCMP who offered his endorsement in requesting reinforcements for his units. Finally there was Lieutenant Colonel McMullin of the British Columbia Provincial Police whose men would replace city constables at the piers.

In his letter to McGeer, Colonel Foster indicated that

> I am informed that Ottawa is not cooperating to any great extent in the matter of providing a concentration camp but that it is the intention of the Attorney General to have all men detrain at Kamloops and be looked after there, pending their dispersal to points from which they came.[22]

Mayor McGeer wired Mr. Bennett, arguing against the delivery of the men to his city. "Respectfully request that you cooperate with provincial government in providing for distribution of these men to relief camps before they arrive in Vancouver."[23]

No doubt, Colonel Foster and Mayor McGeer shared Colonel Wood's belief that the Trekkers, once in Vancouver, would seek to join the waterfront strike which had been underway since 4 June. At the heart of that strike was the disagreement between the Shipping Federation and the Vancouver and District Waterfront Workers' Association as to which organization had jurisdiction over the dispatch or assignment of longshoremen to jobs. The 1934 contract had given this authority to the federation, but the union had come to believe that this inevitably led to discrimination. The weeks of April and May had passed with the added tension created by the possibility of a general strike and by the likely alliance between the waterfront workers and the relief camp strikers. But the waterfront strike did not begin until the Trek had left the city. On 4 June, VDWWA stevedores refused to unload a ship from Powell River and so the federation announced that it was breaking the contract and signing a new agreement with the Canadian

Waterfront Workers' Association. On 18 June, a parade of one thousand VDWWA loyalists marched to the docks, ostensibly to make an appeal to those whom the federation had employed in their place. A police force met them, a riot ensued, sixty were injured and twenty arrested. With this violence, the strike essentially collapsed although the VDWWA stayed out for another five months. By the time the Trekkers returned, port traffic was back to normal.[24]

To the very end, Colonel Foster was under the impression that the men would detrain in Kamloops. Blankets and other supplies were being sent to that city; arrangements to register the men were under way; an agreement had been reached whereby all the men except known agitators would be accepted back into the camps. But the Chief Constable had also learned that men on board the trains were seeking to persuade their comrades not to leave at Kamloops but to go on to Vancouver "in order to promote difficulties there."[25]

On 6 July, Mayor McGeer received a telegram from Prime Minister Bennett who stated that the Trekkers were now simply legitimate passengers on the trains, not trespassers. "Under what lawful authority do you suggest we may interfere with their journey? If you know of any I would be glad to be advised."[26]

At 12:35 A.M. on 7 July, Brigadier D.J. MacDonald of Military District 11 called the Chief of the General Staff to inform him that both trains had just passed through Kamloops and that strikers' pickets had prevented men from dismounting.[27]

Somewhere along this last lap, one of Foster's "operators" joined the trains; by 8 July, his report was in the hands of his superior who reported to Mayor McGeer that this man's experience "corroborates the other reports of a very truculent attitude amongst the men...they stated that they had their new leaders and were going to cause all the trouble they could in Vancouver. They were going to join the striking longshoremen and do picket duty with them." Moreover, they were not going back to the relief camps.[28]

But in a letter to the Mayor on that same day, Foster made it clear that he believed that many of the men did not identify with the position that they should reinforce the waterfront strike, "a great many feeling that they had demonstrated their position pretty successfully, and that to stay here is simply to get into trouble."[29]

The trains rolled into Vancouver shortly after dawn on 7 July; Colonel Foster saw to it that the men were removed immediately in order to avoid entanglement with a rally in their behalf set for 10:00 A.M. A few men produced banners and attempted to start a parade but the police would have none of this and so they all, 787 by count, trooped to an RCWU office on Hastings Street where they left their baggage. Then, Foster's agent notwithstanding, 751 of these registered for relief and signed an agreement to check in to the Employment Service for return to the camps.[30]

With the arrival of the men, Colonel Foster called them "deserters," RCMP Constables Kusch and Graham returned to work. On 8 July, one of them attended a meeting at the Empress Theatre on Hastings Street where "considerable dissension arose" after the Strike Committee urged the men to stay in Vancouver and carry on the fight. But a vote by show of hands turned this idea down in favour of registration for the camps. Smokey Cumber spoke to this last decision: "He urged that they consider their own position and struggle above all else." Return to the camps, Cumber recommended, and resume the union's work there.[31]

After all the anxiety and dread about the possible reinforcement these camp men might give the waterfront strikers, they had "ordered" themselves out of the city. Granted, one motive was simply to secure a fresh suit of clothes. But there was another, so alleged one of Foster's men who was at the Empress Theatre gathering:

> a great majority applauded the statement of one of their number...when he said it was no use getting killed in Vancouver for a bunch of longshoremen.[32]

By 10 July, three hundred had left the city, most for the camps, the remainder for the prairies. More would follow in the next two days.

On the night of the tenth, a rally at the Arena attended by some one thousand strikers and citizens listened to a group of speakers led by Malcolm Bruce, Red Walsh and Mike McCaulay, who described the Trek, recalled with considerable passion the specifics of the riot and the death of Detective Millar who, they claimed, had been struck down by the RCMP who thought he was Arthur Evans, and generally called for further vigilance and the continuation of the RCWU. Colonel Foster's men were there, busily taking notes, actually recording the entire proceedings on phonograph discs. Both Foster's men and the RCMP agent mentioned the lacklustre response from the audience. Though a donation was taken up, it was not enough to pay for the rental of the hall.[33]

To all intents and purposes, the strike was over. But there was still work to be done. Among those who returned to the camps were loyal Trekkers who resumed their harassment of rules and regulations. A few, like Frank Bobby, sought to help the longshoremen; Bobby was promptly arrested and sent to jail for a few weeks.[34] Others went to work in behalf of the Trekkers' reputation, since the trials in Regina were still to take place and therefore the defendants were in need of support and justice. Many of the men, it might be assumed, fled into anonymity, content to subsist in the camps quietly or else to return to the tedious job of looking for a job. Whatever they chose to do, perhaps they took some brief comfort in the prospect that a second Trek was being studied by their friends in Winnipeg.

The leaders of the Trek knew all along that there was an effort under way in Winnipeg to put together a new expedition bound for Ottawa should the On-To-Ottawa Trek, in its original incarnation, be stopped. Throughout the month of June, unemployed men and relief camp workers descended on Winnipeg to wait for the Trek to pass their way. Just how many men might have climbed on board will never be known, but it is likely that as many as two thousand would have been mustered. On 20 June, the *Winnipeg Tribune* described the registration there of 550 men into a regional relief camp workers' union. Tom McCarthy was said to be a leader; the Vancouver example of organization by divisions was in place.[35] Evans's associate in Winnipeg, Jim Litterick, wired on 27 June the prospect of a truck convoy being put together that would race to Regina and bring the boys east across the provincial line.[36] A reinforcement of sixty RCMP was said to have been dispatched to that city.[37] All in all, the prospects for an expanded Trek seemed likely, as did the prospect for the confrontation with the authorities who probably did not want a repetition of the 1919 General Strike.

But the Trek did not arrive, would never arrive. As soon as it was evident that the 27 June truck convoy led by the Reverend Mr. East had not succeeded, Evans wired Winnipeg urging that a march east out of the city be organized if only to take pressure off of his own predicament.[38] Colonel Wood learned on 29 June that a significant movement of camp men from Manitoba and western Ontario was about to enter Winnipeg, presumably to mount trains for the journey to Ottawa. The RCMP wanted to know on what grounds these men could be arrested and if arrested, where might they be lodged?[39]

The answer came the next day when six hundred men all bearing packs tried to board the eastbound freight out of Winnipeg. Police immediately halted the train and managed to draw the crowd into a column and march them off to the Exhibition Grounds. The Manitoba government hastily agreed to provide these strikers with tent camps and two meals a day. Despite the fact that a workers' dining hall was occupied for a few hours on 2 July, the situation in Winnipeg eased for a time.[40]

Whatever the reasons, poor planning, inept leadership, fatigue, subsequent attempts by Winnipeggers to march east failed utterly: on 10 July an advance party of eight made it as far as Kenora where they became stranded. On 16 July, a party of some four hundred set out on foot but soon enough they too turned back. But after all, in the end, a Trek of sorts did make it to Ottawa.

On 17 July, over three hundred men and women, led by Ewart Humphries, secretary of the National Unemployed Council, set out from Toronto, also on foot. They spent the first night camped on the grounds of Scarborough Collegiate and the second night in Pickering. Then on again for twenty-two days until they arrived in Ottawa. There, they threw up tents, lean-tos and wig-wams in Plouffe Park where they were visited by several thousand friends and the curious.[41] On 10 August, Prime Minister Bennett gave their delegation a fifteen-minute audience during which he said, ''You want to embarrass the government.''[42] On 12 August, a summer storm blew the tent camp away. Somehow, the party stayed together despite this symbolic sign, for on 22 August, it set out for Toronto, on foot. Several miles south of Ottawa, at Kemptville, the expedition finally fell apart and its survivors scurried off to phone friends, to entreat for train and bus fare, to go home.[43]

Epilogue
"They might yet be won by humanity."
— *Fred Griffin, Regina* Leader-Post

Once the On-To-Ottawa Trek left Vancouver on 3 June, Canada woke up to the prospect of a great story about to unfold, truly a national story. The range of judgements about the efficacy of the march was as broad as the country itself. No doubt, many citizens worried and wondered, as did Irven Schwartz's friend, "Is this the revolution!" *The Montreal Gazette* recommended to its readers that "the government should make a determined stand and now!"[1] *The Ottawa Morning Citizen,* on the other hand, said of the Trekkers that "the fact cannot be explained away that they are an active and significant manifestation of the economic palsy that has this nation in its grip."[2] *The Citizen's* competitor, *The Ottawa Morning Journal,* did think that the government should talk with the marchers, try to develop some solution, but in any case, "the men should be halted for discussion in the west, where they belong."[3] By the time the Trek had reached Regina, the *Hamilton Spectator* was ready to assert that "articulate protest against the breakdown of human intelligence" was what the expedition was all about... "a protest against our corporate inefficiency...."[4]

The press was interested, as well, in the views of its leaders. The *Leader-Post* quoted Mayor Cornelius Rink of Regina: "They had better keep away from here if they figure the city is going to feed them and look after them while they are here."[5] That same newspaper heard from a Winnipeg astrologer who opined, "This uprising of the people is coming in due time and the planets will help them succeed."[6] *The Ottawa Evening Journal* reported that Mayor P.J. Nolan had received offers from his constituents to form a citizens' guard.[7]

Prime Minister Bennett heard from voters in Belbutte, Saskatchewan; Cochrane, Ontario; Taber, Alberta; London, Ontario; Montréal, Québec, who really thought the boys had a point. But he also heard from a man in Saskatoon, Saskatchewan:

> I am 64 years old and if you will give the word and stand them up against some stone wall in Regina or here or elsewhere, I will be glad to be one of the fellows that will stand in the firing line and let them have it. There is nothing would please me more.[8]

The meanest cut came from the Toronto *Telegram.* The Reverend Sam East and Matt Shaw had gone to Toronto to raise money for the arrested Trekkers. At a rally in Maple Leaf Gardens attended by delegates from the CCF, the CPC, the League Against War and Fascism, the CLDL and the League for Social Reconstruction, on the platform with socialist Graham Spry and communist Sam Carr, the Reverend Mr. East let it be known that "if the blues and pinks and yellows wouldn't lead the strikers, who else was there but the reds to lead them?"[9]

The *Telegram* sniffed and then dismissed the Reverend Mr. East because of the "obscurity of his pulpit."[10]

There might not have been a wide-spread fear of revolution in Canada that summer, but doubtless many citizens wondered whether the great concept of peace, order and good government had not really been placed in jeopardy by this march of men. Was this, might this have been, *the* revolution?

However angry Evans might have been in his pursuit of justice for the working class, he did not take the Trek east with the hidden assumption that their appearance in Ottawa would spring loose the revolution that was thought to be on the agenda of the Communist International. If the caution expressed by *The Worker* as the strikers left Vancouver can be taken as an expression of the CPC leadership, "the fight of the B.C. workers is in Vancouver," then the Trek was not really sanctioned at that level though it was not utterly disavowed. Of course, Tim Buck might have preferred that the relief camp men stay on the west coast and help the longshoremen.

And while there were a number of so-called revolutionaries in the ranks of the Trek, the great majority of the men were not members of the Communist Party of Canada even if they had joined the RCWU, a distinction that probably meant little to the Bennett government. There is little doubt that the Trekkers loathed the system that had relegated them to the camps, but that white passion, that deadly concentration of will and intellect, was simply not in evidence. And more: Evans was not even supposed to take the men over the mountains at the outset; Evans would never have taken his seven associates to Ottawa and left the Trek waiting in Regina had he planned revolution; Evans, with the failure of the truck convoy out of Regina, in effect, gave up the march and began serious negotiations with Premier Gardiner for the dispersal of his followers.

Finally, the Communist Party was neither strong enough in numbers nor its leaders anxious to create a conspiracy across Canada that would have unleashed all sorts of revolutionary cadres should the Trek have reached Ottawa. Evans may have had fun yelling "Moscow Gold, Moscow Gold," but Moscow had no more interest in a revolution in Canada than it would have in Spain, two years later.

On 10 July, five days after the Trekkers had cleared the Queen City, the Lieutenant-Governor of Saskatchewan authorized the creation of the Regina Riot Inquiry Commission and charged it with establishing the origins, the character and the responsibility for the riot. The Commissioners were Saskatchewan Chief Justice James T. Brown, Court of Appeals Judge William Martin and District Court Judge A.E. Doak. But Ottawa immediately objected that its consent or approval had not been secured. Arguments flew back and forth by telegraph and while the Commissioners felt sure that their authorization was clear and legal, they announced that they would defer opening the inquiry until after the general election. Not until 12 November did the proceedings get under way with G.H. Yule and L. Tourigny appointed as counsel for the Commission, F.J.G. Cunningham as counsel for the strikers and B.D. Hogarth and E.C. Leslie as counsel for the Dominion government. Among the 359 witnesses called were James Gardiner, Archie Apps, S.T. Wood, Cornelius Rink, Arthur Evans, John McCarthy and numerous RCMP officers, including the two men who had joined the Trek late in its career, several city constables, various strikers, members of the CEC, and eyewitnesses to the riot, including Steve Fustas who thought he had lost his daughter in the melee. When the Commission closed on 10 February 1936, 7,860 pages of testimony, reports, factotum and 309 exhibits had been entered into 53 volumes. The report of the Commissioners was published two months later and concluded that the riot was the responsibility of the Trekkers. In particular, it castigated Evans while reserving compassion for the many young men whom he had led. The police were absolved of any wrong-doing.

But Chief Constable Bruton harboured some doubts. In a memorandum composed during or just after the proceedings, he appraised his own decision to work with the RCMP in bringing about the arrests of the Trek leaders on 1 July. Informed at 6:45 that evening that Wood had warrants in hand and that the city police were requested to take part in their serving,

> it would have been impossible to refuse to assist them when they called on us. I was well aware of the seriousness of making the arrests on Market Square and expressed disapproval but after protesting and pointing out the seriousness, I could go no further. . . . I knew very well that one could not please everybody. . . . I could only do what I considered right, that is, cooperate. The city police were very much misled by the RCMP in the arrangements for the arrests.[11]

The anonymous author of a monograph called *The History of the Regina Police Force: 1892-1945* concluded his brief account of the riot with these cryptic remarks:

> The trek to Ottawa was over and also ended a constitutional question with Assistant Commissioner Wood taking his orders from the Attorney General [of Saskatchewan]. It was this reluctance to share information and collaborate which may have led to the error in instructions and hurried preparations for the arrest of the trek leaders by the RCMP on Market Square. Questions were later posed. Why had Assistant Commissioner Wood decided to arrest the leaders at a public rally? Had Ottawa and Wood prepared for a "showdown"? Regina policemen thought so. They had lost a colleague.[12]

The "error in instructions" seems to have been this: the RCMP thought they and the city police were to wait until Mortimer's whistle was heard and then to wait again until summoned onto the Square. "If the plainsclothesmen were interfered with, in any way, they were to render such assistance that they deemed was necessary in making a safe passage for the prisoner and the plainclothesmen to the van on Halifax Street."[13] McDougall, who took the city police column out of the garage, understood that he was to move *when* the whistle blew.[14]

From all the evidence, it would appear that the shock of McDougall's column following upon the surprise of Mortimer's whistle, drove the crowd into its panic. By the time the Trekkers and their friends had run back on the Square with their bricks and stones, the RCMP were already moving in. The whistle was sufficient to startle, the flurry of leaping and grabbing at the truck, sufficient to cause spectators in that immediate area to turn and bolt. And then McDougall's column.

"The surprise of Mortimer's whistle." Surely this is a factor for none of the citizens in the crowd, and they were in the vast majority, could have known about the impending arrests. As far as they were concerned, this was one more rally. That was John Toothill on the stand, a familiar face, a Reginan, after all. It was a holiday, Dominion Day. Who in his right mind would send police into a rally to make arrests on Dominion Day?

On the other hand, there is Constable Archie Apps's testimony about the Trekkers calling out to friends: "Come on with us and get some rocks and go to Market Square. There is going to be trouble tonight!" What trouble? Did those two men know something was going to happen that Evans, Black and Tellier either didn't know as they mounted the truck in the Square or else knew, and took the risk of arrest anyway? Bruton had sent a detail to Unity Centre at 7:00 P.M., but none of the men for whom the warrants had been issued could be found on those premises. Were the Trekkers alerted by this search? If they were, did they deliberately keep this quiet in order to go ahead with the rally and then see what the police might decide to do?

Could the Trekkers have known about the arrests from some other source? Bruton maintains that he did not learn of the RCMP plans until 6:45 P.M. And Wood only found out about the warrants at 5:00 P.M. Did some law enforcement officer pass the word to a Trekker? Or was there some citizen witness to police preparations who might have leaked the news? The Reverend J.F. Stewart, it will be remembered, wandered into the Police Station as the rally was about to begin, saw McDougall's men lining up, was told by a constable, "We are very busy" and so left. But the Reverend Mr. Stewart does not speak of any suspicion that an arrest was about to be made. Was there a Trekker or friendly Reginan loitering near the Police Station who saw McDougall's men, had a hunch and went off to warn the Trekkers?

The point of these last questions is that the police later argued that when the riot began and Trekkers and citizens ran off and then back on the Square, that they returned with armloads of rocks and stones and bricks which they had previously hidden behind the buildings adjacent. (Legend has it that a local boy was seen pedalling his bicycle back and forth, the bike basket filled with rocks which he dumped at the feet of the angry Trekkers.)

When had those stones been hidden? Why were they hidden? Were they put there in anticipation of this particular uproar? Were they squirreled away days before, just in case? The Regina Riot Inquiry Commission concluded: "The speed and spontaneity of the attack is evidence of some preparation."

Several Reginans later testified to having seen rioters taking bricks and other débris away from sites in the centre of the city: from behind a billboard at the corner of Smith Street and Eleventh Avenue; from behind a shop in the 1800 block of Lorne Street, near the New Wonder Cafe, a spot frequented by Trekkers over the past two weeks; from behind the King's Hotel on Scarth Street, north of Eleventh Avenue. Florence Dean, who had so valiantly defended her home, claimed she saw children bringing bricks and stones to men hidden in an alley in the rear.[15]

Given the tension of the previous two or three days, the failure of the truck convoy, the speculation that some sort of move might be made by the police, it would not be unthinkable for men to nose around the area for just such missiles.

Once the Trekkers had cleared out of the Exhibition Grounds, police and maintenance crews found dozens of home-made clubs left behind. These seem to have been prepared after the truck convoy incident in case efforts were made by police to roust the men from their quarters.

The Regina Riot Inquiry Commission concluded that the Trekkers on the Square that night were from Division Three, allegedly populated by men from the original Vancouver blacklist who were prone to be vicious.[16] However, there is no real evidence that such was the case. Evans might have made sure a group of his men was on the Square, but he was also determined to wait for Premier Gardiner to meet with his cabinet and prepare their response to Evans's request that his men disperse under their own organization. It stands to reason that he was not about to initiate a struggle.

Scarcely had Regina picked itself up from the Riot, scarcely had the Trekkers left the city, than a series of stories began to circulate that eventually formed a mythology. This mythology told of the clean well-favoured youths who had made the march, of their good humour and steadfast discipline. The police were always brutes, as John Matts's cartoons had proposed once upon a time. This mythology, needless to say, grew out of the Trekkers' resentment:

- An RCMP constable in Regina, recognizing his son among the marchers, is supposed to have resigned from the Force then and there rather than fight with the boy in the streets.
- A number of city police are supposed to have stripped off their tunics rather than advance on the Trekkers.
- The RCMP who came out of the vans were drunk.
- The RCMP killed Millar, mistaking him for Evans.

The first story is beyond verification since no name has ever been supplied.

No constable is known to have taken off his uniform, and if even one had, then his colleagues' indignation over the RCMP orders would have been greatly diluted. Their chagrin and despair over the whole situation are summed up in those sad words: "They had lost a colleague."

As for the charge of drunkenness, Wood later said that his men had been at the RCMP training depot all day and that, moreover, there had not been a wet canteen there in twenty-three years.[17] Surely, no commander is about to let his men go into this sort of action, or any sort, for that matter, in a state of inebriation for all the world to see.

Finally, there are many witnesses to the attack on Millar by men dressed in civilian clothes. None puts a uniformed RCMP constable at the scene. Other than Mortimer's men who were already off the

Square, there is no evidence of any plainclothes RCMP assigned to the arrests.

There is another element to this mythology that is not likely to be verified though it is not likely to be completely disproved: Trekkers were killed in Regina that night and their bodies buried secretly, one version has it, beneath a flower bed at the RCMP barracks. For instance, there was "the boy from Victoria" who went on the Trek and whose family never heard from him again. But many men disappeared that night, fleeing the city in order to avoid arrest. The Trekkers who were arrested and who later testified to the Commission do not speak of friends being beaten to death in their cells which is where any deaths would likely have occurred. The local hospitals do not record the deaths from injuries of any Trekkers. The *Leader-Post* of 19 October 1935 did report the death of Nicholas Schaack who had taken a beating on 1 July, who had been released from hospital in August, who came back weeks later suffering from a "nervous condition" and who died of pneumonia resulting from a coronary problem. Schaack was thought to be in his early fifties.[18]

Some fifty men were brought up on charges stemming from the clash on Dominion Day. Evans, Shaw, Cosgrove, Ivan Bell and Ernest Edwards were all said to have membership in an illegal organization, the Relief Camp Workers' Union. The rest, it was claimed

> *Did with diverse other persons unlawfully, riotously and in a manner causing measurable fear of a tumultuous disturbance of the peace, assemble together and being so assembled together, did then and there make a great noise and thereby began and continued for meantime to disturb the peace simultaneously.*

The Citizens' Emergency Committee disbanded and a number of its members turned to create the Citizens' Defence Committee and then launched a considerable campaign to draw public attention and opinion to the cause of the men lodged in the Regina jail. Released on his own recognizance, Arthur Evans led the attack on the police for their part in the riot. And when the Regina Riot Inquiry Commission began to hold its hearings, Evans turned on it as well, alleging a biased investigation. The Commission took note, in its Report, that Evans "is constantly 'demanding' and never 'petitioning'. He is constantly declaiming against those in authority and never saying anything praiseworthy about them."[19]

The original group of defendants was gradually whittled down with some having their charges withdrawn, with those arrested under Section 98 being discharged *nolle prosque* early in 1936. Twenty-two men finally came to trial in April 1936, a year after the exodus from the camps. Of these, nine were soon released, five were acquitted and eight were sentenced to terms in jail.

The search for Millar's killers had gone ahead, meanwhile. Chief Constable Bruton issued a wanted poster which described three men of very ordinary appearance as possible suspects. Over the next eighteen months, his office received the occasional response from colleagues around the country who had brought in men matching the descriptions. In one instance, a man actually confessed to the crime but it was soon determined that this poor soul had not been in Regina that night. No one has ever been charged with the assault.

By the time of the trial, of course, a new Liberal government was in office in Ottawa with 171 seats. R.B. Bennett, whose party won only thirty-nine seats, had had "a presentiment that he was facing defeat."[20] He blamed his loss on H.H. Stevens's Reconstruction Party which had broken ranks with the Tories. But the measure of the Liberals' majority suggests that Canadians had ceased to have any faith in Bennett. The former Prime Minister remained leader of his party until January 1939, when he resigned his seat and set sail for a new home in England. He died, Viscount Bennett of Calgary, on 26 June 1947.

In those last years as a parliamentarian, Bennett, it might be supposed, looked across the floor with some distaste at the features of James Gardiner and Gerry McGeer who had won seats in the 1935 election. He would have learned of the Riggs Commission created by the new government and charged with the appraisal of the relief camp scheme. While essentially supportive of that programme, the Commission nonetheless must have known that it was in doubt for it recommended that the camps be kept open only on a temporary basis.[21] And, indeed, on 30 June 1936, all works projects then active were shut down.

A new crisis arrived that summer, one that would absorb the attention and the participation of a number of Trekkers: the Spanish Civil War. Arthur Evans became a principal spokesman in British Columbia for aid to the Republican cause. Although many of his younger compatriots set out to join the International Brigade, Evans stayed behind, no doubt because of his age, his family and his lame leg. In the summer of 1938, he was appointed an organizer for the International Union of Mine, Mill and Smelter Workers with the mission of bringing employees of the Consolidated Mining and Smelting Company of Trail, British Columbia, into the union's embrace. A year later, Evans resigned from that job after having served a week in jail for drunkenness. This unfortunate episode, suggest his biographers, "was undoubtedly a factor in the decision.'' Evans next took his family to Lillooet, British Columbia, were he went to work panning for gold in the Fraser River. When World War II broke out, Evans returned to Vancouver and to his old vocation as a carpenter. Thereafter, he worked in the shipyards and was on the verge of re-entering union work when he was struck and killed by a car in the streets of Vancouver in 1944.[22]

If Evans could not go to Spain, hundreds of his friends did, thirteen hundred in all. Ronald Liversedge went to Spain. So did Red Walsh, Tony Martin, Louis Tellier. Stewart "Paddy" O'Neil went to Spain and died in 1937 assaulting a town near Madrid. Charles Sands went to Spain, Evans's captain of the railyard pickets, Walsh's estimable sergeant at arms. Sands fell in the fighting for a town named Belchite. Survivors of the Mackenzie-Papineau Battalion of the Fifteenth International Brigade think that as many as four hundred Trekkers served in Spain. They fulfilled the promise which *Leader-Post* reporter, Fred Griffin, saw in them as they left Regina on 5 July:

> *They have a gospel which they will now spread no matter where*
> *they will go, where they are scattered.*[23]

That gospel has lived on, after Spain, World War II, across the past fifty years. The men who went on the Trek are old men now, those who are alive. It may be supposed that this one adventure still looms large and clear in their memories. It was, after all, something of an epic march, great forces and ideas and ambitions clashing on and off stage, that stage itself, magnificent natural terrain.

And one last word from Joe McKeown, who had come into Regina with the Trek and who stayed on to live there. Mr. McKeown, small and energetic, burst into my hotel room at the first meeting in 1967, introduced himself and said, his arms sweeping back and around, east and west, "We were the salt of the earth!"

Glossary

CCF	Co-operative Commonwealth Federation
CEC	Citizens' Emergency Committee
CLDL	Canadian Labour Defence League
CNR	Canadian National Railway
CPC	Communist Party of Canada
CPR	Canadian Pacific Railway
DND	Department of National Defence
IWW	Industrial Workers of the World
OBU	One Big Union
RCMP	Royal Canadian Mounted Police
RCPD	Regina City Police Department
RCWU	Relief Camp Workers' Union
TLC	Trades and Labour Council
VCPD	Vancouver City Police Department
VDWWA	Vancouver and District Waterfront Workers' Association
WESL	Worker's Ex-Servicemen's League
WUL	Workers' Unity League
YCL	Young Communist League

Bibliography

Archival Material
Public Archives of Canada
  Department of Labour
  A.G.L. McNaughton Papers
  R.J. Manion Papers
  William Lyon Mackenzie King Papers
  Co-operative Commonwealth Federation Papers

City Archives, Vancouver
  Office of the Mayor
  Police Commissioners Board

University of British Columbia Archives

Saskatchewan Archives Board
  Report, Record and Exhibits of the Regina Riot Inquiry Commission

British Columbia Archives

Public Library of Toronto
Public Library of Regina

Books

Abella, Irving, ed. **On Strike: Six Key Labour Struggles in Canada: 1919-1949.** Toronto: James Lewis and Samuel, 1974.
Angus, Ian. **Canadian Bolsheviks: An Early History of the Communist Party of Canada.** Montreal: Vanguard, 1981.
Avakumovic, Ivan. **The Communist Party in Canada: A History.** Toronto: McClelland and Stewart, 1975.
Avery, Donald. **"Dangerous Foreigners": European Immigrant Workers and Labour Radicalism in Canada, 1896-1932.** Toronto: McClelland and Stewart, 1979.
Beaverbrook, Max Aitken, Baron. **Friends.** London: Heinemann, 1959.
Bercuson, David Jay. **Fools and Wisemen: The Rise and Fall of the One Big Union.** Toronto: McGraw-Hill Ryerson Ltd., 1978.
Canadian Annual Review, 1930-35.
Drake, Earl. **Regina: The Queen City.** Toronto: McClelland and Stewart, 1955.
Eayrs, James. **In Defence of Canada: From the Great War to the Great Depression.** Toronto: University of Toronto Press, 1964.
Grayson, L.M., and Michael Bliss, eds. **The Wretched of Canada: Letters to R.B. Bennett, 1930-1935.** Toronto: University of Toronto Press, 1971.

The History of the Regina City Police Force: 1892-1945. N.p., n.d.

Horn, Michiel, ed. **The Dirty Thirties: Canadians in the Great Depression.** Toronto: Copp Clark, 1972.

Larrowe, Charles. **Harry Bridges: the Rise and Fall of Radical Labor in the United States.** New York: Lawrence Hill and Co., 1972.

Leacy, F.H., ed. **Historical Statistics of Canada.** 2nd ed. Ottawa: Statistics Canada, 1983.

Lipton, Charles. **The Trade Union Movement of Canada: 1827-1959.** Toronto: NC Press, 1973.

Liversedge, Ronald. **Recollections of the On to Ottawa Trek.** Toronto: McClelland and Stewart, 1973.

Logan, H.A. **Trade Unions in Canada, Their Development and Functioning.** Toronto: Macmillan of Canada, 1948.

McEwan, Tom. **The Forge Glows Red.** Toronto: Progress Books, 1974.

Neatby, H. Blair. **The Politics of Chaos: Canada in the Thirties.** Toronto: Macmillan of Canada, 1972.

Osborne, Kenneth W. **Hardworking, Temperate and Peaceable: The Portrayal of Workers in Canadian History Textbooks.** Winnipeg: University of Manitoba, 1980.

Safarian, A.E. **The Canadian Economy in the Great Depression.** Toronto: McClelland and Stewart, 1970.

Schultz, H.J. et al. **Politics of Discontent.** Toronto: University of Toronto Press, 1967.

Struthers, James. **No Fault of Their Own: Unemployment and the Canadian Welfare State, 1914-1941.** Toronto: University of Toronto Press, 1983.

Swankey, Ben, and Jean Evans Sheils. **Work and Wages: A Semi-Documentary Account of the Life and Times of Arthur H. (Slim) Evans 1890-1944.** Vancouver: Trade Union Research Bureau, 1977.

Watkins, Ernest. **R.B. Bennett: A Biography.** Toronto: Kingswood Press, 1963.

Wilbur, J.R.H., ed. **The Bennett New Deal: Fraud or Portent?** Toronto: Copp Clark, 1968.

Young, Walter. **The Anatomy of a Party: The National CCF, 1932-1961.** Toronto: University of Toronto Press, 1969.

Articles

Borsook, Ben. "The Workers Hold a Conference." **The Canadian Forum** (September 1932): 449-451.

"Experiences of a Depression Hobo." **Saskatchewan History** 22, no. 2 (Spring 1969): 60-65.

McCandless, R.C. "Vancouver's 'Red Menace' of 1935: The Waterfront Situation." **B.C. Studies** 22 (Summer 1974): 56-70.

Ormsby, Margaret. "T. Dufferin Pattullo and the Little New Deal." In **Politics of Discontent,** by H.J. Schulz et al. Toronto: University of Toronto Press, 1967.

Theses and Dissertations

Brown, Lorne, "The Bennett Government, Political Stability and the Politics of the Unemployment Relief Camps: 1930-1935." Ph.D. dissertation, Queens University, 1980.

LeFresne, G.M. "The Royal Twenty Centers: The Department of National Defence and Federal Unemployment Relief: 1932-1936. B.A. Thesis, Royal Military College, 1962.

Tanner, Thomas William. "Microcosms of Misfortune: Canada's Unemployed Relief Camps Administered by the Department of National Defence." Master's Thesis, University of Western Ontario, 1965.

Interviews

Black, Margaret Hogg. Interview by Victor Howard. May 1967, Vancouver, B.C.

Bobby, Frank. Interview by Victor Howard. May 1967, Vancouver, B.C.

Boor, Fred. Interview by Victor Howard. May 1967, Victoria, B.C..

Cross, James. Interview by Victor Howard. June 1967, Regina, Sask.

Cunningham, Terry. Interview by Victor Howard. May 1967, Victoria, B.C.

Cruickshank, Elizabeth. Interview by Victor Howard. June 1967, Regina, Sask.

Davis, William. Interview by Victor Howard. May 1967, Victoria, B.C.

Fraser, Fred. Interview by Victor Howard. June 1967, Regina, Sask.

Fraser, K.C. Interview by Victor Howard. June 1967, Regina, Sask.

Gray, James. Interview by Victor Howard. June 1967, Calgary, Alberta.

Halaburd, Frank. Interview by Victor Howard. June 1967, Regina, Sask.

Hilton, Perry. Interview by Victor Howard. May 1967, Vancouver, B.C.

Johnson, J.G. Interview by Victor Howard. May 1967. Vancouver, B.C.

Liddell, Kenneth. Interview by Victor Howard. June 1967, Calgary, Alberta.

Liversedge, Mildred. Interview by Victor Howard. May 1967, Lake Cowichan, B.C.

Liversedge, Ronald. Interview by Victor Howard. May 1967, Lake Cowichan, B.C.

Madsen, Nels. Interview by Victor Howard. May 1967, Vancouver, B.C.

McCauley, Mike. Interview by Ben Swankey. May 1983, Vancouver, B.C.

McKeown, Joseph. Interview by Victor Howard. June 1967, Regina, Sask.

Rush, Morris. Interview by Victor Howard. May 1967, Vancouver, B.C.

Savage, Robert. Interview by Victor Howard. May 1967, Vancouver, B.C.

Schwartz, Irven. Interview by Victor Howard. May 1967, Vancouver, B.C.

Swinnerton, Frank. Interview by Victor Howard. June 1967, Regina, Sask.

Tellier, Gerry. Interview by Victor Howard. May 1967, Vancouver, B.C.

Tellier, Louis. Interview by Victor Howard. May 1967, Victoria B.C.

Walsh, James. Interview by Victor Howard. May 1967, Vancouver, B.C.

Notes

Prologue

1 William Davis, interview by Victor Howard, May 1967, Victoria, British Columbia.
2 Public Archives of Canada (hereafter PAC). A.G.L. McNaughton Papers. MG30 E 133, Vol. 99, IV. **Final Report of the Unemployment Relief Scheme for the Care of Single, Homeless Men Administered by the Department of National Defence.** Hereafter, **Final Report.**
3 Thomas William Tanner, "Microcosms of Misfortune" (M.A. Thesis, University of Western Ontario, 1965), 10-12.
4 Holograph memoir of Cecil Fobert in author's possession.
5 "Experiences of a Depression Hobo," **Saskatchewan History** 22, no. 2 (Spring 1969): 60-65.
6 Ibid., 64.
7 William Davis, interview.
8 Ibid.
9 Ibid.
10 Morris Rush, interview by Victor Howard, May 1967, Vancouver, British Columbia.

Chapter One
The Camps and the Union

1 James Struthers, **No Fault of Their Own: Unemployment and the Canadian Welfare State 1914-1941** (Toronto: University of Toronto Press, 1983), 45ff.
2 Canada, Report of the Department of Labour for the Fiscal Year ending 31 March 1934 (Ottawa: King's Printer, 1934), 74-75.
3 Struthers, **No Fault of Their Own,** 71-74.
4 Tom McEwen interview in University of British Columbia Archives; see also: Ian Angus, **Canadian Bolsheviks: The Early Years of the Communist Party of Canada** (Montreal: Vanguard, 1981); Ivan Avakumovic, **The Communist Party in Canada** (Toronto: McClelland and Stewart, 1975).
5 Ben Barsook, "The Workers Hold a Conference," **The Canadian Forum** (September 1932): 449-51.
6 Baron Beaverbrook, **Friends** (London: Heinemann, 1959), 73-76.
7 **Final Report,** Vol. I, Pt. I: 1.
8 G.M. LeFresne, "The Royal Twenty Centers: The Department of Defence and Federal Unemployment Relief: 1932-1936." (B.A. thesis, Royal Military College, Kingston, Ontario, 1962), 15-30.

9 James Eayrs, **In Defence of Canada: From the Great War to the Great Depression** (Toronto: The University of Toronto Press, 1964), 126-27.

10 Ibid., 133-34.

11 **Final Report,** Vol. I, Pt. II: 17-23.

12 Ibid., Vol. I, Pt. I: 8.

13 Eayrs, **In Defence of Canada,** 134.

14 **Final Report,** Vol. 99, V. III: 1-80.

15 PAC. Correspondence and Reports of Colonel D.W.B. Spry, Vol. 1. RG 24, Vol. 3046 HQ 1376-11-13-83. Vancouver Office, Department of Labour, Unemployment Relief Branch.

16 **Final Report,** Vol. 99, V. II and III: 1-80.

17 **Final Report,** Vol. I, Pt. II: 24.

18 Ibid., 45.

19 Louis Tellier, interview by Victor Howard, May, 1967, Vancouver Island, British Columbia.

20 **Final Report,** Vol. I, Pt. II:24.

21 Ibid., Vol. 99, V. III: 50-80.

22 Premier Simon Fraser Tolmie's government created a system of camps that could house fifteen thousand men in the winter of 1931-2, but mismanagement, high costs and the refusal of the Dominion to assume responsibility forced a collapse.

23 Regina Riot Inquiry Commission (hereafter RRIC), Exhibit 294, "Constitution of Relief Camp Workers' Union, B.C. District."

24 Ronald Liversedge, **Recollections of the On to Ottawa Trek** (Toronto: McClelland and Stewart, 1973), 35-55.

25 Liversedge, **Recollections,** 47.

26 **Final Report,** Vol. 99, V. III: 50-57.

27 **Relief Camp Worker,** 31 October 1934.

28 RRIC, **Report.** 32-34; see also Exhibit 94, "Report of Camp Workers Delegation to Victoria."

29 PAC. R.B. Bennett Papers. MG 26K Vol. 800: 495558-495634.

30 D.W.B. Spry Correspondence and Reports.

31 RRIC, **Record,** Vol. 13: 87.

32 J.R.H. Wilbur, ed., **The Bennett New Deal: Fraud or Portent?** (Toronto: Copp Clark, 1968), 80-81.

33 **Relief Camp Worker,** 7 February 1935.

Chapter Two
The Walk-Out

1 RRIC, Arthur Evans Cross-Examination, 16.

2 RRIC, **Record,** Vol. 9: 114.

3 RRIC, Arthur Evans Cross-Examination, 46.

4 City Archives, Vancouver (hereafter CAV). Office of the City Clerk. Vol. 198. Relief File E-574.

[5] Ben Swankey and Jean E. Sheils, **Work and Wages: A Semi-Documentary Account of the Life and Times of Arthur H. (Slim) Evans, 1890-1944** (Vancouver: Trade Union Research Bureau), 75.

[6] William Davis, interview.

[7] CAV. Relief File E-574.

[8] RRIC, **Record,** Vol. 11: 4.

[9] James Walsh, interview by Victor Howard, May 1967, Vancouver, British Columbia. The details of the conference have been reconstructed from the Walsh, Davis, Tellier and Rush interviews; the 19 March 1935 issue of **Relief Camp Worker** and the testimony of Arthur Evans in RRIC, **Record,** Vol. 7, 66-69.

[10] CAV. 33-B-6. File 10. VCPD memo, 22 March 1935.

[11] PAC. **Outline of Events Relating to Anticipated Strikes, Disturbances, etc., on April 4, 1935.** MG 30 E 133 Vol. 61. M.D. 11 to Attorney General, 25 March 1935. (Hereafter, **Diary**).

[12] PAC. R.B. Bennett Papers. MG 26 K Vol. 801: 495677, Pattullo to Perley, 25 March 1935.

[13] Ibid., 495678, Perley to Pattullo, 26 March 1935.

[14] Ibid., 495679, Pattullo to Perley, 27 March 1935.

[15] Canada, House of Commons, **Debates,** 29 March 1935, 2253.

[16] RRIC, **Record,** Vol. 13: 25.

[17] Irven Schwartz, interview by Victor Howard, May 1967, Vancouver, British Columbia.

[18] Louis Tellier, interview.

[19] Nels Madsen, interview by Victor Howard, May 1967, Vancouver, British Columbia. See also Walsh and Schwartz interview.

[20] James Walsh, interview.

[21] **Relief Camp Worker,** 12 April 1935.

[22] RRIC, **Record,** Vol. 14: 132.

[23] Frank Bobby, interview by Victor Howard, May 1967, Vancouver, British Columbia.

[24] **Diary,** M.D. 11 to Attorney General, 30 March 1935.

[25] (Vancouver) **Sun,** 1 April 1935.

[26] (Vancouver) **Sun,** 4 April 1935.

[27] (Vancouver) **Sun,** 5 April 1935.

[28] (Vancouver) **Sun,** 1 April 1935.

[29] Ibid. See also Margaret Ormsby, "T. Dufferin Pattullo and the Little New Deal," in **Politics of Discontent** by H.J. Schultz et al. (Toronto: University of Toronto Press, 1967), 28-48.

[30] Louis Tellier, interview.

[31] (Vancouver) **Sun,** 5 April 1935.

[32] CAV. 33-B-6. File 10. VCPD memo, 9 April 1935.

[33] Perry Hilton, interview by Victor Howard, May 1967, Vancouver, British Columbia. The table of organization given here is based on interviews with Hilton, Walsh, Davis, Tellier and Schwartz and on testimony given by Evans and Shaw in RRIC.

[34] CAV. 33-B-6. File 10.

[35] William Davis, interview.
[36] These assignments are recalled in the Hilton, Walsh, Davis and Schwartz interviews along with interview with Robert Savage, May 1967, Vancouver, British Columbia.
[37] CAV. 33-B-6. File 10. VCPD memo, undated, but from internal evidence drafted between 23 April and 29 April 1935.
[38] RRIC, **Record,** Vol. 13: 71-179.
[39] (Vancouver) **Sun,** 9 April 1935.
[40] William Davis, interview.
[41] Mildred Liversedge, interview with Victor Howard, May 1967, Lake Cowichan, British Columbia; (Vancouver) **Sun,** 26 April 1935.
[42] (Vancouver) **Sun,** 10 March 1935.

Chapter Three
April in Vancouver

[1] PAC. RG 24, Vol. 3047, File: C-18-34-1-1B (Vol. 1). The first report available is dated 24 April 1935. Both Kusch and Graham later testified before RRIC, (hereafter, RCMP).
[2] CAV. 33-B-6. Files 7-10.
[3] Correspondence of William Gilbey, to author, 6 July 1984, Regina, Saskatchewan.
[4] (Vancouver) **Sun,** 9 April 1935.
[5] CAV. 33-B-6. File 10. VCPD memo, 9 April 1935.
[6] (Vancouver) **Sun,** 10 April 1935.
[7] RRIC, **Record,** Vol. 8: 12-20.
[8] CAV. 33-B-6. File 10. McGeer-Pattullo exchange, 10-13 April 1935.
[9] Ibid.
[10] RRIC, **Record,** Vol. I: 36.
[11] Liversedge, **Recollections,** 60.
[12] Ibid., 62; RRIC, **Record,** Vol. 7: 123.
[13] (Vancouver) **Sun,** 12 April 1935.
[14] (Vancouver) **Sun,** 15 April 1935.
[15] (Vancouver) **Sun,** 16 April 1935.
[16] RRIC, **Record,** Vol. 8: 41.
[17] (Vancouver) **Sun,** 11 April 1935.
[18] (Vancouver) **Sun,** 16 April 1935.
[19] **Daily Province,** 16 April 1935.
[20] (Vancouver) **Sun,** 16 April 1935.
[21] (Vancouver) **Sun,** 17 April 1935.
[22] (Vancouver) **Sun,** 18 April 1935.
[23] **Diary,** M.D. 11 to Attorney General, 9 April 1935.
[24] R.C. McCandless, ''Vancouver's 'Red Menace' of 1935: The Waterfront Situation,'' **B.C. Studies** 22 (Summer 1974): 56-70.
[25] RRIC, **Record,** Vol. 7: 144.
[26] CAV. 33-B-6. File 10. VCPD memo, 21 April 1935.

[27] **Diary,** C.G.S. to M.D. 11, 14 April 1935. There were four telegrams exchanged between McNaughton and Ashton regarding this matter.

[28] Ibid., M.D. 11 to C.G.S. 18 April 1935.

[29] Ibid., C.G.S. to M.D. 11. 19 April 1935.

[30] Eayrs, **In Defence of Canada,** 145.

[31] Ibid., 145-46.

[32] **Diary,** M.D. 11 to C.G.S., 20 April 1935.

[33] Ibid., C.G.S. to M.D. 11, 22 April 1935.

[34] CAV. 33-B-6. File 10. VCPD memo, 21 April 1935.

[35] (Vancouver) **Sun,** 9 May 1935.

[36] RCMP, 24 April 1935.

[37] CAV. 33-B-6. File 10. Lyons to Foster, 26 April 1935.

[38] RCMP, 24 April 1935.

[39] RRIC, **Record,** Vol. 51: 34.

[40] Ibid., 151.

[41] CAV. 33-B-6. File 10. Lester to Foster, 16 April 1935.

[42] RRIC, **Record,** Vol. 51: 115.

[43] Ibid., 93-97.

[44] Ibid., 7.

[45] RCMP, 24 April 1935.

[46] The Riot Act had been read in Vancouver in 1912 before a belligerent group of unemployed. (Vancouver) **Sun,** 24 April 1935.

[47] RRIC, **Record,** Vol. 51: 8-9.

[48] (Vancouver) **Sun,** 24 April 1935; RCMP, 24 April 1935.

[49] RRIC, **Record,** Vol. 51: 39-53.

[50] William Davis, interview.

[51] CAV. 33-B-6. File 10. McGeer-Perley exchange, 23-24 April 1935.

[52] (Vancouver) **Sun,** 27 April 1935.

[53] **Diary,** M.D. 11 to C.G.S., 25 April 1935; CAV. 33-B-6. File 10. "Minutes of Conference of Unemployed Relief Camp Strikers."

[54] CAV. 33-B-6. File 10. "Proposals for the Camp Strikers, Endorsed by the Four Divisions."

[55] Ibid., VCPD memo, 25 April 1935.

[56] Ibid., RCMP, 26 April 1935.

[57] (Vancouver) **Sun,** 26 April 1935.

[58] CAV. 33-B-6. File 10. "Citizens Resolution," 25 April 1935.

[59] Ibid., McGeer to Perley, 16 April 1935.

[60] RCMP, 26 April 1935.

[61] RRIC, **Record,** Vol. 11: 22.

[62] CAV. 33-B-6. File 10. VCPD memo, undated; see also James Walsh interview; Liversedge, **Recollections,** 65.

[63] CAV. 33-B-6. File 10. VCPD memo, 28 April 1935.

[64] Ibid.

[65] Ibid.

[66] (Vancouver) **Sun,** 29 April 1935; RCMP, 29 and 30 April 1935.

[67] RCMP, 30 April 1935.

[68] Ibid.

[69] There are four reports filed by RCMP on 30 April. It is clear that Constable Kusch was the witness to Evans's "highly inebriated condition." Evans's biographers indicate that Evans was a drinking man and that his last job as an organizer in 1938 was taken away from him after he spent a week in jail on a drunk charge. See Swankey and Sheils, **Work and Wages,** 276.

[70] RCMP, 30 April 1935.

[71] **Diary,** M.D. 11 to C.G.S., 30 April 1935.

[72] Liversedge, **Recollections,** 65.

Chapter Four
May in Vancouver

[1] CAV. 33-B-6. File 10. VCPD memo, 27 April 1935.

[2] Ibid., Foster to McGeer, 1 May 1935.

[3] Ibid., "Special Duties — May Day Demonstration." The memo is signed by A.G. McNeill, Chief Inspector, C.I.D.

[4] (Vancouver) **Sun,** 2 May 1935; RCMP, 2 May 1935.

[5] RCMP, 2 May 1935.

[6] Ibid.

[7] CAV. 33-B-6. File 9. Foster to McGeer, 2 May 1935.

[8] Ibid.

[9] (Vancouver) **Sun,** 2 May 1935.

[10] **Daily Province,** 2 May 1935.

[11] CAV. 33-B-6. File 9. MacInnis to McGeer, 3 May 1935.

[12] **Diary,** M.D. 11 to C.G.S., 4 May 1935.

[13] (Vancouver) **Sun,** 6 May 1935.

[14] CAV. 33-B-6. File 9. VCPD memo, 6 May 1935.

[15] Liversedge, **Recollections,** 72-73.

[16] PAC. R.B. Bennett Papers. MG26K Vol. 802: 495890; see also (Vancouver) **Sun,** 16 May 1935.

[17] CAV. 33-B-6. File 9. Perley to McGeer, 13 May 1935.

[18] Ibid., "Mayor-Trekker meeting" memo, 10 May 1935.

[19] Ibid., VCPD memo, 16 May 1935.

[20] (Vancouver) **Sun,** 13 May 1935; see also Liversedge, **Recollections,** 71.

[21] (Vancouver) **Sun,** 14 May 1935.

[22] (Vancouver) **Sun,** 21 May 1935.

[23] CAV. 33-B-6. File 9. Foster memo, "Arrangements for Thursday, 16 May 1935."

[24] Ibid., VCPD memo, 16 May 1935; see also (Vancouver) **Sun,** 17 May 1935.

[25] RCMP, 17 May 1935.

[26] CAV. 33-B-6. File 9. VCPD memo, 16 May 1935.

[27] RCMP, 17 May 1935.

[28] CAV. 33-B-6. File 9. McGeer to Bennett, 16 May 1935.

190

29 (Vancouver) **Sun,** 18 May 1935.
30 CAV. 33-B-6. File 9. Taylor to Foster, 18 May 1935.
31 Liversedge, **Recollections,** 77. See also RCMP, 20 May 1935 and (Vancouver) **Sun,** 20 May 1935.
32 RRIC, **Record,** Vol. 51: 204.
33 Ibid., 199-203.
34 Liversedge, **Recollections,** 80.
35 Louis Tellier, interview.
36 RRIC, **Record,** Vol. 51:13.
37 CAV. 33-B-6. File 9. VCPD memo, 19 May 1935.
38 Liversedge, **Recollections,** 81.
39 RRIC, **Record,** Vol. 51: 14-15.
40 Liversedge, **Recollections,** 82.
41 RRIC, **Record,** Vol. 51: 199-203.
42 Liversedge, **Recollections,** 83.
43 CAV. 33-B-6. File 9. McGeer to Bennett. 19 May 1935.
44 Ibid., Bennett to McGeer, 20 May 1935.
45 RCMP, 20 May 1935; see also (Vancouver) **Sun,** 20 May 1935.
46 RCMP, 21 May 1935.
47 RCMP, 23 May 1935.
48 **Diary,** M.D. 11 to C.G.S., 19 May 1935.
49 Ibid., 23 May 1935.
50 CAV. 33-B-6. File 9. VCPD memo, 24 May 1935.
51 (Vancouver) **Sun,** 25 May 1935.
52 (Vancouver) **Sun,** 27 May 1935.
53 CAV. 33-B-6. File 9. Foster to McGeer, 27 May 1935.
54 Ibid. VCPD memo, 28 May 1935.
55 Ibid., Grundy to Foster, 31 May 1935.
56 Ibid., VCPD memo, 28 May 1935; see also **Diary,** M.D. 11 to C.G.S., 29 May 1935.
57 **Diary,** M.D. 11 to C.G.S., 31 May 1935.
58 (Vancouver) **Sun,** 27 May 1935.
59 (Vancouver) **Sun,** 29 May 1935.
60 (Vancouver) **Sun,** 29 May 1935.
61 CAV. Pamphlets #1935-69 "Citizens League: Organizational Memorandum," 23 May 1935.
62 PAC. RG 24, Vol. 2967. File: "Unemployment Relief, Meeting 28 May 1935 re B.C. Situation." Memo: A.G.L. McNaughton to Deputy Minister of Labour, 29 May 1935.
63 RCMP, 31 May 1935.
64 CAV. 33-B-6. File 9. VCPD memo, 30 May 1935.
65 RCMP, 30 May 1935.
66 Ibid.
67 Liversedge, **Recollections,** 83.
68 RCMP, 31 May 1935.
69 **Diary,** M.D. 11 to C.G.S., 1 June 1935.
70 CAV. 33-B-6. File 9. VCPD memo, 30 May 1935.

71 (Vancouver) **Sun,** 30 May 1935.
72 CAV. 33-B-6. File 9. Foster to McGeer, 1 June 1935.
73 **The Worker,** 1 June 1935.
74 Liversedge, **Recollections,** 69.
75 William Davis, interview.
76 **Daily Province,** 6 June 1935.
77 The report is included in RRIC.

<h2 style="text-align:center">Chapter Five
The Trek</h2>

1 RRIC, **Record,** Vol. 2: 59-64. see also (Vancouver) **Sun,** 4 June 1935.
2 Ibid.
3 Irven Schwartz, interview.
4 (Vancouver) **Sun,** 6 June 1935.
5 RRIC, **Record,** Vol. 8: 68-69.
6 Ibid.; (Vancouver) **Sun,** 7 June 1935.
7 (Toronto) **Daily Star,** 5 June 1935.
8 Kingsbury left the Trek once it reached Regina.
9 (Toronto) **Daily Star,** 5 June 1935.
10 RRIC, **Record,** Vol. 8:69.
11 Irven Schwartz, interview.
12 RRIC, **Record,** Vol. 8: 72-73.
13 Ibid., 70.
14 James Walsh, interview.
15 Ibid.
16 RRIC, **Record,** Vol. 8: 74.
17 RRIC, **Record:** 252-55.
18 RRIC, **Record,** Vol. 8: 80.
19 Ibid., Vol. 15: 39.
20 Irven Schwartz, interview.
21 RRIC, **Record,** Vol. 14: 144ff.
22 Liversedge, **Recollections,** 94.
23 Ibid., 96. MacLeod later served as the CPC's liaison with the Mackenzie-Papineau Battalion in the Spanish Civil War, making three trips into that country.
24 Ibid., 97.
25 RRIC, **Record,** Vol. 52. The whole of this volume is given over to interviews with participants in and witnesses to the siege.
26 Liversedge, **Recollections,** 99-100.
27 RCMP to Bruton, 11 June 1935. A tape recorded transcript of this message is in the possession of the author.
28 Liversedge, **Recollections,** 101.
29 (Toronto) **Daily Star,** 10 June 1935.
30 Ibid., 11 June 1935.

31 Liversedge, **Recollections,** 102.
32 (Toronto) **Daily Star,** 11 June 1935.
33 RRIC, **Record,** Vol. 8: 88-89.
34 (Toronto) **Daily Star,** 11 June 1935.
35 Ibid.
36 William Davis, interview.
37 **Diary,** M.D. 13 to Attorney General, 4 June 1935.
38 Ibid., 8 June 1935.
39 Ibid., 9 June 1935.
40 PAC. R.B. Bennett Papers. MG26K Vol. 802: 496566.
41 RRIC, Exhibit 158, MacBrien to Wood, 11 June 1935.
42 RRIC, **Record,** Vol. 7:3-15; see also (Toronto) **Daily Star,** 14 June 1935.
43 RRIC, **Record,** Vol. 3: 146-59.
44 Ibid., Vol. 4: 96-97.
45 Irven Schwartz, interview.
46 RRIC, Exhibit 109, Shaw to J. Matts, undated.

Chapter Six
Regina

1 Earl Drake, **Regina: The Queen City** (Toronto: McClelland and Stewart, 1955), 185-96.
2 RRIC, **Record,** Vol. 4:30.
3 Ibid., Vol. 36: 119.
4 Ibid., Exhibit 20, Gardiner to Bennett, 12 June 1935.
5 Ibid., Exhibit 21, Bennett to Gardiner, 12 June 1935.
6 Ibid., Exhibit 22, Mather to Gardiner, 12 June 1935.
7 Ibid., Exhibit 25, Hungerford to Gardiner, 12 June 1935.
8 Ibid., Exhibit 24, Gardiner to Mather, 12 June 1935.
9 Ibid., Exhibit 29, Mather to Gardiner, 13 June 1935.
10 Ibid., Exhibit 30, Gardiner to Mather, 13 June 1935.
11 Ibid., Exhibit 31, Mather to Gardiner, 13 June 1935.
12 Canada, House of Commons, **Debates,** 13 June 1935, 3884-3885.
13 RRIC, Exhibit 150, Wood memo to Inspectors and Sergeants, 12 June 1935.
14 Ibid., Exhibit 168, Wood to MacBrien, 13 June 1935.
15 Ibid., Exhibit 258, Bruton to Regina City Police Force, 14 June 1935.
16 Ibid., **Record,** Vol. 8: 120-26.
17 Ibid., Exhibit 59, "Minutes of Citizens Emergency Committee," 13 June 1935.
18 This account of the Trek's arrival is based on coverage in the (Regina) **Leader-Post** and the **Regina Daily Star,** 14 June 1935.
19 (Regina) **Leader-Post,** 15 June 1935.
20 RRIC, Exhibit 60, "Minutes of Citizens Emergency Committee," 14 June 1935.
21 RRIC, **Record,** Vol. 35: 32-34.
22 (Toronto) **Daily Star,** 16 June 1935.

[23] Based on coverage in the (Regina) **Leader-Post** and the **Regina Daily Star,** 15 June 1935.

[24] PAC. CCF Records. MG 28. IV-I, Vol. 107, File: "J.S. Woodsworth 1933-36".

[25] **Diary,** M.D. 12 to Defensor, 15 June 1935; see also (Regina) **Leader-Post,** 14 June 1935.

[26] **Regina Daily Star,** 17 June 1935.

[27] (Regina) **Leader-Post** 17 June 1935.

[28] Ibid.

[29] PAC. R.J. Manion Papers. MG 27 III B1 Vol. 33. Memo, 17 June 1935.

[30] RRIC, **Record,** Vol. 4: 101-103.

[31] Manion Papers. "Minutes of a Conference Held at the Canadian Room of the Hotel Saskatchewan, Regina, Saskatchewan on Monday, 17 June at 3:15 P.M."

[32] Ibid., Manion to Bennett, 17 June 1935.

[33] James Walsh, interview.

[34] RRIC, Exhibit 204, Wood to MacBrien, 19 June 1935.

[35] (Regina) **Leader-Post,** 18 June 1935.

[36] Manion Papers. Memorandum, 17 June 1935.

[37] (Regina) **Leader-Post,** 18 June 1935.

[38] Manion Papers, Manion to Bennett, 17 June 1935.

[39] RRIC, Exhibit 204, Wood to MacBrien, 19 June 1935.

[40] RRIC, Exhibit 193, Wood to MacBrien, 18 June 1935.

[41] PAC. William Lyon Mackenzie King Papers. MG 26 J1 Vol. 205: 176493.

[42] RRIC, Exhibit 64, "Minutes of Citizens Emergency Committee, 18 June 1935."

[43] Ibid., Exhibit 65, 19 June 1935.

[44] Ibid., Exhibit 67, 24 June 1935.

[45] K.C. Fraser, interview by Victor Howard, June 1967, Regina, Saskatchewan.

[46] RRIC, **Record,** Vol. 16: 3-4.

[47] RRIC, **Record,** Vol. 15: 178.

[48] Ibid., Vol. 16: 40; see also (Regina) **Leader-Post,** 25 June 1935.

[49] Ibid., Vol. 16: 22.

[50] Ibid., Vol. 12: 82.

[51] Ibid., Vol. 5: 43.

[52] RRIC, Exhibit 258, Bruton to Regina City Police Force, 14 June 1935.

[53] Frank Bobby, interview.

[54] RRIC, **Record,** Vol. 4: 3-28.

[55] Ibid., Vol. 3: 62.

[56] James Walsh, interview.

[57] RRIC, **Report,** Vol. II: 92-126. Report of Interview between Delegation of Strikers and Dominion Government, June 22, 1935 Transcript.

[58] James Walsh, interview.

[59] RRIC, **Record,** Vol. 9: 29-32.

[60] Canada, House of Commons, **Debates,** 24 June 1935, 3899-3900.

[61] RRIC, **Record,** Vol. 9: 29-32.

[62] RRIC, Exhibit 206, Wood to MacBrien, 25 June 1935.

63 (Regina) **Leader-Post,** 26 June 1935.
64 RRIC, **Record,** Vol. 3: 71-73.
65 Ibid., Vol. 9: 38.
66 Based on coverage by (Regina) **Leader-Post** and **Regina Daily Star,** 27 June 1935.
67 RRIC, **Record,** Vol. 36: 137.
68 (Regina) **Leader-Post,** 27 June 1935.
69 RRIC, **Record,** Vol. 37: 62.
70 **Regina Daily Star,** 28 June 1935.
71 Based on (Regina) **Leader-Post** and **Regina Daily Star** coverage, 28 June 1935.
72 **Record,** Vol. 37: 78-79.
73 Ibid., Vol. 37: 96.
74 (Regina) **Leader-Post,** 29 June 1935.
75 RRIC, **Record,** Vol. 4: 125-29.
76 Ibid., Vol. 4: 175.
77 Ibid., Exhibit 222, Wood to MacBrien, 29 June 1935.
78 Ibid., Vol. 37: 89.
79 Ibid., Vol. 37: 99-101.
80 Ibid., Vol. 4: 175-77.
81 Ibid., Vol. 37: 106.
82 Ibid., Vol. 37: 114-15.

Chapter Seven
The Regina Riot:
Market Square

1 RRIC, **Record,** Vol. 48:88.
2 Ibid., Vol. 46: 125-30.
3 Ibid.
4 Ibid., Vol. 46: 125.
5 Ibid., Vol. 15: 120-21.
6 Ibid., Vol. 21: 163-68.
7 Ibid., Vol. 17: 22.
8 Ibid., Vol. 19: 98-110; Vol. 21: 50-68; Vol. 23: 156-67; Vol. 20: 183-99, 30-60.
9 Ibid., Vol. 16: 106-28.
10 Ibid., Vol. 34: 43-65.
11 Ibid., Vol. 20: 96-143; Vol. 18: 96-169; Vol. 25: 141-57; Vol. 23: 3-40; Vol. 19: 110-55.
12 William Davis, interview.
13 RRIC, **Record,** Vol. 27: 38.
14 Ibid., Vol. 27: 39.
15 Ibid., Vol. 25: 32-46.
16 Ibid.

[17] Ibid., Vol. 41: 42-94.
[18] Ibid., Vol. 25: 24-32; Vol. 47: 3-140.
[19] RRIC, **Report:** 121.
[20] RRIC, **Record:** 117-22.
[21] Ibid., Vol. 42: 111-58; Vol. 44: 13-40; Vol. 43: 24-95; Vol. 42: 52-160; Vol. 43: 129-53.
[22] Ibid., Vol. 18: 88-89.
[23] Ibid., Vol. 47: 9-10.
[24] Ibid., Vol. 42: 52-160.
[25] Ibid., Vol. 48: 24.
[26] Ibid.: 29-38.
[27] Ibid.
[28] Ibid., Vol. 26: 28-29.
[29] Ibid., Vol. 21: 164-65.
[30] Ibid., Vol. 17: 99.
[31] Ibid., Vol. 21: 44-49; Vol. 21: 130-39.
[32] Ibid., Vol. 17: 3-69.
[33] Ibid., Vol. 20: 33.
[34] Ibid., Vol. 47: 72-91.
[35] Ibid., Vol. 43: 24-95.
[36] Ibid., Vol. 45: 59.
[37] Ibid., Vol. 44: 72-73.
[38] Ibid., Vol. 44: 91-105; Vol. 44: 106-17; Vol. 44: 117-25.
[39] Ibid., Vol. 46: 33-44.
[40] Kenneth Liddell, interview with Victor Howard, June 1967, Calgary, Alberta; see also RRIC, **Record,** Vol. 44: 41-57; Vol. 44: 91-105.
[41] Ibid., Vol. 34: 48-49.
[42] Ibid., Vol. 34: 49.
[43] Ibid., Vol. 47: 152-69.
[44] Ibid., Vol. 48: 3-15.
[45] Ibid., Vol. 45: 3-21; Vol. 45: 40-101.
[46] Ibid., Vol. 45: 102-31; Vol. 20: 183-99; Vol. 21: 50-68; Vol. 25: 63-70; Vol. 25: 6-7; Vol. 19: 98-110.
[47] Ibid., Vol. 43: 3-24; **Report:** 223-25.
[48] Ibid., Vol. 43: 24-75; Vol. 35: 151-60; Vol. 43: 129-53; Vol. 45: 102-31; Vol. 42: 52-160.
[49] Ibid., Vol. 16: 76-106.
[50] Ibid., Vol. 18: 91-93.
[51] Ibid., Vol. 23: 58.

Chapter Eight
The Regina Riot:
City Centre

[1] RRIC, **Record,** Vol. 48: 78-93.
[2] Ibid., Vol. 24: 156-64.

3 Ibid., Vol. 29: 81-99; Vol. 25: 85-114; Vol. 27: 116-38.
4 Ibid., Vol. 26: 10-34; Vol. 21: 139-58; Vol. 21: 169-73; Vol. 30: 75-83.
5 Ibid., Vol. 26: 15.
6 Ibid., Vol. 29: 159.
7 Ibid., Vol. 36: 21-58.
8 Ibid., Vol. 30: 84-116.
9 Ibid., Vol. 45: 131-47.
10 Ibid., Vol. 26: 47.
11 Ibid., Vol. 32: 14-22.
12 Ibid., Vol. 29: 25.
13 Ibid., Vol. 45: 102-31.
14 Ibid., Vol. 26: 58-60.
15 Ibid., Vol. 29: 30-57.
16 Ibid., Vol. 29: 57-74.
17 Ibid., Vol. 23: 73.
18 Ibid., Vol. 21: 126.
19 Ibid., Vol. 28: 17-43.
20 Ibid., Vol. 29: 113-32; Vol. 24: 115-47.
21 Ibid., Vol. 47: 9-10; Vol. 28: 99-116; Vol. 32: 136-60.
22 Ibid., Vol. 32: 3-13.
23 Ibid., Vol. 24: 10-16; Vol. 23: 3-25; Vol. 23: 25-49; Vol. 20: 143-83; Vol. 35: 151-65.
24 Ibid., Vol. 21: 159-63.
25 Ibid., Vol. 35: 120-30.
26 Ibid., Vol. 47: 26.
27 Ibid., Vol. 25: 3-5; Vol. 50: 54-63; **Report:** 234-36.
28 Ibid., Vol. 24; 150-56.
29 Ibid., Exhibits 267-68; Vol. 17: 184.
30 Ibid., Vol. 43: 24-95.
31 Ibid., Vol. 23: 54-60.
32 Ibid., Vol. 27: 4.
33 Ibid., Vol. 50: 113-15; Vol. 50: 108-13.
34 Ibid., Vol. 20: 96-143.

Chapter Nine
After the Riot

1 (Regina) **Leader-Post,** 3-4 July 1935; see also RRIC, Exhibit 288.
2 RRIC, Exhibit 267. ''Rioters Hurt in Riot July 1, 1935. Brought to Grey Nuns Hospital.''
3 **Regina Daily Star,** 5 July 1935.
4 RRIC, **Record,** Vol. 38: 19-22.
5 Ibid.
6 Ibid., Exhibit 48, Gardiner to Bennett, 1 July 1935.
7 Ibid., Exhibit 51, Bennett to Gardiner, 2 July 1935.
8 Ibid., **Record,** Vol. 6: 44.

⁹ Ibid., **Record,** Vol. 4: 140-42.

¹⁰ Ibid.

¹¹ **Diary,** Boak to C.G.S., 3 July 1935; see also RRIC, **Record,** Vol. 6: 53.

¹² RRIC, **Record,** Vol. 33: 34-39.

¹³ Ibid., Vol. 5: 52.

¹⁴ Ibid.

¹⁵ Ibid., Vol. 38: 29.

¹⁶ PAC. RG24. Vol. 3047. "Unemployed Relief Disperal of Strikers, B.C." Cdg. 12 to C.G.S., 5 July 1935. Two Strikers, Walter Hellund and Gerry Winters, stayed behind in Regina to continue the search for missing colleagues.

¹⁷ **Regina Daily Star,** 5 July 1935.

¹⁸ (Regina) **Leader-Post,** 6 July 1935.

¹⁹ Ibid.

²⁰ Ibid.

²¹ Ibid.

²² CAV. 33-B-6. File 7. Foster to McGeer, 4 July 1935.

²³ Ibid., McGeer to Foster, 5 July 1935.

²⁴ McCandless, "Vancouver's Red Menace," 56-70.

²⁵ CAV. 33-B-6. File 7. Foster and McGeer, 5 July 1935.

²⁶ Ibid. Bennett to McGeer, 6 July 1935.

²⁷ **Diary,** M.D. 11 to C.G.S., 7 July 1935.

²⁸ CAV. 33-B-6. File 7. Foster to McGeer, 8 July 1935.

²⁹ Ibid.

³⁰ Ibid., Foster to McGeer, 9 July 1935; RCMP, 7 July 1935.

³¹ RCMP, 9 July 1935.

³² CAV. 33-B-6. File 7. Foster to McGeer, 9 July 1935.

³³ Ibid. "Notes and Recordings Made From Mass Meetings of Camp Strikers Held in Arena, 10 July 1935."

³⁴ Frank Bobby, interview.

³⁵ **Winnipeg Tribune,** 20 June 1935.

³⁶ RRIC, **Record,** Vol. 9: 30.

³⁷ **Winnipeg Tribune,** 22 June 1935.

³⁸ RRIC, **Record,** Vol. 10: 116.

³⁹ Ibid., Vol. 38: 86.

⁴⁰ Ibid.: 91.

⁴¹ **Ottawa Evening Citizen,** 8 August 1935.

⁴² (Toronto) **Telegram,** 10 August 1935.

⁴³ Ibid., 22 August 1935.

Epilogue

¹ (Montreal) **Gazette,** 11 June 1935.

² **Ottawa Morning Citizen,** 8 June 1935.

³ **Ottawa Morning Journal,** 11 June 1935.

⁴ **Hamilton Spectator,** 17 June 1935.

[5] (Regina) **Leader-Post,** 4 June 1935.

[6] Ibid., 25 June 1935.

[7] **Ottawa Evening Journal,** 7 June 1935.

[8] PAC. R.B. Bennett Papers. Vol. 803, 496934.

[9] (Toronto) **Daily Star,** 6 July 1935.

[10] (Toronto) **Telegram,** 13 July 1935.

[11] RCPD Archives. Transcription on tape in possession of the author.

[12] **The History of the Regina City Police Force: 1892-1945.** N.p., n.d. A copy of this history is on file in the library of the Regina City Police Station.

[13] RRIC, **Record,** Vol. 41: 58.

[14] Ibid., Vol. 46: 129. See also RRIC, **Report:** 283.

[15] Ibid., **Report:** 206-208.

[16] Ibid., 126.

[17] Ibid., **Record,** Vol. 39: 110.

[18] (Regina) **Leader-Post,** 19 October 1935.

[19] RRIC, **Report,** 251.

[20] Ernest Watkins, **R.B. Bennett** (Toronto: Kingswood Press, 1963), 223.

[21] The Report of the Riggs Commission is included in RRIC.

[22] Swankey and Sheils, **Work and Wages,** 283.

[23] (Regina) **Leader-Post,** 5 July 1935.

INDEX

Other Publications
from the Canadian Plains Research Center

Canadian Plains Studies
1. Richard Allen, ed., *A Region of the Mind: Interpreting the Western Canadian Plains*, 1973. $7.40
2. Martin Louis Kovacs, *Esterhazy and Early Hungarian Immigration to Canada*, 1974. $7.40
3. Richard Allen, ed., *Religion and Society in the Prairie West*, 1975. $6.35
5. Clinton O. White, *Power for a Province: A History of Saskatchewan Power*, 1976 $8.90
6. Richard Allen, ed., *Men and Nature on the Prairies*, 1976. $6.35
7. Wilhelm Cohnstaedt, *Western Canada 1909; Travel Letters by Wilhelm Cohnstaedt*, translated by Herta Holle-Scherer; Klaus H. Burmeister, ed., 1976. $6.00
8. Martin L. Kovacs, ed., *Ethnic Canadians: Culture and Education*, 1977. $12.00
9. David G. Mandelbaum, *The Plains Cree: An Ethnographic, Historical and Comparative Study*, 1978. $14.50
10. Alan F.J. Artibise, ed., *Town and City: Aspects of Western Canadian Urban Development*, 1961. $15.00
11. Gaston Giscard, *Dans la prairie canadienne/On the Canadian Prairie*, 1982. $14.00
12. L.A. Sulerzhitsky, *To America with the Doukhobors*, translated by Michael Kalmakoff, 1982. $13.00
13. Gordon C. Church, *An Unfailing Faith: A History of the Saskatchewan Dairy Industry*, 1985. $29.95

Occasional Papers
1. B.Y. Card, *The Expanding Relation: Sociology in Prairie Universities*, 1973. $1.00
2. Robert C. Cosbey, *All in Together, Girls: Skipping Songs from Regina*, 1980. $3.50

Canadian Plains Proceedings
6. W. Davies, ed., *Nature and Change on the Canadian Prairies*, 1978. $7.00
11. M. Douglas Scott, ed., *Third Biennial Plains Aquatic Research Conference: Proceedings*, 1983. $16.00
12. A.E. Smith, ed., *Wild Oats Symposium: Volume One*, 1983.
    A.E. Smith and Andrew I. Hsiao, eds., *Wild Oats Symposium, Volume Two: Use and Mode of Action of Wild Oat Herbicides*, 1984. $12.00
13. J. William Brennan, ed., *"Building the Co-operative Commonwealth": Essays on the Democratic Socialist Tradition in Canada*, 1985. $15.00
14. Kenneth J. Alecxe and G. Wayne McElree, eds., *Saskatchewan Labour Market: Issues, Politics and Opportunities for Change*, 1984. $11.50

Canadian Plains Reports
2. Jill M. Robinson, *Seas of Earth: An Annotated Bibliography of Prairie Literature as it Relates to the Environment*, 1977. $6.00
3. Dorothy Hepworth, ed., *Explorations in Prairie Justice Research*, 1979. $7.00
4. Shirley Skinner, Otto Driedger and Brian Grainger, *Corrections: An Historical Perspective of the Saskatchewan Experience*, 1981. $12.00
5. Robert Stock, *Monitoring Migration in the Prairie Provinces: Administrative Date Sources and Methodologies*, 1981. $17.00

Canadian Plains Bibliographies
1. John P. Miska. *Canadian Studies on Hungarians, 1885-1983: An Annotated Bibliography of Primary and Secondary Sources*, 1985. $28.00
2. George Arthur, *A Buffalo Roundup: A Selected Bibliography*, 1985. $35.00

Prairie Forum
Multidisciplinary regional journal issued twice a year, commencing 1976. $15.00

Prepayment of order would be appreciated. Our discount policy is as follows: libraries—20%; retailer—40%; all sales of 5 or more copies of same title—40%. Please send orders to the Canadian Plains Research Center and make cheque payable to the University of Regina. All income from the sales of publications will be returned to the Center's publication fund. Canadian Plains Research Center, University of Regina, Regina, Saskatchewan, Canada S4S 0A2.